THE
STUDENT'S ONLY SURVIVAL GUIDE TO ESSAY WRITING

Steve Good & Bill Jensen

ORCA BOOK PUBLISHERS

Canadian Cataloguing in Publication Data
 Jensen, Bill, 1941–
 The student's only survival guide to essay writing

 Includes bibiliographical references and index.
 ISBN 1-55143-038-X

1. English language—Rhetoric. 2. Essay. I. Good, William Stephen, 1950–
II. Title.
PE1471.J46 1995 808'.042 C95-910444-5

Every effort has been made to trace ownership of all copyrighted material and to secure permission from copyright holders. In the event of any question arising as to the use of any material, we will be pleased to make the necessary corrections in future printings.

Cover design by Suburbia Studios

Printed and bound in Canada

Orca Book Publishers   **Orca Book Publishers**
PO Box 5626, Station B   PO Box 468
Victoria, BC Canada   Custer, WA   USA
V8R 6S4   98240-0468

10   9   8   7   6   5   4   3   2   1

To Sue and Winona,
who put up with dinners
of white wine, fresh salmon
and interminable rhetorical blather.

It's done — we'll be home soon.

Table of Contents

INTRODUCTION

We have, between the two of us, about thirty-four years of teaching experience. During our careers, we've always tried to be responsive to our students' suggestions and concerns. The problem that our students most often voice has to do with their dissatisfaction with whatever composition text we might be using. The most common complaint is that composition texts tend not to address directly and consistently the skills the students need to deal effectively with the undergraduate expository essay as a testing device. They also complain that the texts are verbose and pedantic, and that most of them seem to be written for instructors rather than students. In *The S.O.S. Guide to Essay Writing*, we've attempted to address our students' concerns. The material we've developed has been tested in our classes for five years now, and has been so successful that former students come back to us (months and even years later) to pick up new copies of our multiple unit model templates and guides for use in other classes and other institutions. We hope that our system will help you with your own writing.

Although we've generated an artifact (the book you're looking at right now), we see this text as a work in progress. Our intention is to be as responsive to our readers as we try to be with our students. To this end, both we and our publisher welcome any suggestions, comments or criticisms you as a student may have. You can write to us at Orca Book Publishers; we look forward to hearing from you.

Good luck with your essay-writing!

Steve Good & Bill Jensen

1
DEFINING YOUR AUDIENCE

If you look through texts or listen to many lectures on composition, you'll certainly be advised that you should give careful consideration to your audience. An audience is usually characterized in one of two ways: horizontally or vertically. The most common characterization describes an audience horizontally (*see highlighted row, figure 1-1*). This view deals in broad brushstrokes and looks at generalized considerations like educational level, income, and ethnic or religious background. When writing for college or university classes, you'll usually deal with this horizontal view of an audience. Given this point of view, you should assume that your audience is bright, moderately educated, and literate. Its members are concerned about current events and take a vital interest in the world around them. They have no patience with a writer who displays inadequate subject knowledge, expresses himself in an awkward manner, is illogical, or proofreads poorly. This audience's *general* characteristics are more important to you than any special interests its members may have (*see the vertical columns in figure 1-1*). Examples of horizontally directed communications are television news broadcasts; magazines like *Time, Maclean's,* and *Newsweek*; many best-selling novels like *The Silence of the Lambs*; and most biographies.

The second characterization looks at an audience from a vertical perspective (*see highlighted column, figure 1-2*). This audience is composed of specialists or well-informed amateurs in the field. They are capable of understanding any well-organized, intelligently written composition dealing with their specific content area. They are probably not interested in references to anything outside their specialized sphere of interest.

When you're addressing this audience, you'd be well advised to

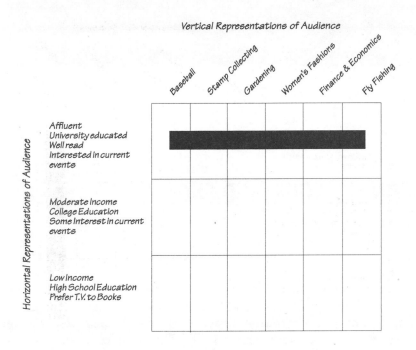

Figure 1-1: Horizontal and Vertical Audiences

research their characteristics before beginning to write. A miscalculation regarding their interests or knowledge base could result in disgruntled readers. This audience is very carefully cultivated by the magazine industry, as you'll see. If you check the variety of titles offered at a magazine rack, you'll find publications that target model-airplane builders, computer users, fishers, RV owners, etc. In fact, you'll find that there are publications catering to World War I model-airplane builders, laptop computer users, fly-fishers, and owners of four-by-fours who use their vehicles for off-road camping. You'll notice in figure 1-2 that the audience's special interest in fly-fishing moves across the horizontal considerations of income, education, etc. In other words, a fisher may be a PhD or a high-school dropout. A well-written essay dealing with fly-fishing is likely to appeal to individuals from both educational extremes. You may object that the linguistic expectations of the PhD are significantly different from those of the high-school dropout, and that those expectations are sure to affect the reader's acceptance of the essay. But as the audience becomes more narrowly verticalized (fly-fishers rather than fishers generally), you'll usually find that there is a specialized vocabulary associated with the area of interest that is shared by all members of the special interest group. Care in addressing these special requirements will solve problems created by horizontal polarization.

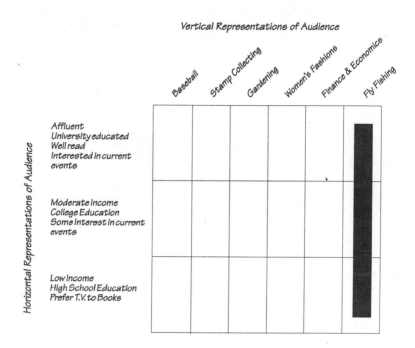

Figure 1-2: Horizontal and Vertical Audiences

You must remember that these two characterizations of an audience are generalized, and there are always exceptions to them. It's not uncommon to find an audience that is specific both horizontally and vertically (*see figure 1-3*). A magazine devoted to *haute couture* is focused vertically on women's fashions and horizontally on women with high income.

Although approaching an audience in this mechanical manner has its uses, trying to tailor your essay to meet these kinds of audience requirements too soon in the writing process will make things more difficult for you. In fact, there's a simple rule governing the writer's relationship with the audience.

> *Deal with the content of the essay in a non-trivial, thorough and specific manner, and you will usually have dealt effectively with your audience.*

This isn't always true; but even in instances where difficulties arise, if you've followed this rule, you'll need to make only minor adjustments to your work to bring it in line with your audience's special requirements. Thus, from your point of view as a writer beginning to work on an essay, it is of primary importance that you understand

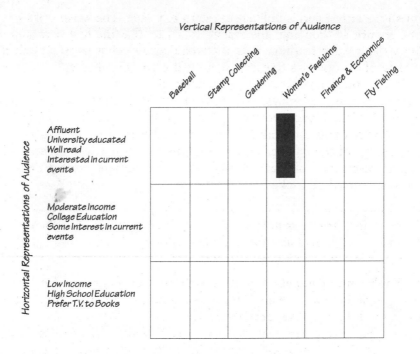

Figure 1-3: Horizontal and Vertical Audiences

the issues, concepts, and procedures surrounding a content area. As you clarify your own sense of what is important, you will also begin to get a feel for the audience.

If you look at the work of professional essayists, particularly in the popular media (magazines, newspapers, television editorials, etc.), you'll find a number of confusing approaches to solving the problem of the audience: essays where the thesis is hidden or misrepresented; essays where the thesis appears in the middle or at the end; essays where the conclusion is in the first paragraph. If you pay close attention to the popular media and begin to read critically, you'll find the essay form squeezed and stretched into every possible shape.

There is a very good reason for this. These writers are competing for audiences. If you think about how most people read a magazine, you'll realize why it is necessary to manipulate essay form so drastically. The average person picks up a magazine and then flips through it. She looks at the photographs and the "heads and decks" (the essay titles and the short descriptions of the content), and if her interest is piqued during this flipping process, she will stop and read the first paragraph of the article. If this introductory paragraph does not hold the reader's interest, she will not finish the article and is unlikely to return to it later. The writer only gets one chance at "hooking" the reader; it is vital that the first paragraph keep the reader reading. It is this requirement that causes such a variety of approaches to essay form in the popular media.

As a student writing for an academic audience, as a writer of formal expository essays, you have a much different audience to contend with. Unless you're expressly told otherwise, one of the assumptions you can make about your audience is that it has some knowledge of the subject area and is interested in a well-organized, logical discussion of that subject area. Your audience doesn't want to be surprised or tricked.

⇨ > *Your audience wants to know what you are going to do, why you're going to do it, and how you're going to accomplish it.* ⇦

You're not competing with salacious blue-jeans ads for your reader's attention. What you are competing with are other well-structured, informative, academic essays.

In preparing these materials, we talked with a friend who is in charge of the composition program at a local university. He said he is very clear with his composition students about the nature of the expository essay: "The expository essay, within the academic community, is like a secret handshake." It's not something with which you should merely be familiar; it's a part of what defines you as a member of the community of scholars. The ability to express yourself clearly, using proper essay form, is expected of you. Your audience has learned this secret handshake and expects that you have also learned it. There's no place for awkwardness or fumbling. If you read academic journals, doctoral dissertations, essay work in courses, or chapters in your course texts, you'll find examples of carefully written, properly structured expository essays. Your audience, as long as you're operating within the academic world, expects the same from you.

⇨ > *The platform from which you operate as a student of composition is the expository essay. It is a fundamental expectation of your audience that you have control of essay form.* ⇦

However, for most students, control of essay form is the easy part. There is a much more subtle and difficult audience-based problem. This problem (and the solution to it) hinges on your ability to understand that *what you write is a communication* intended to be read by someone other than you: an audience. It has been claimed that when we talk to people, only about 20 percent of our communication is conveyed by the words we use. The other 80 percent is imparted through tone, gesture, facial expression, and body language. Suppose you're having coffee with a close friend, and in the course of the conversation, he claps you on the back, smiles reassuringly, and says, "You halfwit, what's the matter with you?" You have no doubt as to his meaning. He's used an insult to demonstrate intimacy; friends do this all the time. He'd be very surprised if you were hurt or angry. In fact, this exchange will likely leave you feeling close to the person. Using an insult as part of friendly banter can actually underline the depth of a friendship.

Let's assume, now, that you come from class and find a piece of paper folded under the windshield wiper on your car. You unfold it and find the following note: "You halfwit, what's the matter with you?"

What's the intention of the note writer? Are you being insulted? Have you done something stupid? Is the note a friendly jab in the ribs? What is your reaction going to be? The words on the paper are not enough. The words, by themselves, are insulting. If the intention of the writer was the same as your friend's intention during coffee, then something went wrong.

Did the writer misjudge you as an audience? She didn't misjudge your knowledge of some esoteric subject area; she didn't overlook your marital status, income level, political affiliations, or educational background. Her mistake was in forgetting that you are a separate, independent consciousness with separate feelings, experiences, expectations, and interpretive biases. She forgot that you don't have access to her knowledge or intentions. She wrote a note that *she* understood. She put it on your windshield and assumed that, because she understood it, *you* would understand it. She made the biggest mistake a writer can make. She assumed that the reader and the writer are one.

> *The most important thing you must learn about the members of your audience is that they are separate from you. The problem is not necessarily that they do not know what you know, but that they often know it differently.*

Let us give you a real example. Bill worked for a number of years with a Cree Indian Elder. The Elder was quite old, and he was concerned that much of the knowledge he had acquired during his life would disappear when he died. He was particularly distressed by the thought that the teaching stories he knew might be lost. He often said he wanted to tape the stories so that they could be written down and published. Unfortunately, he had such a busy schedule that he never sat down to tape them, and he died without any of them being documented. Bill always felt badly about this loss. He eventually decided to write a series of traditional fables that grew from the experience of working with the Elder. Although he didn't know the specific stories, he was familiar with the lessons they taught and the techniques they used. He felt he could echo the Elder's tradition, if not the exact words.

In a short time, the first of the stories was completed; it was titled *How Raven Found a Wife*. Bill was quite pleased with his work. In fact, when he was invited to read at a college-sponsored symposium, he included the tale of *Raven*. The story was very well accepted, and Bill was convinced that he had done a superlative job.

Sometime later, Bill became friends with a native student at the college. In conversation, Bill discovered that the student was involved in finding and preserving examples of traditional native stories and art. Bill explained the background of the Raven fable and asked the student if he would provide some feedback. When the student returned with the manuscript, he was laughing so hard that he could hardly explain the problems he'd found. It appeared that Bill had made two incredibly stupid errors—from a native point of view. At one point, Raven arrived at a village "at exactly noon"; and, earlier in the story, Orca demanded a gift from Raven. The student told Bill that both of these errors would be hilariously funny to any native reader. He explained that no native person would deal with time in terms of hours and seconds; that kind of punctuality was a non-native concept. He also explained that payment and gifts are never demanded in Native culture. They may be given for a variety of reasons, but a sense of appropriate behavior renders a demand for payment or gifts unacceptable.

The fixes to the story were simple. In the revised version, Raven arrived at the village "when the sun was at its highest point in the sky," and, although a gift was given to Orca, it had not been demanded. The events in the story were the same, but the details had to be slightly altered because part of the intended audience "knew differently."

At first, this may seem irrelevant to you when you're writing an essay comparing Freud's theories on dreams to Jung's. However, you'll be up against the same difficulties that Bill had with *Raven*. You're going to absorb a body of knowledge, rethink it in terms of your own experience and understanding, and then try to communicate that understanding to an audience—most likely an instructor, who will then give you a grade based on the depth and precision of your communication. You must always keep in mind that you have an audience. It is the awareness of, and concern with the existence of your audience that is vital. Though some may tell you otherwise, there is no homogeneous mass audience—other than in the mind of some half-mad grammarian. Individuals (sometimes very large groups of individuals) read your work. Each of these individuals is unique, despite the potential for shared interests, and each of them is not you.

> *Beyond simply dealing with your content in an effective manner, you must always remember that you are communicating with a reader who is separate from you. That is your primary definition of "audience."*

Remember that the analyses of horizontal and vertical audiences are tools for you to work with, nothing more.

You must think carefully about how you can most effectively communicate your opinions, your ideas, and your understanding to another person. This involves more fundamental problems than are normally considered when an audience is discussed. You must be sure that your use of language is appropriate. You must construct precise, readable sentences. Your paragraphs must be logical and controlled. Your essay must clearly lead the reader from the introduction and presentation of your central focus, through the development and support of your arguments or position, to your conclusion. When you have done all of this, you may be left with a few details of jargon or specialized knowledge to clean up; but your primary obligation to your audience will already have been met and the reader's expectations of you as a writer will have been satisfied.

Writing (in the abstract) isn't significantly different from what happens during a conversation, save that you, as a writer, lack many of the clues that would be available if you were confronting a live audience. This makes your sense of the reader's needs much more critical. As with the note under the windshield, the only thing your audience has to rely on is the document—the words on the paper. If your words aren't a complete and precise communication of your ideas, then you have failed to deal appropriately with the question of your audience.

Exercise

Obtain three or four magazines that appear to address significantly different audiences. Read some articles from each magazine. Try to answer the following questions about the articles:

1. Is the audience that the article addresses horizontal, vertical, or horizontal/vertical?

2. Based on your answer to question 1, how would you describe the qualities and/or interests of the audience?

3. Identify characteristics of the article (language, tone, etc.) that you feel are the result of audience considerations.

2
How to Read Topics & Generate Ideas

When you're getting ready to write, you'll have to address some important issues right away. First, you must have something to write about. You may be free to select a focus or subject, or you may have to write to specific requirements. If you have some choice open to you, the material you choose and the approach you decide to take must be appropriate and non-trivial. Before you start writing, you must ensure that you understand any limitations imposed on you by the assignment. You'll also need to spend some time thinking about your reader and about how to make your subject clear to him or her. These are concerns any writer must address. It doesn't really matter what form the writing will take; even a decision to write a simple paragraph involves responding to these issues. In a given assignment, you may be relatively free to handle these concerns according to your own sense of appropriateness, or you may have to comply with stringent requirements as to the form and content for a particular paper. In either case, you must be clear in your own mind about the "rules" for the particular assignment.

⇨   *When you approach the subject of the essay, you'll need to know what you want to say about the subject, why you're dealing with it in a particular way, and how you'll deal with it in terms of concept and structure.*   ⇦

To get what you need to know in order to begin working on an essay assignment, you must first recognize that all your essay topics will fall somewhere between two extreme types: closed and open topics.

CLOSED TOPICS

You may be assigned a very specific subject, one that is closed. A closed topic offers you little or no apparent room to make choices. You're restricted as to the topic area and specific focus, the nature and extent of any required research, and the particular approach you're to take in attacking the topic. You must write to the instructor's expressed expectations in order to get the kind of result you want on the assignment. Because closed topics may impose many limitations, you must also examine the wording of such assignments very carefully in order to be sure that your understanding of the assignment is complete and accurate. Sometimes this can be a problem: you may need to seek clarification as to specific aspects or requirements. How well you'll do on such assignments will depend on a number of factors: your command of the skills needed to meet the technical criteria for the paper; your level of interest and knowledge; your ability to understand the vocabulary of the subject area; your willingness to ask relevant questions; and your sense of the instructor's expectations.

Below are some sample closed topics. For the moment, don't worry about the specifics of each topic, the particular approaches required, or the ways you might go about dealing with each. Simply look at the level of specificity and the requirements expressed in each sample, and recognize that the samples may not be closed to the same degree.

Literature: You have been reading Edgar Allan Poe's "The Tell-Tale Heart." For your next essay, you will write an analysis of the narrator's viewpoint in the story, being certain to examine the change in pacing as the narrator grows more agitated. In particular, you are to identify excerpts in which you think the author intended to demonstrate the extent of the narrator's guilt, and the impact of that guilt on him as time passed. You may, if you wish, discuss any technical "tricks" Poe used to heighten the suspense for you, the reader. Your paper should be approximately 1,000-1,200 words.

Composition: For your next assignment, you will be writing a comparison/contrast essay of approximately 750 words. You are to consider your favorite sport or hobby, in terms of the kinds of equipment required to engage in the activity. For example, if your favorite sport is skiing, think about the various makes and models of skis that skiers at your level of expertise generally use. You are to select from the range of equipment the two most likely choices (makes and models) for people wanting to get involved in the activity, and you are to compare or contrast them. You must use at least three different characteristics or questions as your standards for comparison. In your conclusion, you must make a recommendation to your reader as to which equipment option is most suited to the reader's needs.

Political Science: For your next paper, you will be examining some of the statements made by politicians in your district in the recent congressional election. In particular, you will be identifying and analyzing one specific "plank" in a party platform and discussing it in terms of the issue(s) it purports to address. You may use statistical information and other secondary material in addressing the issues in your paper. Your paper must be at least 1,000 words, and must deal very clearly with the issues as you have outlined them to your reader.

OPEN TOPICS

Occasionally, you may get an assignment that seems to be open-ended. An instructor may mention a subject or issue and leave you to take some specific part of it that interests you and that you can explain well in the space available. You may be given an opportunity to "find something that interests you, and write about it." As a result, open topics such as the ones below will force you to take a more active role in your own writing process. In considering these topics, don't worry about specifics; look at each in terms of the latitude afforded the writer. How might you deal with such topics?

Literature: Choose a short poem by a living American poet whose work interests you, and analyze it. You may take any approach you wish, as long as your approach is clear to your reader. Your paper should be about 750-1,000 words long.

Composition: You will write an essay in which you will explain or teach a process of some kind to the reader. The process you select may be an instructional process, a natural process, or a mechanical process. For example, you might be explaining the process by which one tunes a guitar; you might be telling the reader about the steps in photosynthesis, the process by which plants extract energy from sunlight; or you might be explaining what happens inside your computer when you tell it to save a file to disk. Your process essay should be 500-750 words.

History: For your first paper, you will select an historic event that occurred in the twentieth century and speculate as to its most significant effect or effects. You must choose a single important event that you can describe to your reader. Your paper should be approximately 1,000 words.

Political Science: For your first paper, you will select an established economic or social policy of the state government, and discuss it in terms of what you see as its merits or disadvantages for various citizens' groups in the state. Your paper should be approximately 1,000 words.

These topics allow so much latitude that many student writers may have problems identifying clearly what they are supposed to do. An open topic may not provide many express clues to help you refine it so that it will be manageable. As a result, you may have to take extra time *before* you start working on the paper in order to be certain about specifics.

You'll probably have to write essays that span the range between closed and open topics. You'll find that you're able to cope more effectively with an assignment once you have learned to assess the degree to which the topic is open or closed. Your sense of a topic and its requirements will determine how you should proceed with your planning and writing. In order to determine your starting point and to be able to generate useful ideas, you must learn to read topics properly. Only then will you be able to work with effective idea-generating strategies.

READING TOPICS

Have you ever been annoyed by the ease with which some people seem to generate ideas? It doesn't seem to matter whether they are speaking or writing; it doesn't even matter what subject or focus they are considering. They just seem to be able to think on their feet, and to develop and express interesting ideas clearly and logically. They point out connections between concepts or events; they make meaningful comparisons from which you learn valuable lessons. They explain so clearly how to do something that you feel you could do it right away, without difficulty.

Most of us aren't able to generate ideas quite so easily, and it isn't unusual for student writers to feel some anxiety when they have trouble generating ideas on a subject. You shouldn't be too worried about this, since you can overcome it by taking a more active and inquiring role in the writing process. Many of us have been conditioned to be passive learners and writers; consumers of ideas rather than producers of ideas. This is a pattern we can change. The way to deal with the anxiety and get the ideas flowing is to adopt some strategies you can use consistently in developing your subject. You might need an actual topic idea, or you might need some ideas you can use to elaborate on a point or topic you already have in hand. Your topic might be open or very specific.

So, how should you begin the process of identifying topics?

⇨ *You can't do anything meaningful with an essay assignment until you understand clearly what the assignment requires of you.* ⇦

You must find answers to critical questions. You must be very careful to define essential terms of reference and to find an approach that suits the topic. All of these things will depend on your reading of the assignment. Reading assignments accurately is a skill which involves carefully examining the structure and wording of assignment topics. It also requires you to interpret topics in light of the material you have been covering in the course, and to avoid making unwarranted assumptions about key aspects of the subject or question you're to address. Your reading will allow you to determine the degree of openness in the topic. Based on your understanding, you must be willing to ask for clarification when you need it, since the success of your essay depends on the accuracy of your reading.

Read the assignment carefully and objectively; avoid assumptions

When you're given an assignment, read it carefully. Try to explain the topic to yourself clearly, in terms an unsophisticated audience might understand. You might even want to try writing a paraphrase of the assignment—a kind of translation in which you put the assignment into your own words. If you can't do this, ask for immediate clarification. In your reading, be open-minded, even if you already have some opinions about the subject matter.

⇨ *Try to avoid making assumptions based on your current knowledge or opinions of the material.* ⇦

If you make incorrect assumptions about key aspects of the assignment even before you've started to prepare it, your efforts may be wasted. Remember that the assignment actually sets up a kind of testing situation—part of the test is to determine whether you'll approach the assignment objectively.

Let's consider an example. Suppose you're given the following topic in a literature class:

> The Romantic poets gave being to the vision of the archetypal Hero—not only in their poetry, but in their own lives. They were preoccupied with dark and mysterious journeys, and with the hidden magic in the natural world and in the realms of imagination and emotion. Blake's eidetic vision, Byron's undying passion, the lyrical music of Shelley and Keats—all exemplify the magic and mysticism of the Romantics. In your next paper, you will select a single work by one of the Romantic poets on your reading list and do a critical analysis of it. You will find it useful to make some inquiry into the life of the poet in order to have a clear sense of the intent of the poem.

Some students may become intimidated when they see a topic like this one in a literature course. The assignment uses some difficult and potentially confusing words and phrases. Some of the words have specific meanings in literary study, though you may not recognize the special meanings on your first reading. There seems to be a clear bias expressed in the assignment as well: it expresses acceptance of the view that a knowledge of the poet's life is important to your appreciation of the poet's individual works. This is a clear cue to you, the prospective critic; you would be foolish to ignore it. Similarly, the instructor seems to think highly of the poets named in the assignment. They won't be the only poets on your reading list, so you're going to have to decide whether there is an advantage to be gained by choosing a work by one of the named poets. The assignment also reflects some other assumptions about the subject matter—assumptions you might have to test before you try to write anything. What exactly is "eidetic vision?" Why has the assignment characterized the works of the Romantics in terms of "magic and mysticism?" Why have the works of Shelley and Keats been characterized as "lyrical?"

Reread the assignment; highlight important or confusing words and phrases

Let's look at the topic again. This time, we will emphasize critical or potentially ambiguous terms. These are terms which you should recognize as important to your grasp of the assignment, whether or not you know what they actually mean at this point.

The <u>Romantic</u> poets gave being to the <u>vision</u> of the <u>archetypal Hero</u>—not only in their poetry, <u>but in their own lives</u>. They were <u>preoccupied</u> with <u>dark</u> and <u>mysterious journeys</u>, and with the <u>hidden magic</u> in the <u>natural world</u> and in the realms of <u>imagination</u> and emotion. <u>Blake's eidetic vision</u>, <u>Byron</u>'s undying passion, the <u>lyrical</u> music of <u>Shelley</u> and <u>Keats</u>—all exemplify the <u>magic and mysticism</u> of the Romantics. In your next paper, you will select a single work by one of the Romantic poets on your reading list and do a <u>critical analysis</u> of it. <u>You will find it useful to make some inquiry into the life of the poet in order to have a clear sense of the intent of the poem.</u>

There's quite a bit going on here. You should have flagged in your reading the terms that are underlined, as these are the terms that will help you understand the bases from which the instructor prepared the assignment. An understanding of the expressions used can help you get a sense of the period and the poets.

You've read—and reread—the assignment, and you've identified the key terminology. If your vocabulary in the subject area and your sense of the material are good enough that you can explain the key words to yourself clearly and accurately, that's fine. If not, your next step should be to define all key terminology. This means looking up words in the dictionary; in the example, it also means some preliminary reading about the Romantic poets and the characteristics or qualities that made them Romantic. You must also develop an understanding of the conventions (the currently accepted ways of doing things) governing a "critical analysis" of a literary work. None of this material is hidden; in fact, it's easy to find, if you bother to look for it. Remember that this preliminary reading is not a waste of time. It's actually part of the assignment. Moreover, in the case of this example, even a little reading is going to provide considerable material that will alter your perspective and understanding, and actually provide you with multiple focal points for the assignment.

Review the assignment again; determine its degree of openness

Let's suppose that you have defined the important terms in the example. You now know what an archetype is. You know that the archetypal Hero is always on a quest; a journey that requires him to act in ways that set him apart from other people. You've discovered that the archetypal Hero often has contact with magic, black and white, and that from the Romantic point of view, there exists hidden in the wonders of the natural world a kind of spiritual, universal magic that sometimes interferes with the destiny of human beings.

You've figured out that Blake was a very strange and gifted man whose ability to "see" with his imagination separated him from other poets; but you haven't decided whether you agree with the statement that Blake actually had "eidetic vision." You understand what a lyric is, and you know that Shelley and Keats were famous for lyrical work. You've taken a book of literary criticism from the library and have read some critical analyses (admittedly by professionals), and you understand that you can't get away with simply telling what a poem says on the literal level. You're thinking about a certain poem and poet you might want to write about, but that is as far as you've gone.

Here is the next step:

> ⇨ *Determine whether, on its face, the assignment appears to be closed, or whether there is latitude for further selection and refinement.* ⇦

In the assignment, you have some expressed and implied guidelines to which you must adhere. However, you've also been allowed considerable latitude in terms of your choice of primary material, perspective, and approach. You have already chosen a poem you like, and you know you must analyze it—but from what perspective and with what critical approach? Will you look at the poem from the standpoint of technique, imagery, and metaphor? Will you approach the poem by trying to tie events and images within it to specific times or events in the poet's life? Will you focus on the Hero (if there is one) in order to examine and discuss the ways in which the poet has given form to the Hero's role in the work? All these possibilities exist—and more.

Reread the assignment yet again, being sure to think about its implied scope based on the actual words used. If your reading of the assignment suggests at least three or four possible answers or avenues of investigation, you'll usually be allowed to choose only a single avenue. You need to confirm the expected length and make a realistic assessment of your ability to provide the answers required in the space available. If you think you can't make such an assessment on your own, or if you see the possibility of the sort of latitude that exists in this assignment, you should go back to the instructor with some questions or suggestions about possible topics that fall within the assignment's scope as you see it.

> ⇨ *Even when the instructor clearly intends to provide you with options, you still need to know that the specific option or approach you decide to take is one that is appropriate.* ⇦

After all, you might choose an appropriate variation or option and handle it badly, because your understanding of it was inaccurate or incomplete. Alternatively, you might do a brilliant job with an inappropriate option or approach. Eventually, through a combination of reading, questioning, and thinking, you'll be able to decide on a specific topic and a specific approach. Once you have developed a sense of the approach you'll take, don't be shy about going back to the instructor at regular intervals. This is crucial if you lack confidence in your ability to keep refining your focus appropriately.

Ask more questions; do some directed reading

"Directed reading" means reading that is focused on the specifics of your topic or issue. In the sample assignment, you might have done some general reading on the Romantics in order to understand the wording of the assignment. If you were to choose to write about Blake's poem "The Tyger," you would focus your outside reading on material dealing only with Blake and his works. The more specific your approach and the more limited your subject or topic become, the more focused you should make any outside reading you do. As for the questions you ask your instructor (or yourself), it's natural for each question you have to give rise to several more. If you could understand everything without having to ask questions, you wouldn't be taking any courses in the first place. However, your questions should arise from reading and inquiry, or from confusion about the nature or wording of the assignment, rather than from the fact that you haven't done the assigned reading or have skipped the last four classes. Moreover, your questions should be directed toward making your subject clearer and more specific. Remember that, at this point, you're still not looking for "The Answers" to the assignment question. Those will come later, after you've figured out how (or how much) you can narrow the question or topic to get a workable focus— that is, an issue or subject or premise that is clear enough to work with. At this point, you're still refining your understanding of the situation giving rise to the question or topic.

Determine the basic writing strategy you will use

Given the wording of the assignment, determine the approaches available to you in terms of basic writing strategy. Within your critical analysis, you'll have several approaches with which you can work. On a given assignment, the instructor may direct you to a particular approach to your subject: you may be asked to compare or contrast; you may be asked to determine causes or effects; you may be asked to classify items or to explain how something works;

you may be asked to define, narrate, or describe. Each of these approaches is a basic strategy that you can use in different situations, as we'll explain in chapter 6. In our example, you might decide to compare two related images in a poem, one of which occurs at the beginning of the work and the other at the end. Using the comparison, you could analyze the poem based on the poet's treatment of the related images and the differences or similarities between them. If an assignment topic is open-ended, you'll need to make an informed and conscious decision to adopt one of these approaches as your controlling model, so that your intentions will be clear to the reader.

The skill of reading topics accurately in order to determine expectations and generate ideas is one you must practice. It depends on your sense of urgency and excitement about the subject area and on your commitment to the process of gathering, analyzing, and conveying meaningful and important information about your subject to the reader.

Exercise: Topic Reading

Below, we've restated some of the topics we presented to you when we were talking about closed and open topics at the beginning of this chapter. If you're going to develop your assignment-reading skills, you need to practice on a range of potential assignment topics and materials. These samples will provide you with a place to start; you should add them, together with any notes you make for purposes of this exercise, to your note files. We'll explain how to set these files up later in this chapter. For now, simply hang on to the material you generate for this and other exercises.

Review the steps and procedures outlined above, and then work through these topics at your own speed, being sure to focus on accurate reading and interpretation. Don't go out and do research, although some of the topics seem to require it. What you're trying to do is to develop your sense of the actual nature of the task assigned to you. So highlight key words, define terms, and go through all the other steps to arrive at what you think is an informed reading of the topic. Once you have done this, get together with at least one other student to compare your sense of each of the topics. Then try the exercise together.

Composition: For your next assignment, you'll be writing a comparison/contrast essay of approximately 750 words. You are to consider your favorite sport or hobby, in terms of the kinds of equipment required to engage in the activity. For example, if your favorite sport is skiing, you should be thinking about the various makes and models of skis generally used by skiers at your level of expertise. You are to select from the range of equipment the two most likely choices for people at your level in the activity, and you are to compare or contrast them. You must use at least three different criteria as your standards for comparison. In your conclusion, you must make a recommendation to your reader as to which option or choice is best for the purpose(s) you have discussed in your paper.

History: For your first paper, you will select an historic event that occurred in the twentieth century and speculate as to its most significant effect or effects. You must choose a single important event that you can describe to your reader. The event should be one that is significant, but not so sweeping that you can't do it justice in your essay. For example, the effects of the bombing of Hiroshima would be too much to write about, but you might be able to address a single, immediate, and very specific political repercussion of America's final military withdrawal from Vietnam. Your paper should be approximately 1,500 words.

Political Science: For your first paper, you will select an established economic or social policy of the state government, and discuss it in terms of what you see as its merits or disadvantages for particular citizens' groups in the state. Your paper should be approximately 1,000 words.

Sociology: For your next paper, you will be examining some of the pronouncements made by politicians in the recent federal election. In particular, you will be identifying and analyzing one specific social policy "plank" in a party platform and discussing it in terms of the issue(s) it purports to address. You may use statistical information and other secondary material in addressing the issues in your paper. In addition, you are expected to interview at least two members of a special interest group affected by the policy and analyze their comments within your paper. Your paper must be at least 1,500 words in length and must deal as fully as possible with the issue as you have outlined it to your reader. Thus, you must be clear and specific in describing the issue and the policy that addresses it.

STIMULATING THE FLOW OF IDEAS

Writing is work; so is the planning stage you go through when you're preparing to write. Many students find that ideas will begin to flow smoothly and easily once they understand an assignment or subject clearly. At other times the ideas don't flow painlessly, and some students may be tempted to abandon a central idea or approach as a result. Don't give in to this temptation too easily—even seasoned professional writers wrestle with false starts, crumpled notes, headaches and mental blanks. This problem will continue to plague writers, though changes in technology have made it easier for some writers to overcome aspects of the problem. For others, the advent of word-processing software has meant simply that they can enjoy their frustration in a more streamlined way.

Composition textbooks are full of techniques and strategies you can use to stimulate the flow of ideas, whether you're looking for a generalized subject within which to focus, or working to develop ideas to flesh out the structure of a paper. You may bring some ideas of your own to the writing task because you're interested in the subject or have done some work with it in the past. If you're working on an actual essay assignment, you may have developed some good ideas during your reading of the topic. Even if you haven't, you can use the techniques discussed below to "unfreeze" your mental muscles. These techniques actually work; and the more you work with them, the better they work.

Prepare brainstorming lists

"Brainstorming" is a commonly used term. It refers to a technique you can use in any subject area or discipline to develop ideas, define approaches, and test or determine relationships. When you're having trouble determining the specifics or scope of your subject in a paper, you can try brainstorming.

Brainstorming involves making idea lists based on a single idea or concept as a starting point. You aren't concerned with exploring each and every idea that occurs to you or with refining any particular point. What you want to do is to keep the list growing, without regard for grammar and punctuation. The ideas in your brainstorming lists will be particularly useful when you're looking for material to insert into the model we will show you in chapter 5.

Exercise: Brainstorming

This exercise requires you to brainstorm in order to generate lists of ideas around three key words or phrases. You want at least three lists, and you should allow yourself five minutes to generate each list. When you have finished, don't throw your lists away—save them for storage in the note files we'll be discussing in a moment. Your key words are: (1) welfare; (2) procrastination; and (3) housing.

When you prepare your lists, don't get fancy—use the key words as the headings. If you decide you need a subheading, keep it to one or two words. List your ideas vertically under the key-word headings in point form. You can create as many lists as you need.

Keep note files

Unless you have a very disciplined and orderly mind, you'll find ideas occurring to you at the most inconvenient times—in the middle of the night, while you're taking your morning shower, during that lunch date you've been anticipating, or in the middle of a class. You may promise yourself to remember the ideas that occur at these moments, but most people rarely seem to keep the promise. Even if you can remember the general outline of an idea for a paper, your memory of it is never as clear, immediate, or forceful as the original idea at the moment it occurred to you.

It's also very easy, especially when you're under pressure, to get caught up with re-inventing the wheel in approaching essay assignments. You may have already found that assignments given in a subject from year to year tend to overlap or have striking similarities. You may have had the experience of searching frantically through that old cardboard box into which you dumped all your materials from last year or the year before. You were hot on the trail of an old paper, some course notes, some material in a text, or a journal entry you made. You may have been given a new assignment, and it suddenly occurred to you that if only you could find that particular piece of material, you could easily adapt it for your current purposes. Sometimes you find it—and sometimes you don't. Why leave it to chance?

➪ | *When it comes to writing, be reluctant to throw anything away.* | ⬅

Unless they're illegible or unintelligible, keep all your rough notes, outlines, plans, course materials, rough scratchings, old assignment questions, clippings, and the like. When you begin to have too much stuff to handle easily, you can summarize key points and rewrite more tersely, and you can go through the material to eliminate duplication.

Whatever you decide to keep, you should put into note files. Organize the material in any way that seems logical: by course, by subject, by time, by type of material. Update your note files regularly, and keep a separate section for new assignments. There's nothing wrong with "lifting" from these note files of your own material and applying or adapting it for purposes of another assignment. You might be using it for generating new ideas, choosing or clarifying a subject or specific topic, gathering support, or developing key points. Whatever you use it for, you'll find that it will drastically short-cut the time you would otherwise have spent on the idea-generation phase. You'll also find that you can keep a large file with notes about ideas that were interesting, but that did not relate to any particular assignment.

A word of caution is appropriate here. When you use any material that you personally did not write, you're always under an obligation with respect to proper citation of sources. We'll deal with this issue in more detail when we discuss research and citation systems, but you should be aware of at least one basic fact: plagiarism constitutes academic misconduct in *every* post-secondary academic institution. So use your stored material to generate ideas, to find topics, and to identify support, but NEVER let your reader come to the conclusion that the material originated with you if that is not actually the case.

Use a series of free-writing sessions

Free-writing is similar to brainstorming, though it's actually less structured. It involves a kind of forced writing, in which you set a time-frame for yourself. During the predetermined period, you write non-stop about anything that pops into your head, even if you think it's absolute garbage. It's a bit like searching through a junkyard: buried with the rubble and junk, you're likely to find some valuable material.

Begin free-writing without any preconceptions. Set an egg-timer or a wristwatch alarm for five minutes. Once the timer starts to run, don't take your pen from the page, <u>and don't stop</u> during the entire period. Don't stop or slow down to change what you've written. When you've finished, examine the results—they should provide you with several possibilities.

Exercise: Free-writing

Students are frequently surprised by the material they generate in free-writing sessions. Free-writing tends to be like a kind of written free-association exercise, in which you get to relate ideas without constraint or structure. You can generate material that may ultimately supply you with several potential topics or areas of consideration, so most of your free-writing notes should end up in one of your note files. In this exercise, you're to go through the free-writing experience. Remember that, for this technique, you'll need a clock or kitchen timer.

<u>Initial free-writing session</u>: You'll start with a five-minute session. Set the timer, start it running, and begin your session. Write down anything that occurs to you. If a particular subject seems uppermost in your mind, that's fine, as long as you keep writing. It doesn't matter if most of what you say turns out to be nonsense—just keep going.

<u>Second free-writing session</u>: This time you'll reduce the session length to three minutes. Before you start, read over your notes from the first session. Choose a single idea that appeared in your material from the first session. This will be your focus. Set the timer; get on with it. Continue to write down whatever occurs to you, but have as your one control the need to make connections (however bizarre or illogical) with the area you identified from your first-session materials.

<u>Third free-writing session</u>: Repeat the process, keeping the length of the session at three minutes and focusing on one of the ideas from the second session. Remember: review your notes from all three sessions in order to decide what should go into your note files.

Use diagrams

Diagrams provide an alternative approach to the problem of idea generation. Diagramming looks different from brainstorming and free-writing, although to some extent the differences are created with smoke and mirrors. Diagramming will get you to the same place in terms of idea generation—it just gets you there by a different route. It involves using a visual model to identify and relate concepts, groups, individuals, items, attributes, qualities, experiences, or characteristics. Some students seem to feel more comfortable with a visual model because it lets them see all the components they are working with.

When you diagram, you're essentially starting with a bare visual layout which will let you fill in information and establish connections between ideas. If you start by working with a large square on a sheet of paper, you can divide the square into quadrants, with a key concept from your reading of an assignment in the center as your starting focus. From there, you can take the same approach that the brainstormer takes. Develop four aspects of the central idea, and assign one of the four to each quadrant of the square. In each quadrant, list as many related ideas as you can. If you discover that you have too many ideas or not enough room on your diagram, then either use a bigger piece of paper, or choose the key word or concept from the most promising quadrant of your dia-

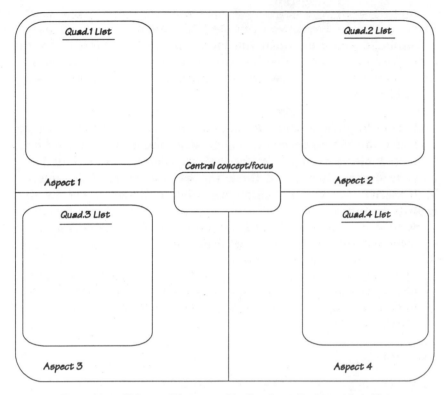

Figure 2-1: Using a Diagram with Quadrant Brainstorming Lists

gram and make it the core of a new diagram. If you use the technique correctly, you'll find that you will soon reach a point at which you want to begin using phrases or sentences rather than key words. That's good—that's what is supposed to happen.

When you diagram properly, you'll find that each diagram you produce will reveal scores of ideas, some of which will be general and some particularized. You should keep reminding yourself to do two things. First, expend the most energy on those parts that seem to be the most promising in terms of the subject area. Otherwise, you're going to end up trying to cover everything, and this is a temptation you must resist. Second, keep your best diagrams—including those you did not use for the current assignment—in your note files. These will often save you from having to start from scratch on other apparently unrelated assignments.

Exercise: Using Diagrams

In order to see whether you can use diagrams effectively, try a diagramming exercise in which you focus on three key words of your own choosing. Select individual words, not phrases. Prepare a diagram for each of the key words; and remember that you'll be doing something very similar to brainstorming. The point is to see if the visual model works better for you in fulfilling the same purpose as brainstorming. Make your own copy of the blank diagram in figure 2-1, and don't be shy about using all available space or adding lines and divisions that you feel are appropriate. Once you have completed diagrams for all three key words, compare the quality and usefulness of the result with what you developed in the brainstorming exercise.

Remember that the use of diagrams is another device you have at your disposal. It doesn't control your writing process. You can do much with it, as with brainstorming and free-writing, as long as you keep it in perspective: you're generating ideas for the purpose of shaping and refining your message to your reader. The clarity and the accuracy of that message are, as always, your ultimate goals.

3
The Need For Narrowing

Narrowing means you can discuss <u>thoroughly</u> the material you are writing about in the space that you have to write about it.

Narrowing refers to the process by which you take a general subject area, an open topic, or a partially closed topic and make it both clearer and more specific. Familiarity with this process is critical to your success as a writer of essays. Sometimes, you may be given a broad essay topic and told that you must write on the topic exactly as it is presented to you. Except in such cases, you should proceed on the following assumption:

> *Your essay requires a subject small enough to define clearly and precisely. You can then take a position with respect to it and discuss that position completely and in detail, according to conditions you set for yourself and your reader.*

Why should I narrow?

There are many reasons why you should want to make certain that the focus of your paper is narrow, clear, and specific. Most of the reasons flow from the nature and purposes of the college or university undergraduate essay and the conventions and expectations governing essay form. Remember what we said earlier: the essay is, among other things, an artificial testing device. It provides a structure or form through which you may show your ability to analyze, explain, or interpret particular bodies of subject knowledge and express your views on a subject.

The essay tests you on how accurately you read, how well you write, and how intelligently you respond to key issues. In order for you to satisfy the requirements of an essay assignment, you must have sufficient grasp of your subject to be able to discuss it thoroughly in the space available to you. You also have to be curious about unexplored questions related to the subject. You must ask intelligent questions of yourself, as part of the assignment. You'll have to focus on a single issue or series of issues within the essay framework. Without the ability to narrow your material or your focus properly, you may have some trouble convincing your reader that you have a sound command of the subject matter. For example, one of your obligations is to do a thorough and complete job— will you be able to fulfill this obligation if you try to discuss the major theories of the origins of the universe in 1,000 words? Given the centuries of thought and writing devoted to the problem of the origin of the universe, it's unlikely that you'll resolve it in so short a space. Effective narrowing will help you start your essays from a clear, detailed and specific premise.

On its face, narrowing sounds like a simple process, and it can be. Unfortunately, some students have been conditioned to write in a way that interferes with the narrowing process and is counterproductive in the college or university setting. For example, if you were able to get an "A" on a high-school assignment requiring you to discuss the three major effects of World War II in 500 words, you would have learned what NOT to do in a freshman essay.

At the university level, you can be sure that your instructors know more than you do about the subject; you can't snow them with vague or unsupported generalizations. Because your instructors know their subject areas and were themselves successful as students, they'll approach reading and evaluating your work with certain expectations. They'll expect you to meet two thresholds, or minimum levels of competence—one concerned with grammar, punctuation, and structure, and the other with content. At the very least, they'll expect your analysis, explanation, or treatment of a topic to be an examination of a clearly defined issue, presented in concise and specific terms, and based on specific evidence or supporting material. They'll also expect that you have narrowed to a level of meaningful inquiry.

⇨   *If you have narrowed your focus properly, you will probably have reached the edge of your subject knowledge.*   ⇦

That is, you'll have to deal with aspects of content that you have not yet mastered, or find out about things you don't yet know, in order to write the essay. After all, if you already knew everything the course required of you, you wouldn't be taking the course. Moreover, college and university instructors are unlikely to be impressed with simple parroting of lectures or material from the course text. They expect to see you working with specific issues in constructive ways and supporting your views clearly and sensibly. They'll expect you to use an essay assignment to prove that you are an active learner and writer, rather than a passive one.

Obviously, if you accept the premise that a narrow focus is a requirement, you're going to have concerns about any assignment topic that doesn't absolutely lock you in to a narrow and clearly worded issue or question. (You should remember what we said earlier about the nature of open and closed assignments, and think back to the discussion of how to read an assignment.) As you develop skill in the area of topic reading, you'll realize that even those assignments that are quite structured still allow some slack for topic refinement. Thus, you'll often have to exercise your ability to narrow your focus appropriately. Where the assignment is clearly open, the issue of narrowing may be one of the primary criteria on which you will be evaluated. If you don't narrow, you can't do the assignment—and your instructor knows it. Thus, you must always address the question of narrowing.

How narrow is narrow?

This is a difficult question because the answer to it may change depending on subject, course level, your current skills levels, the emphasis in the course, and other factors. The best we can say is that, after years of teaching and reading undergraduate papers, we have yet to see an undergraduate essay in which the focus was both appropriate *and* too narrow. On the other hand, we have seen a great many papers in which the focus was too broad or too vaguely expressed.

Looking for a narrow focus within a given subject area is something like peeling an onion. There are layers built upon layers, and the layers tend to come off in your fingers one at a time. The onion keeps shrinking, but you are never quite certain exactly how many layers are left or exactly what they look like. It's easy to give in to the temptation to stop peeling too soon, especially if it looks like the onion is getting too small to be useful. Most students make some attempt to narrow the focus of their inquiries; but they frequently stop narrowing too soon. They identify a focus that looks as if it will fit with the model or conceptual structure required by a given assignment, but they fail to look at their own assumptions about the subject or their reader's current knowledge and need for specificity.

For example, suppose you have been reading Arthur Miller's play, *Death of a Salesman*. If you are given a 750- to 1,000-word open assignment on the play, you might find yourself trying to discuss "what leads to Willy Loman's downfall." It's true that this focuses on a single character who meets a tragic end; but there is so much going on in the play that you would need quite a bit more than 1,000 words to discuss everything that led to Willy's downfall. Your assumption that limiting your discussion to a single character will be sufficient is, in fact, incorrect. You would be far better to pick a single moment in the play as your focus, like the moment in the kitchen scene near the end of the play when Biff embraces Willy and the latter is unable to return the embrace. This is a significant moment that you could examine in a variety of ways, and it would provide a real means of limiting the scope of your discussion.

There isn't an absolute standard for narrowness. You'll learn through practice just how far you need to go in order to be able to meet your obligations. You'll come to understand that your degree of focus will depend on the level of content knowledge and the extent of inquiry expected of you, and on the level of your readers' knowledge about and understanding of your topic. Given the lack of any kind of objective, quantifiable standard for narrowing, you might want to follow this simple rule:

> *When you're trying to narrow your focus, keep going until you think you're overdoing it. When you think you are nitpicking, you have probably narrowed your focus sufficiently.*

NARROWING & YOUR OBLIGATIONS TO YOUR READER

When you write an essay in college or university, you must meet some basic standards or obligations to your reader that have little to do with specific courses or disciplines; the standards apply to all your essays. Before you can learn to narrow your subjects consistently and appropriately, you must have a clear sense of these obligations.

Just what are your obligations to your reader, and how do they relate to the issue of narrowing your focus? There are several key qualities or attributes that must be present in your work. Each essay must have a single clear focus; your work must be credible or believable; it must reflect your sense of appropriateness in the subject area; it must be thorough and complete; it must be internally consistent; and it must provide the reader with relevant and non-trivial information. While these standards tend to overlap to some extent, you'll see that it is impossible to meet any one of them unless you can effectively narrow the scope of your work. We're going to consider each one of these elements; and in our discussion, we'll use examples drawn from a single topic. Here is the topic:

> Write a 750-word essay in which you discuss some aspect of the problem of computer viruses for today's home computer users.

You need a single, clear focus

Have you ever read a paper or article in which the author appeared to jump from subject to subject in such a way that you ended up unsure of what the work was about? If you have, or if you've ever had an instructor write on your own work that you were trying to cover too much material, you've had problems with this standard. The terms "unity" and "specificity" are often used to refer to this attribute of effective writing. Your essay meets this standard when it focuses on one clearly defined subject and addresses the topic and purpose you suggest to the reader in your introductory material. Your obligation to your reader is to provide a meaningful discussion around a single, clear focus which you must be able to cover in the space available to you. You must express your specific subject precisely, so that you don't create uncertainty in the mind of the reader about what you're really trying to do. If you express your focus vaguely, your reader may misunderstand your intentions or conclude that your subject is too broad.

Think for a moment of our computer virus example; this is an open topic. If you try to write about computer viruses generally, you could get caught discussing the various viruses that can attack a home computer, the forms of damage the viruses might do, and the reasons why the home computer user should care about all these problems. If you did some reading on the subject, you would find that 750 words wouldn't even be enough to list the names of currently existing viruses. The topic isn't limited yet. In order to say anything meaningful and useful about this topic to your reader, you would have to confine it in some way. You might choose a single virus and try to deal with it in terms of three or four areas of importance to a particular group of home users. For example, you might decide to tell home users of small-business accounting packages about three ways in which the "Joshi" family of viruses can ruin their programs and data. The virus and its importance to these users would become the single focus of your paper. The features or effects you chose to discuss in the main part of the essay would have to convince your reader that the virus does create some particular problems for the specified group. If, during the course of your essay, you went into a lengthy discussion of the best places to buy virus-free software, then you would have created a unity problem, since this issue does not directly relate to the importance of the virus to the user group. It would be inappropriate to broaden the scope of your discussion in this way. Similarly, if you were to introduce a body of supporting material that had more to do with video displays than with the virus, you would be creating further problems.

> *If your essay deals with some subject or subjects other that the one you present to the reader as your focus, then it will lack unity and specificity.*

If one of your supporting units or paragraphs deals with material that isn't relevant to your central focus in some direct way—or supports some point other than the one you're trying to make—your paper will lack unity and specificity. Nor would these deficiencies be the only ones created by the lack of a single, clear focus.

The broader and less defined your focus is, the more likely you are to encounter such problems. Troubles with unity and specificity arise as a direct result of a writer's lack of adequate narrowing before she started to write the paper. On the other hand, if your focus is narrow, clear, and coherent, you'll have met the first of your obligations to the reader. In every essay, define a single focus that you can actually cover in the space available to you, and be certain to make the reader aware of the intended scope of your discussion.

Your work must be believable

In planning your essays, you may occasionally find yourself pursuing an inappropriate approach or an idea that isn't really relevant for the purpose of a particular assignment. You may be considering a focus for which there is no meaningful evidence or support available. Even if you can express a proposition narrowly and clearly, you may find yourself trying to argue for a proposition that no one in his right mind would accept. If you do this, your work will lack credibility—that is, it won't be believable. For example, if you were to narrow the computer virus topic so that your focus was the idea that only cloned computers (computers compatible with the products of the biggest manufacturers) could be afflicted with viruses, you would be dealing with a subject for which there is no evidence or support. If you argued that computer users who took aspirin were less likely to have viruses invade their computer systems, you would have selected a focus that no reasonable reader would consider seriously. In either case, your work would not be credible, even though it might be clearly written and grammatically perfect.

A lack of credibility is serious, and will hurt you in two ways. If your paper lacks credibility, the reader may assume that nothing you say in the paper can be trusted. A lack of authenticity or believability will quickly spread from one part of an essay to the other parts, and you won't get the kind of reader response you wanted. This is serious enough; but if the same readers are likely to be seeing your work again and again, those readers may begin to make judgments about your credibility as a writer and may begin to form expectations about any written work you do. Thus, if the focus of your first paper isn't credible, and the supporting material you offer in your second paper isn't credible, you'll be sending a clear message to the reader: "Don't believe what I say in my writing—my arguments are suspect, my evidence is shaky."

You can ensure that your work is believable by selecting and refining specific topics that your reader will see as acceptable in the subject or course, and by spending time carefully selecting supporting materials and presenting them accurately, in context. This may mean relying on statements by established authorities or doing research—even where none is required under an assignment's terms. It may also mean choosing specific topics that have some real, acknowledged meaning and validity, even if such topics are difficult. We're not saying that your focus or viewpoint must always be correct or that your supporting material or examples must always be perfect and unassailable. We are saying that when you write an essay, you must appear to be realistic and honest, and you must try to take a defensible position for which you can offer reasonable arguments, evidence, and details.

Your selection and handling of subject and material must be appropriate

It's important to have a clear understanding of just what constitutes appropriateness. Appropriateness relates to your obligation to provide something believable or credible for your reader, and your obligation to deal with a real subject in a non-trivial, meaningful way. It also relates to grammar, tone, punctuation, and style. Appropriateness is what you get when the focus of an essay and the approach you took in handling it seem to fit together in communicating your message to your audience. Your work also shows appropriateness when the body of the essay provides the best possible support for your focus or position, given your specific purpose and the characteristics of your audience.

Appropriateness relates to believability, especially with respect to the basic nature of your topic on a given assignment. Except in circumstances where you're expressly told by an instructor that you can invent evidence or work with a nonsense topic, your choice of focus must also be appropriate in the context of the subject discipline. That is, your topic must be one that readers recognize as addressing a legitimate issue or question in the subject area, a question or issue that reflects important points of emphasis in your course materials. Thus, it's inappropriate for you to narrow an open English assignment on "Animals" by focusing on alternative methods of teaching porcupines to fly, or on raising piranha by feeding them domestic pets. Neither of these issues is worthy of serious consideration within the specified area. Neither is credible; neither is appropriate. A platitude-filled discussion of "why the dog is man's best friend" is also likely to be considered inappropriate because it seems (at least on first glance) to be clichéd and trivial. In our computer virus topic, it would be appropriate to narrow to the single most dangerous virus, and to discuss it in terms of its most significant effect on the systems of a particular group of users. Since you're dealing with home users, it would also be appropriate to avoid computer jargon, and to use a level of language that would be clear and non-technical.

When you write an essay, your ability to select appropriate topics and supporting material is part of the task on which you'll be evaluated by instructors. You also must ensure that grammar, diction, and tone are appropriate to the subject and to your reader's level of knowledge and sophistication. Effective narrowing doesn't guarantee a well-written and appropriate essay; but lack of effective narrowing does guarantee lack of essay quality and appropriateness.

You must cover your subject thoroughly and completely

Students are regularly told that their written work must be complete; they must cover their essay topics or themes thoroughly. This is admirable advice, since no reader is impressed with a partial job, sketchy facts, inadequate evidence, or unanswered questions. Many students interpret this advice to mean that they must answer every question and say absolutely everything they can find regarding a given topic. This often creates unity problems; worse still, if you don't narrow properly, then by definition you <u>can't</u> do a complete and thorough job. Common sense suggests that if you narrow only to the level of a subject or question on which there are dozens of books and articles available, you may have a problem providing the reader with something meaningful, believable, and complete in 500 or 1,000 words. Thus, in the computer virus assignment, if you decided to write about "Computer Viruses and Their Dangers" in a 500-word essay, it would be impossible for you to cover your subject thoroughly and completely.

You must be very clear that completeness will be measured against the task you set for yourself when you narrow and define the focus of the paper.

> *If you do not narrow the focus to something clear and specific which you can discuss fully in the space available, then you cannot do a thorough job or meet the standard of completeness.*

When you let the reader see the focus of your paper, the reader is entitled to expect that you'll cover all aspects of that focus that you haven't ruled out. The more hidden areas there are, the less likely it is that your paper will be complete.

Your writing must be logical and internally consistent

When you take a position on an issue, discuss a particular idea, or present a point of view in an essay, your reader's acceptance of that position or point of view will depend largely on your ability to present logical arguments in a logical sequence. If the reader is unable to see the logic in the writer's development of major points, or if material is presented in an illogical order, the reader may not accept your position. For example, if you begin your essay on the premise that a particular computer virus is intended to attack only certain kinds of data files, and the first part of your discussion sets out a conclusion that a particular program is more virus-resistant than other programs, the reader won't grasp the logic that led you to that conclusion at that point in your essay. You can't afford to draw conclusions unrelated to the evidence presented or to the premise of the essay; nor can you make unexplained, contradictory statements.

You must take pains to ensure that the logic behind your presentation in an essay is clear to your reader, that the ideas and evidence are in a logical sequence, and that the paper is internally consistent. This basic principle or standard remains true even for those assignments in which an instructor has expressly asked you to take an odd or unrealistic position, address an implausible topic, or use made-up evidence or supporting material. Even in such cases, the internal logic of your paper must appear to the reader to work. You must deliver on any commitments you make to your readers, and you can't rely on the implausibility of a topic or the invention of false evidence to validate or justify for inclusion anything that pops into your head. Thus, if you've been assigned an essay that focuses on the correct procedure for putting diapers on large mammals, you must rely on support or argument that is logical within the context of that topic. Your reader must be able to conclude that if your premise were real and true, your discussion, support, and conclusion would follow logically and naturally from that premise.

Your subject must be relevant and non-trivial

Relevance relates to both appropriateness and credibility. Many times in your career as a student, you may have picked up some material to read and become annoyed because the material addressed a trivial or irrelevant issue, or didn't tell you anything you didn't already know. You're right to become annoyed—your time is valuable to you, and you're entitled to expect that what you read will give you information you need. At the very least, the things you read should provide you with new or alternative viewpoints about things you do know or are currently studying. Your reader is, of course, entitled to the same consideration from you. Therefore, you should make it a rule never to waste the reader's valuable time. When you're writing for a large or diverse audience, you have to look carefully at your focus and your supporting material, and consider your basic approach. Are you giving your readers meaningful information? That information might not change their minds about an important, contentious area of concern, but it should certainly get them thinking about what you see as key issues.

What about content value when the reader is actually your instructor? The likelihood that you'll surprise your instructor with some totally new and hitherto undiscovered information about your topic is slim. However, in view of the nature of the essay as a testing device, you must build into each assignment enough content value to convince the instructor that you understand and can apply the concepts and operative principles relating to your focus. In essence, the essay provides you with a vehicle by which you'll demonstrate your ability to offer insights and to work with new and relevant concepts in a meaningful way. As we said earlier, if you're working with the process properly, essay assignments will regularly bring you to the edge of your content knowledge. To give the reader some meaningful material, you may have to explore areas that are new to you. When you "go over the edge," you'll be much more likely to convince your instructor that you're dealing appropriately with content issues in your work and that you're learning something in the course.

These are your obligations to your reader; you should try to address them in each essay you write. In order to do so in a meaningful and consistent way, you must have properly narrowed the focus in each assignment.

HOW DO I NARROW?

Occasionally, you may read an assignment and conclude that it's too broad for you to handle, or that you'll have to do some considerable refining in order to complete the work in the required space. There are many techniques you can use to help you narrow your focus, though not all of these techniques work for all students. Some students prefer to work with linear logic; others like to see ideas in terms of images and spatial relationships. Some techniques may work better than others. Some may not work for you at all, depending on your learning style, your present skills levels and your degree of enthusiasm for the task. As long as you understand clearly that you must work on narrowing the focus of your writing, you should be able to find at least one technique that works well for you. We're going to limit our discussion to two techniques or approaches that you might find workable. You'll find that when you apply either of these approaches properly to a given topic area, you can work your way to a narrow focus. In fact, you could apply each of these methods to the same area and end up with the same narrow focus, even though you might have arrived there by different routes.

Ask yourself a repetitive cycle of questions

Once you've done a thorough reading of an assignment, one of the easiest ways to narrow your focus is to use a repeating cycle of questions, applying them to a more and more restricted field of response. You ask questions; you get answers. You select the most promising answer, and ask the questions again—about that answer. The questions are the obvious ones that logic and common sense would dictate: who, what, where, when, why, for whom, to whom, under what circumstances? However, you're doing more than merely asking questions. You're making deliberate selections as to the answers you get, and you're focusing on individual answers for the purpose of asking the same questions over again—about those specific answers.

Let's consider an example. We'll start from the premise that your English instructor, who happens to be interested in ecology and conservation, has asked you to do a short essay on some issue relating to the forestry industry in British Columbia in terms of conservation practice or policy. This is a sensitive subject at the time of your assignment, and the American press has been covering related issues—especially in the Pacific Northwest. The topic is open, and you have determined, by analyzing the wording of the assignment and speaking with the instructor, that no particular approach is required. You're simply to find an issue within the topic area and deal with it effectively in 750-1,000 words. You begin from the premise that your paper will be about some aspect of the forest industry's logging practices. We'll also assume that you are the sort of person who listens to the daily news, reads newspapers, and is in possession of some basic information about current events.

What forest industry logging practices will you address? This is the easiest question to start with. Given the technological sophistication of modern forestry and the needs of differing markets, you can be certain that there will be more than one well-defined and controversial logging practice in use in B.C. Because there has been so much controversy about forestry and conservation generally, you won't have a difficult time finding out the current buzz-words for the sorts of logging practices that might be suitable. You can also be certain there will be more than one large company engaged in forestry in British Columbia, especially since the industry is recognized as one of the province's most important resource industries. Who is doing what? Is there one company whose practices you could examine, based on the names you've heard in the news? Has someone allegedly committed some flagrant violations of policy or practice? Is there, in fact, a company or group that acts as a kind of public relations agency for one or more of the forestry companies in the province? Is there a dispute about whether some practice or practices should be implemented or permitted in the province? Given our assumptions about your familiarity with current events and your willingness to read about the broader issues, you should be able to answer "yes" to each of these questions. However, you don't want to deal with all of them—after all, you are trying to narrow. You recall hearing on a news broadcast that some companies engage in a practice called clear-cutting, and that this particular practice has created considerable controversy. You aren't exactly sure what clear-cutting is or why it has so many people upset; but you know that you can find out easily, especially because there has been so much controversy about it.

What exactly is clear-cutting? When you visit the library to do some preliminary reading, you'll probably look through the subject index to find information about the forest industry and its practices; you might look in the dictionary or in a general encyclopedia. You're after some information about the nature of clear-cutting, so again you engage in a cycle of questions: how does clear-cutting work and why is it considered problematic? You find that the process involves the effective stripping, right to the ground, of the area to be logged. It also involves the building of roads through rugged areas. You also find that there are usually old-growth trees and mountain rivers or streams in the areas to be logged. These areas tend to be the habitat of a variety of animal or avian species (some of them said to be endangered). You discover that clear-cutting makes the logged area look terrible; but you also find that some reforestation does occur and that some industry authorities say the results of clear-cutting "look worse than they really are."

Who has been engaging in clear-cutting, and what is their rationale for doing so? Your preliminary reading and the daily news will provide you with information, as will a call to any local branch of a conservation group. There are several major companies and a large number of smaller companies engaged in clear-cut logging in the province. You ask more questions: who are the major players, and who is the most obvious, prominent, or important? Who has publicly defended the practice? Who has expressed a determination to continue to use it? We'll suppose that you pick on ABC Company, a huge corporation whose name has long been associated with forestry in the province. You quickly discover that ABC has used clear-cutting as one of its standard methods for many years, and they still use it today. If you're going to focus on ABC's clear-cutting practices, you'll need to confine your discussion by time and location in order to have something you can handle.

Where has ABC been using or attempting to use the clear-cutting method, and when have they been attempting to do this? Which locations have been targeted? Has the clear-cutting already occurred, or is it likely to occur soon? When? With what other interests will it conflict, and at which times and locations? Because you may be getting nearer to the edge of your subject knowledge at this point, you'll need to get some real information, even if your instructor has suggested that you needn't do any research. As we've already noted, the process of narrowing, if performed properly, will quickly bring you to this point. If you're going to meet your basic obligations to your reader, you'll have to address things you don't already know in order to provide new or meaningful information that is complete on its own and is supported credibly. Along the way, you'll learn something about the scope of the larger problem of clear-cutting; this will allow you to discuss a specific instance intelligently in a limited space.

A review of the clippings file in the library provides you with a series of newspaper articles, and you find one or two journal articles by looking through the periodical indices. You discover that there are several allegedly sensitive locations or regions in which clear-cutting has occurred or is proposed. You also find that a particularly hot controversy is raging about the logging of old-growth forest in one specific area in a region known as the Carmanah. It appears that ABC is scheduled to begin logging in the area in a matter of weeks, having received the necessary permits from the government; but several environmental groups are staging protests and there might be some serious confrontations.

Why are the opponents of clear-cutting so upset about the intended logging in this particular area of the Carmanah at this particular time? The materials you have read, while not addressing the issue in quite this way, provide you with ample information to answer this question in your own words. In fact, you find that the area to be logged happens to be the habitat for a rare and possibly endangered species of bird which can only survive in undisturbed old-growth forest, and that the population of the bird species is approaching a critical level. You also discover that there is some sort of conflict with a previously enacted provincial law dealing with parks in an adjacent area. There are immediate problems with soil erosion, other animal habitats, timber waste, and other matters. Some of these are issues on which you feel capable of expressing your opinion as a concerned individual who has a vested interest in both the environment and the health of the North American economy. You decide that you can deal effectively in about 1,000 words with the two most important reasons or justifications offered by a particular environmental group as the rationale for their opposition to clear-cutting by ABC Company in this particular area of the Carmanah at this particular point in time. This will be the focus of your paper:

> *The Carmanah Valley is an ecologically sensitive area of old-growth forest in which ABC Company should be forbidden to engage in clear-cut logging for the foreseeable future. The provincial government must act immediately in order to preserve the old-growth habitats of two rare and endangered avian species: burrowing murrelet and the Fraser owl.*

Exercise: Questioning

You have to practise questioning to make it work consistently for you. We've set out, at the end of this paragraph, three open subject areas. You should address each of these areas by using a cycle of repetitive questions, remembering that the idea is to make the issue narrower, not larger. If you keep turning the answers you get into further questions, you will find that the answers to those questions have more and more qualifiers attached to them. The qualifiers may relate to time, place, persons, circumstances, and other matters. Don't be put off: the qualifiers in your answers are supposed to be there, and the more qualifiers there are, the narrower your answers are. Here are your subject areas: (1) gender relations in education; (2) communication skills in the information-processing era; and (3) the impact of taxation.

Make a chart

Charts are visual representations of organization and content and are frequently used in the sciences to depict the interrelationships between components in a device or steps in a process. They're also used in business to show corporate structure and management relationships. You can use them in your writing preparation to help you break larger ideas into groups of more tightly focused ideas and to express to yourself the relationships between the ideas you've developed around a specific subject. In terms of the narrowing process, you can select one of the narrowed ideas and break it down even further. Eventually, you'll be able to select one of these component ideas as the focus for a paper. Have a look at figure 3-1 in order to see the relationship between larger and smaller ideas.

Every area of thought has its own coherence, its own internal rhythm and order. When you develop ideas or narrow your focus, you need to understand the logical connections between the ideas you're working with, in order to create a coherent discussion. Charting is very good for this because it provides a visual model for the process. Charting allows you to show how each large component breaks down into a series of smaller components, each of which can itself be broken down further. You can use the logical requirements of the chart to figure out where you should go from where you are and to determine the appropriateness of your ideas in context. When you're identifying components, you may find that it's something like filling in the blanks in a puzzle.

Figure 3-1 shows a generic chart; figure 3-2 presents you with an example in which charting has been used to narrow a topic from open (women's aerobics shoes) to specific (the best type or model of shoe for a specific category of user with particular needs). In the example, you can see a breakdown of the basic idea into a series of smaller units, each of which has its own box. You might also notice that, because there appears to be more than one "path," you could find more than one specific focus to write about. So charts that you make for a particular assignment should always go into your note files, since you might be able to get more than one essay out of your initial charting session. In this particular case, the student

Making A Chart

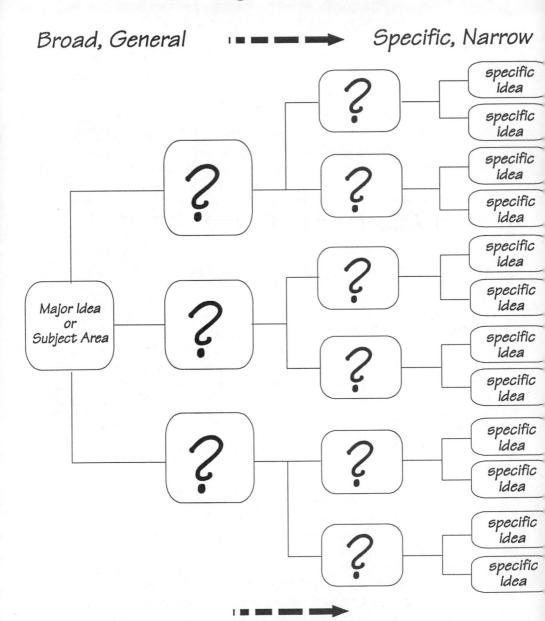

Broad, General ▪ ▪ ▪ ➡ *Specific, Narrow*

▪ ▪ ▪ ➡

Break Larger Ideas Into Smaller Ideas

Figure 3-1: Using a Chart for Narrowing

Making A Chart

Broad, General ▪ ▪ ▬ ▬ ➡ Specific, Narrow

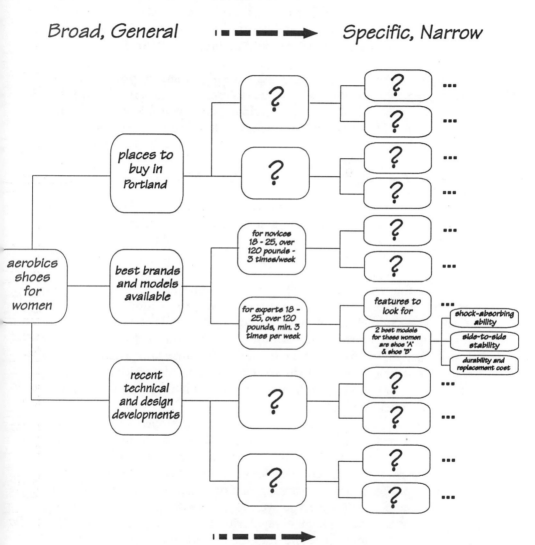

Break Larger Ideas Into Smaller Ideas

Figure 3-2: Using a Chart for Narrowing - Sport Shoes

chose to pursue a path that would allow her to write a comparison/contrast essay about which of two specific aerobics shoes would be best for a female between the ages of 18 and 25 who weighed more than 120 pounds and who wanted to engage in intensive aerobics at least three times a week. The student decided, based on the material in her chart, that the most relevant points of comparison would be: the ability of the shoes to absorb shock; their ability to provide side-to-side stability; and their durability in relation to replacement cost.

Examine the chart in figure 3-2 carefully; then try your hand at the exercise below. When you try to use a chart for narrowing, think about the different kinds of relationships you might be looking for: cause/effect, classifications, part/whole, chronological sequence, and the like.

Exercise: Charting

In this exercise, you'll try to create your own chart. The object is not to pick some difficult or esoteric subject in order to see how much you can make yourself suffer. Instead, pick a subject you know and like, even if it doesn't relate to your classes. To become comfortable with charting, you need to work with the visual model in a way that isn't threatening or exhausting. Simply select an area of interest to you and target a broad issue or question within that area. For example, if you enjoy listening to jazz, take as your starting point the characteristics of modern jazz. You might then try to break this down by instrument, style, or musician. Then, try to pursue a logical chain of increasingly narrow, related ideas, issues, or questions. The chart will help you see relationships you might not have noticed before.

Narrowing is a skill that you may have developed well already. If so, don't rest on your laurels; you should continue to work with it to provide better subjects for discussion and clearer insights for your readers. If you haven't developed your skills in this area, or if you have problems with narrowing at first, keep at it. It's a skill you can learn, and it will serve you well in your writing. The message in all this is that the task of essay writing in college or university requires you to develop sound judgment, and to exercise it—appropriately. If you address your obligations to your reader clearly and specifically in a fair, honest, and consistent manner, and if you apply yourself to mastering effective writing skills, you'll find your efforts rewarded in terms of both your growing command of the language and your grades.

4
How to Develop Your Essay's Context, Thesis & Path Statement

Have you ever been introduced to someone who, because of nervousness or a lack of social skills, acted foolishly at the time? If so, you might have immediately characterized the person as a "dork." In future meetings, or in conversations in which that person's name came up, you may always have thought of the person as "that dork." However, you may have had an opportunity at a later date to talk to the person at length about something that was of interest to both of you and discovered that your first impression was completely wrong. It's unfortunate that, based on a brief and misleading first meeting, you dismissed the "dork" as uninteresting or not worth your time. Even worse, you may unknowingly have been the person characterized as the dork, only to find much later that you had been rejected by an individual or group because of your initial awkwardness. On the other hand, you probably know someone who is adept at making good first impressions—every time. This ability provides an advantage in all kinds of relationships. Just as it is difficult for someone who makes a poor first impression to change how he or she is perceived in the future, an individual who makes a good first impression will continue to be perceived positively.

The first unit of your essay introduces your subject (and you) to your reader. If you remember that the college expository essay is a testing device, you'll see that the reader's first impression of your work can be very important. If the first part of your essay is unclear, illogical, incomplete, or mechanically flawed, you'll negatively bias the reader. This bias will affect the way he or she perceives the rest of your paper, even if the rest of your paper is well written. Similarly, if your essay starts in a clear and elegant fashion, the reader will carry a positive bias into the reading of your paper. Over-coming interpersonal inadequacies may take years; overcoming weak introductions to essays is relatively easy.

⇨ | *Always provide your reader with a clear context, thesis, and path statement.* | ⇦

At this point, you're probably going to start thinking about the physical layout of your essay or paper, even though that's still a few steps away. You'll probably be concerned with matters such as margins, spacing, paper, etc. Both the MLA and APA style guides (noted in chapter 8) have very specific requirements in these areas. However, we have found that individual instructors often alter some of the formal requirements for essays in their courses. Therefore, you must <u>always</u> check with your instructor as to his or her preferences or preferred systems if you are uncertain about course requirements in these areas. For instance, in this book our sample materials are all single-spaced; that was our choice. As a student, you'll almost certainly be required to double space all course work you submit for grades. Please bear these points in mind as we begin to create the essay structure for you.

THE CONTEXT

A student in one of our classes wrote a paper about the May 1992 riots in Los Angeles that followed the acquittal of the police officers accused of beating a motorist named Rodney King. The introduc-tion to her essay read as follows:

> The verdict in the King trial was the cause of the recent riots, and if a reoccurrence of these events is to be avoided, the entire judicial system must be overhauled.

We suggested to the student that she had not provided a proper context for the reader. In other words, the student had not provided the reader with the basic information necessary to make sense of what was on the page. Who is King? To what trial is the writer referring? Where did the riots take place? The reader does not even know the country in which the events occurred. The student argued that one would have to have been living at the bottom of a well to be unaware of the answers to these questions, and on the face of it she seemed to have a point. However, only a few hours after the paper was handed in, there were riots in Toronto. Suddenly, what had seemed to be an obvious reference was unclear and confusing—even to the writer.

When you begin to write, you must remember that your audience might not know as much about the issue under discussion as you do. They might live at the bottom of a well. More likely, they may simply need to be reminded of the details surrounding the event or issue under discussion. One of the major functions of the opening remarks in an essay is to give your audience a point of entry, a comfortable place from which to begin their exploration of the specific themes you intend to develop. When you fail to provide your reader with proper, complete, contextual information, you create logic gaps from the very beginning of your discussion—and the reader may fall right through those gaps. At best, logic gaps confuse the reader. At worst, they make your essay completely unreadable. With a little thought, you can provide introductory information to the reader that will minimize the possibility of confusion. Here is our student's rewrite of the "riot" paragraph:

> Almost a year ago, the world was shocked when television news broadcasts aired a videotape showing a black motorist, Rodney King, being brutally beaten by four Los Angeles police officers. The tape, made by a home-video enthusiast, provided the primary evidence in the trial of the four officers for "assault with a deadly weapon," and use of "undue force." Last week, an all-white jury found all four officers innocent of the assault charge and three of the officers innocent of the charge of "undue force." In the case of the fourth officer, the jury was unable to reach a verdict on the second charge and the judge declared a mistrial. Within hours after the trial results were made public, Los Angeles was under siege. Riots had broken out in a number of locations. Hundreds of buildings were burned, stores were looted, and, at last count, the death toll was nearing 50. In order to avoid a repetition of these events in the future, the entire American judicial system must be overhauled.

Although some awkwardness still remains, the information she gives to the reader is complete and provides a point of departure that sets the stage for a discussion of almost any issue connected with the Rodney King case or the riots that followed the trial of the four officers. There is, however, a serious problem still to be solved.

THE THESIS STATEMENT

The last sentence in our student's opening paragraph seems to suggest the primary focus of the essay: "In order to avoid a repetition of these events in the future, the entire American judicial system must be overhauled." In other words, it appears that the paper will discuss, in detail, what is wrong with the American judicial system and what needs to be done to improve it. The reader will probably make this assumption because the sentence, in terms of its location in the paragraph and its wording, appears to be addressing a typical audience expectation—that the writer will inform the reader of the primary issue to be discussed in the essay. This is a reasonable expectation, especially in the context of undergraduate expository essays and the rules governing their evaluation.

Because the expository essay provides a formal writing context, it places requirements on both the reader and the writer. If the writer ignores the reader's familiarity with expository essay form and its proper sequencing, then one of those logic gaps is created. Although, with skill, one can alter the basic structure of the essay, most readers will expect that once you've provided contextual information, you'll then offer them a thesis statement. This is consistent with the conventions and expectations on which the undergraduate essay form rests.

> *The thesis statement is a contract between you and your reader. It is a clear, precise description of the issue you will discuss in the essay.*

It is frequently in the form of an arguable assertion—a statement that your reader might accept as true if you demonstrate its accuracy or make a case for its validity, through analysis and support, in your essay. The contextual material leads up to it; the development material supports it; and the conclusion refers back to it.

> *The thesis statement is the heart of your essay and a promise to the reader.*

If we assume that the last sentence in the student paragraph is the thesis, we might paraphrase it in contractual terms as follows: In this essay I will discuss, in a complete and convincing manner, how a restructuring of the American judicial system will improve race relations in large American cities, using Los Angeles as a point of reference.

We often suggest to our students that phrasing their thesis statements in this way can help them clarify, in their own minds, the nature of their obligation to the reader. This wording would be inappropriate in the essay itself, but it provides you with a clear benchmark for your planning and drafting. As you work with this concept, remember that the expository essay traditionally assumes the writer is relatively unbiased. Thus, your position relative to the central issue in the essay should be the result of research and analysis. If your writing is too personal, you will compromise the objective tone of the paper. So, when you're asked to write a formal essay, you should probably avoid speaking in the first person (as "I") or addressing the reader directly as "you"—not because it is wrong, but because many university markers will view it as amateurish in that context. While there is a growing trend toward acceptance of less distance between you and your reader, it is still safer to assume that such a direct approach is inappropriate unless an instructor tells you otherwise in a specific course or assignment.

Once you have a clearly formulated the thesis statement, you can determine its appropriateness in terms of subject and narrowness. Since the assignment we gave simply required the student to discuss some aspect of the Rodney King case (an open topic), there was no problem with content. However, the discussion was to be limited to 750-1,000 words. Clearly, the potential scope of the discussion, based on the student's thesis, was immense. We pointed out that 1,000 pages wouldn't provide enough space for a discussion of a complete reform of the American judicial system. By neglecting to further qualify the thesis, she took on an implied (but nonetheless real) obligation to cover everything within the scope of the thesis that was not otherwise ruled out.

As we suggested in chapter 3, most non-technical errors in expository writing can be traced to inadequate narrowing. If you aren't clear in your own mind about the extent of the commitment your thesis imposes, it's easy to take on more than you can handle. For this reason, an important function of the thesis statement during the drafting process is to provide a reference point for you as a writer. When our student realized what she had promised to do in her essay, she did some more research. Here is her narrowed thesis:

> The King case clearly suggests that one area which needs immediate reforms, as least insofar as the Los Angeles Police Department is concerned, is the policy governing the application of force to an unarmed accused person, particularly in situations unrelated to drugs.

This appears to be much better, but there may still be problems. In order to address those problems for both the reader and the writer, the student needs more information.

THE PATH STATEMENT

Depending on how the student handles her discussion, the new thesis could be reasonable; or it could be problematic. However, to determine which case applies, we need to know how she will develop her argument. It is the final section of the first unit, the path statement, that provides the needed information. The path statement is a simple concept: it is an explanation (in one or more sentences) setting out the specific areas of discussion by which the writer will demonstrate the accuracy or validity of the thesis.

➪

Your path statement is a table of contents for your essay. The path statement lets the reader know how you intend to organize the discussion of the thesis, how you will sequence that discussion, and what developmental elements you will emphasize.

⇦

Let's take a look at the student's thesis statement, with the path statement (italicized) added:

The King case clearly suggests that one area which needs immediate reforms, as least insofar as the Los Angeles Police Department is concerned, is the policy governing the application of force to an unarmed accused person, particularly in situations unrelated to drugs. *Reform should address three critical areas: standards by which application of appropriate force is determined in specified circumstances; possibilities of civilian dispute-arbitration to address citizen complaints; and educational programming for officers who regularly are called on to use force.*

As we've suggested, the addition of the path statement to the thesis provides the reader with a map to the essay. This map tells the reader, "Here is the point which I wish to make in this essay. I am moving toward a particular conclusion. I will take you to this conclusion via a specific route, and will make x stops along the way. We will thoroughly explore the terrain at each stop. This will lead us smoothly and efficiently to the end of the journey—to the stated conclusion."

Certainly, this content information is of help to the reader. More importantly, once it's properly formulated, the thesis and path statement provide a check for you as a writer. It is imperative that you fully understand where you're going, why you're going there, and how you intend to get there. If you haven't considered all of these factors carefully, despite an intuitive sense that your choices are the best possible in the circumstances, you could end up taking the reader in the wrong direction via a zigzag course. When our student reformulated her thesis and path statement, she began to understand how these elements provided her with both a vital mechanism for determining the appropriateness of her direction in the paper and a platform for further refinement. She felt more secure with the direction she was taking, but she was able to see that the potential scope of her path statement was still too great.

Exercise

The following is a copy of the completed student paragraph: context, thesis statement, and path statement. Although it is much better now than it was in its original form, there is still much work to be done. To further refine your own sense of context, thesis statement, and path statement, try to rewrite this paragraph so that it is complete and properly narrowed, and moves the reader in a logical, direct way toward the conclusion that you choose in your rewritten thesis statement.

> Almost a year ago, the world was shocked when television news broadcasts aired a videotape showing a black motorist, Rodney King, being brutally beaten by four Los Angeles police officers. The tape, made by a home-video enthusiast, provided the primary evidence in the trial of the four officers for "assault with a deadly weapon," and use of "undue force." Last week, an all-white jury found all four offices innocent of the assault charge and three of the officers innocent of the charge of "undue force." In the case of the fourth officer, the jury was unable to reach a verdict on the second charge and the judge declared a mistrial. Within hours after the trial results were made public, Los Angeles was under siege. Riots had broken out in a number of locations. Hundreds of buildings were burned, stores were looted, and, at last count, the death toll was nearing 50. The King case clearly suggests that one area which needs immediate reforms, as least insofar as the Los Angeles Police Department is concerned, is the policy governing the application of force to an unarmed, accused person, particularly in situations unrelated to drugs. Reform should address three critical areas: standards by which application of appropriate force is determined in specified circumstances; possibilities of civilian dispute-arbitration to address citizen complaints; and educational programming for officers who regularly are called on to use force.

If you can remember that the thesis for an essay should usually be in the form of a narrow, clear, arguable assertion (as opposed to an argument), you can construct a workable thesis for almost any subject: the best recipe for lemon pound cake, the best or most crucial play of the final period in a particular Stanley Cup final, the most important image used by a poet in a particular poem, and the like. Until you're comfortable using the device of the thesis and path statement, whether express or implied, you'll have a critical problem reaching your audience from the very outset of your essay.

5
How to Design the Multiple Unit Essay

In a perfect world, there would be a single, perfect model for the undergraduate essay. We sometimes talk about this idealized model as if it were some kind of magical talisman. Unfortunately, the world is not perfect. Thus, over the years, scholars have offered an array of models intended to provide you with different ways to organize essays effectively. Some authorities suggest that the best way to approach the essay is to think of it as having three parts—a beginning, a middle, and an ending. Other authorities prefer to use a model that depends on there being an introductory section, three (or more) development sections, and a concluding section. Still others set out models that depend for their structure on specific rhetorical or critical approaches like process, cause/effect, or comparison.

You can use almost any model effectively, provided that you remember some essential facts. First, models are just that—models. You should not adopt any one of them blindly, since no model relieves you of your obligation to think or of your obligations to your reader. Moreover, no model is perfect for every purpose or assignment; so you have the additional obligation to use common sense in modifying the model you choose in order to meet the requirements of a particular essay. The model you select must be able to flex to your needs; if it won't flex, then it will be of little use to you.

The way you narrow and word your thesis and path statement has much to do with the model you select or develop for your essay.

⇨
> *If you have devised a properly narrowed and structured thesis and path statement, the organizational framework of the essay must flow directly from that thesis and path statement.*
⇦

In other words, the model you use must be appropriate to the specific topic you're working with—and to your proposed path statement. You can't always select the model first and then try to cram your thesis and path statement into it.

A third fact—the most important—is that the various models are only incidentally models for structuring essays. That is not their primary function.

> *They are primarily models for organized thinking. They are intellectual devices or constructs that are intended to allow you to create and express information coherently.*

They are reflections of operative principles in the same way that math theorems or axioms are reflections of operative principles. You can commit them to memory or you can use them in a fill-in-the-blanks fashion; but they're truly useful to you only when you understand them well enough to apply them intelligently.

You may find the use of structural models to be mechanistic or uncomfortable. However, you need to get past your discomfort if you're to use models effectively as tools in your writing toolbox. In this chapter, we're going to try to give you a basic model and some organizational strategies you can use as resources. Provided that you understand the principles involved, you can adapt this material easily for many different writing tasks. As you read through the material on basic structure, remember that it reflects the nature of the thesis statement and path statement. Don't fall into the trap of thinking that you need to memorize all of this stuff. Instead, concentrate on making sure you understand the principles underlying the model and the ways in which you could make the model work for you. If you can do that much, then you'll know what to look for and where to look for it when you're confronted with your next essay assignment.

The Multiple Unit Model

We will refer to our basic working model as the multiple unit model. In this context, the term "unit" means a conceptual unit or part of the essay in which you explore a main branch of your path statement. We use "unit" rather than "paragraph" because some students leap to the erroneous conclusion that each branch of their path statement will be limited to a single paragraph. Clearly, this is incorrect, as common sense ought to suggest.

⇨

> *If you have a complicated thesis and path statement, then each branch*
> *of your path is likely to involve multiple paragraphs, even though*
> *each branch constitutes a single unit in the essay.*

⇦

It should be equally clear that the number of units in an essay will depend on the nature of the assignment, the wording of your specific thesis and path statement, the length within which you have been told to work, and the underlying purpose of the essay. There's nothing magic about a three-part essay; there's nothing magic about a five-part essay. These are simply convenient structures around which to discuss the nature of the undergraduate expository paper. We use what we call the multiple unit model, because it includes (without being limited to) the generic three-part essay and the generic five-part essay.

What's the structure of the multiple unit model, and how does it reflect the thesis and path statement? Essentially, the multiple unit model consists of a series of discrete, logically sequenced components and is structurally a kind of magnified replica of the thesis and path statement for your essay. You'll recall our discussion of this structure in chapter 4. Figure 5-1 is a visual representation of the relationship between the most basic components in the model.

Each of the conceptual units of a typical undergraduate essay is represented in this layout. If we adopt a traditional five-part structure (an introduction containing context, thesis and path statement, three (or more) central units of discussion, and a conclusion), we can see that the introductory unit is comprised of the boxes labeled "audience & purpose," "general topic area," "narrowed topic area," "context & clear, narrow thesis statement," and "path statement." This isn't as complicated as it looks. It simply suggests that to see the validity of your thesis, the reader must be shown the context. We can also see from figure 5-1 that those units of the essay forming the main part of the discussion (paths *A*, *B*, and *C*—units II, III and IV, respectively) are based on the branches or directional pointers contained in the path statement. The progression starting from the arguable assertion contained in the thesis statement develops along each branch of the path and culminates in the conclusion.

The model illustrates the relationship of the first four units to the conclusion, which restates the thesis and shows transference. The concept of transference is at work when you are able to show the reader in your conclusion how she may take the principles or ideas explained in the essay and transfer them to a related area of inquiry not specifically covered in your essay. If the reader can do this, she has learned as a result of the writer's efforts. We can make an analogy

The Multiple Unit Model - Stage One

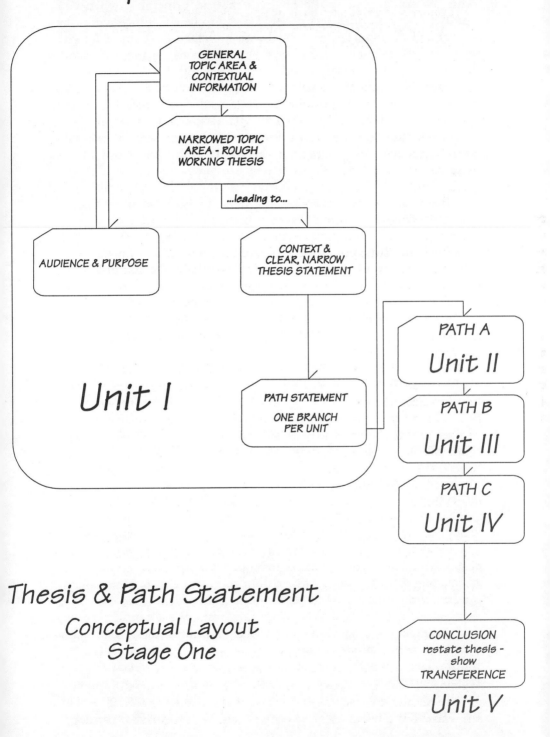

GENERAL TOPIC AREA & CONTEXTUAL INFORMATION

NARROWED TOPIC AREA - ROUGH WORKING THESIS

...leading to...

AUDIENCE & PURPOSE

CONTEXT & CLEAR, NARROW THESIS STATEMENT

Unit I

PATH STATEMENT

ONE BRANCH PER UNIT

PATH A
Unit II

PATH B
Unit III

PATH C
Unit IV

CONCLUSION restate thesis - show **TRANSFERENCE**

Unit V

Thesis & Path Statement
Conceptual Layout
Stage One

Figure 5-1: Basic elements of the Multiple Unit Model.

with the study of scientific or mathematical principles: when you study a theory, the idea isn't merely for you to be able to memorize the theory and the examples associated with it. Rather, the point is for you to learn how to apply the theory to new situations, so that the theory becomes a useful analytical and problem-solving tool for you. When you strive to create transference in the conclusion of an essay, you're trying to create an opportunity for your reader to transfer what she has learned in the paper to some new situation or set of facts.

As we know from what we learned in chapter 4, in your thesis and path statement, you're really saying something like this to the reader:

> Here is an arguable assertion; the point I wish to make in this essay. I'm going to lead you to a particular conclusion; and in my essay, I'm going to take you to the conclusion by one particular route. This route involves several stops at major landmarks along the way. The landmark we'll visit first lies at the end of [path A]; next, we'll follow [path B]; and then we'll follow [path C]. Once we have visited all these landmarks, we'll be ready to finish our journey to the conclusion of this paper, by which point you, reader, will have learned something of value.

Before you can start to write your essay and keep this commitment to the reader, you'll need to expand the model so that most of your paper's content will be reflected in the visual layout. We'll assume that the process of developing a suitable visual layout usually consists of three steps or stages: figure 5-1 would represent stage one; figures 5-2 and 5-3 would represent stages two and three, respectively.

In planning your essays, you should try to develop a regular process by which you can get to stage three—not because it is "right," but because you'll find that if you strive for some consistency in your methods, you'll become secure with the process more quickly. As a result, you'll also develop consistency in terms of the results you achieve on your assignments. Over time, you can work at developing a consistent process of your own. Initially, however, many students find it beneficial to start with a clearly identifiable structure, especially if they're used to working randomly. We'll consider an actual example in a moment. We'll take a sample thesis and path statement and translate it into the layout we used in figure 5-1, altering the labels of each of the components. Once we're certain that the relationship of the components is clear, we'll go through stages two and three, expanding the model by adding more of the elements you would need to begin writing the essay. At the end of the process, we'll have

The Multiple Unit Model - Stage Two

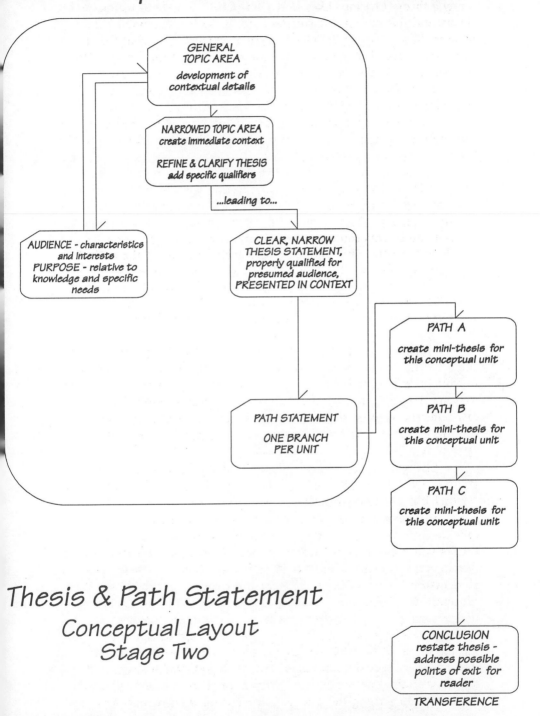

GENERAL TOPIC AREA
development of contextual details

NARROWED TOPIC AREA
create immediate context

REFINE & CLARIFY THESIS
add specific qualifiers

...leading to...

AUDIENCE - *characteristics and interests*
PURPOSE - *relative to knowledge and specific needs*

CLEAR, NARROW THESIS STATEMENT, *properly qualified for presumed audience,* **PRESENTED IN CONTEXT**

PATH A
create mini-thesis for this conceptual unit

PATH B
create mini-thesis for this conceptual unit

PATH C
create mini-thesis for this conceptual unit

PATH STATEMENT
ONE BRANCH PER UNIT

Thesis & Path Statement
Conceptual Layout
Stage Two

CONCLUSION
restate thesis - address possible points of exit for reader

TRANSFERENCE

Figure 5-2: Elements of the Multiple Unit Model - Stage Two

The Multiple Unit Model - Stage Three

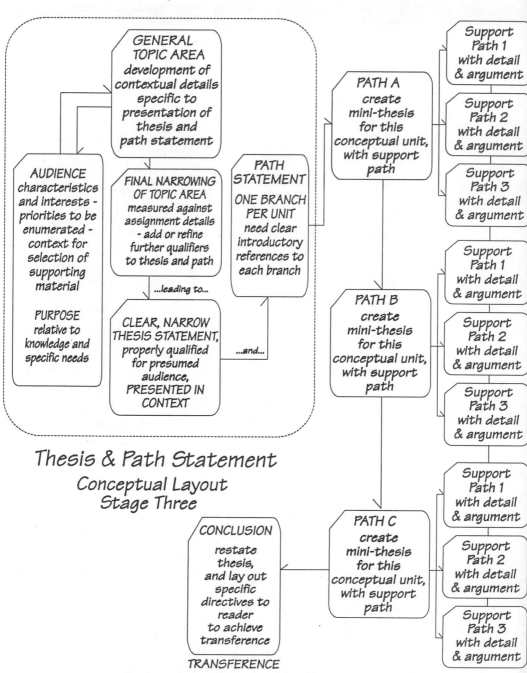

Figure 5-3: Elements of the Multiple Unit Model - Stage Three

something that displays most of the material you'd want to include in the essay, in the order in which you'd want to include it—and all of this will happen before you actually write a draft in coherent sentences and paragraphs.

It is important you understand the extent to which you should use the model to "front-load" your organizational process when you're preparing your essays. Some students try writing a draft much sooner in the organizing and idea-generating process than they should. They assume that their command of spoken English, which is sufficient for their daily needs and social interactions, will provide them with the additional information they need when they attempt to write an essay about a specific subject. This is not true for most people, who aren't up to the task of figuring out exactly *what* they want to write at the same time they are figuring out *how* they want to write it.

> *The stages in the development of the model are designed to help you separate structure and organization from the actual drafting of the paper.*

The idea is to have you separate the planning stages from the writing stage. That way, by the time you write your first draft, you won't have to worry about two things at the same time: "Oh my God, what will I say next?" and, "Hmm—is that a sentence?" This is what front-loading means.

Let's suppose that you've been given an assignment on the benefits of effective time management for first-year college or university students. You've spent some time working on it, and you think you'll probably focus on the following thesis and path statement—though you are not quite sure if it's really narrow enough yet:

> First-year college or university students who have trouble with managing their time effectively can benefit in several ways from adopting an effective time-management system. They will find that they are better able to meet critical course deadlines and handle high workloads; they will maintain their psychological balance more easily; and they will have adequate time to devote to non-academic pursuits.

Based on the information contained in this thesis and path statement, let's look at the structural model we saw in figure 5-1: see figure 5-4.

This level of organizational detail may seem sufficient. Some students, feeling that they have adequately set out the structural

The Multiple Unit Model - Stage One

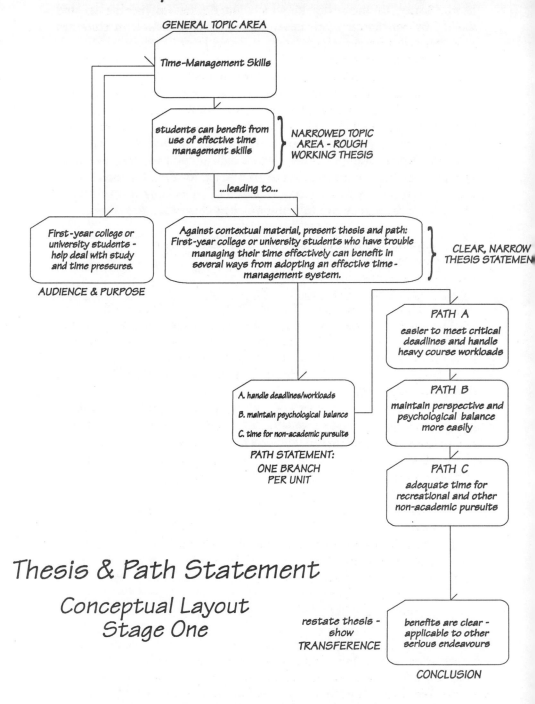

GENERAL TOPIC AREA

Time-Management Skills

students can benefit from use of effective time management skills

NARROWED TOPIC AREA - ROUGH WORKING THESIS

...leading to...

First-year college or university students - help deal with study and time pressures.

AUDIENCE & PURPOSE

Against contextual material, present thesis and path: First-year college or university students who have trouble managing their time effectively can benefit in several ways from adopting an effective time-management system.

CLEAR, NARROW THESIS STATEMEN

PATH A

easier to meet critical deadlines and handle heavy course workloads

A. handle deadlines/workloads

B. maintain psychological balance

C. time for non-academic pursuits

PATH STATEMENT: ONE BRANCH PER UNIT

PATH B

maintain perspective and psychological balance more easily

PATH C

adequate time for recreational and other non-academic pursuits

Thesis & Path Statement
Conceptual Layout
Stage One

restate thesis - show TRANSFERENCE

benefits are clear - applicable to other serious endeavours

CONCLUSION

Figure 5-4: Basic elements of the Multiple Unit Model - Stage One

components for the assignment, might even begin to write at this point. Some will have the skills to complete the assignment on this basis; however, in our experience, this isn't the case for most students. Ask yourself whether, in the course of tackling the assignment, you would regard this visual model as sufficient to enable you to write the essay without having to think up other information, arguments or details. At this point, most of your material is still hidden, even though you have a sense of where it should fit in the model. Even this basic stage will depend for its success on whether your thesis and path statement are properly narrowed. You're going to need to move to the next stage, taking care to ensure that the elements you decide to include accurately reflect the path by which you intend to lead your reader to your conclusion. You'll also have to scrutinize your thesis for clarity and specificity, and you may have to make it narrower still.

To expand the model, you'll have to add further components. A good way to proceed is to pretend that each branch of your path statement is almost like a separate essay itself. Using the same thesis/path statement structure, expand each branch by adding (in point form) a kind of mini-thesis for each branch. You may have to do additional brainstorming or some general reading in the area in order to get some details or specific ideas about where you'll go from this stage. When you're done with this phase, your visual model might look something like figure 5-5.

Figure 5-5 looks even better than the first version, and there's an even greater temptation to launch into a full draft at this point. In order to use the model to greatest advantage, you should resist the temptation, even though your skills and memory may be equal to the challenge. You need to be certain that you can work with the multiple unit model successfully. Then, when you're given an assignment you can't hold in your head while you're writing it, you'll have a viable procedure for structuring your material in such a way that you don't have to hold it in your head. It's one thing to keep control of a 500-word paper without following a formal process. It's quite another to control a 5,000-word research paper and to juggle all the material you need to keep organized in order to write it.

If we consider figure 5-5 carefully, several things will become obvious right away. We already know that the audience for a college or university essay is, at best, artificial; but we'll continue to work on the assumption that many instructors will require you to target a particular hypothetical audience. The profile of this audience does not actually fit the person who will be marking your essay. We also know that if you refine your topic area and thesis properly—that is, bring yourself and your reader to the edge of

The Multiple Unit Model - Stage Two

Time-management skills for first-year college students and mature or returning students

GENERAL TOPIC AREA
development of contextual details

Improving chances of success through time management for specified categories of students with specific pressures

NARROWED TOPIC AREA
create immediate context

REFINE & CLARIFY THESIS
add specific qualifiers

PATH A - mini-thesis
Many students have trouble meeting deadlines and carrying workloads, through inefficient use of time and energy - proper time management can fix.

First-year college students - social pressures, skills weaknesses, many distractions - need motivation to adopt effective method of time management - will create opportunities for academic success.

First-year college or university students who are having trouble achieving academic success because of weak skills, social pressures or outside responsibilities can benefit in several ways from adopting an effective time management system.

PATH B - mini-thesis
Pressures arising from poor use of time create vicious circle of panic and anxiety - better time management can help one maintain perspective and reduce destructive anxiety.

AUDIENCE
characteristics and interests

PURPOSE
relative to knowledge and specific needs

PATH STATEMENT

ONE BRANCH PER UNIT

A. handle deadlines and workloads
B. maintain psychological balance
C. have time for non-academic pursuits

PATH C - mini-thesis
Success requires healthy balance of study, family and personal relationships, and athletics or recreation - only possible through adoption of an effective time-management system.

Thesis & Path Statement
Conceptual Layout
Stage Two

Benefits will apply not only in one's studies - same principles apply to other areas, including business and industry. As pressure increases, benefits become more apparent and related skills more desirable.

Figure 5-5: Elements of the Multiple Unit Model - Stage Two

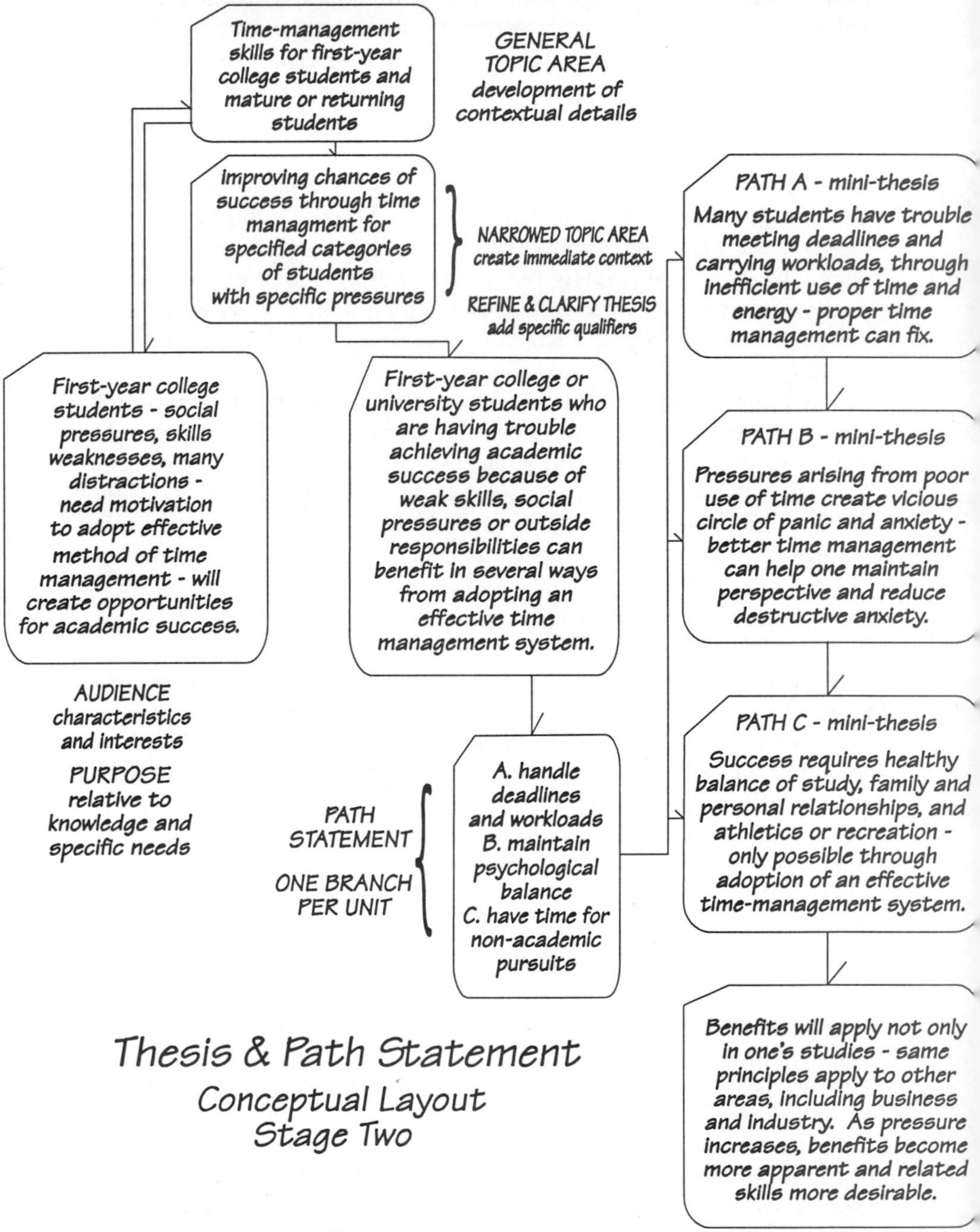

CONCLUSION
TRANSFERENCE

your collective subject knowledge—you'll have dealt with many of the concerns you should have about your audience. Thus, the refinement of the audience/purpose section in the model is tied to the ongoing development of the general topic area, narrowed topic area, and clear, narrow thesis statement. Remember: these components are all part of the first conceptual unit of your essay. They provide the reader with both the context or situation, and the arguable assertion on which you'll focus. In figure 5-5, each of these sections is expanded to include additional details. In fact, it even looks like there has been some duplication. You should expect this, since the thesis flows naturally from the context you create in your essay when you address your audience and general topic area. This is the context to which you were introduced in chapter 4; your thesis is presented against a backdrop of introductory detail with which it has a clear relationship. It's against this backdrop that your audience—and your marker—will measure the validity, accuracy, and narrowness or specificity of your thesis and path statement. So you shouldn't worry about the apparent duplication at this stage in the process, as it will assist you later with proper qualification of the thesis for the presumed audience.

You'll also notice the mini-thesis that appears for each branch of the path statement. In the model, there are three branches; you might be working on a paper in which there are two or five, or more. Since each branch of your path statement reflects a major conceptual unit in your paper, each branch of your path statement must have within it a clearly worded indicator of the matters to be addressed within that unit or branch. Thus, in our time-management example, we see that each branch of the path statement contains a mini-thesis that focuses on one particular aspect of the proposed discussion. However, it may not be possible for you to determine at this stage whether these mini-thesis statements are sufficiently narrowed.

Finally, you'll note that we now start to see in the conclusion some generalized information focusing on transference in terms of this specific topic. You should always assume, unless you're specifically told otherwise by an instructor, that part of your conclusion will be an intelligent restatement of your thesis. Such a restatement may well be sufficient, especially at the first-year level. However, an understanding of the concept of transference is critical to your success and growth as a writer—you shouldn't be satisfied with meeting the minimal requirement. At this point in the model, the transference component is still generalized, mostly because the point-form material in the preceding parts of the model is also generalized. It does, however, provide you with some initial direction. In order to effect transference properly, you'll need to ensure that the conclusion is logical and flows from the discussion preceding it *and* that the area of transference is one the reader will see as related to the general topic area. Otherwise, the value of the transference will be lost on the audience.

Figure 5-6 is a layout of stage three in the development of our time-management example. You'll see that it includes all the material we included in stage two (figure 5-5); but there are now some additional boxes down the right side of the model. Because our path statement consisted of three units, we've chosen to break each branch into a further three units or components that we've labeled "Support Paths." However, there's nothing magic about that number, even at this stage in the model's development. You might well find that one or more branches of the path would require you to develop more than three support paths. Each support path might be the topic sentence in a paragraph within the unit, or each might be a key sentence within a single paragraph, depending on the nature and complexity of your subject matter.

You'll have noticed that we've left you with a series of question marks instead of providing you with the specific information you would want for each support path in our example. This stage is critical in terms of your understanding of the individual bits and pieces of the model. When you get to this point, you're creating for the reader the actual steps in the journey she will take from your introduction through your path statement to your conclusion. You need to experiment with generating the specific ideas and supporting arguments or details you think you would use in fulfilling the mini-thesis in each branch of your path. This is how you test the mini-thesis in each branch of your path. Is it narrowed sufficiently? Can you express meaningful ideas which logically develop your main thesis? If you find that you either cannot generate anything meaningful or are left with interesting but unsupported generalizations in these steps, this is a clear indicator that you haven't narrowed enough or been clear enough in setting out your thesis and path components.

In a moment, we'll help you cope with the support paths for branch *A* of the time-management example; but we want you to be clear about what is going on at this stage. If, for example, you were using the model to plan a research paper, at this stage you should be able to create a further set of boxes to the right of the support-path components. These boxes would include pointers to the specific quotations or research data you'd want to integrate into each branch of the path. If the relationship between each support path and its supporting material wasn't clear and obvious, even in point form, or if you could see an immediate problem of logical sequencing, you could be certain you had not narrowed and clarified your path statement and

The Multiple Unit Model - Stage Three

Time-management skills for first-year college students and mature or returning students

GENERAL TOPIC AREA
development of contextual details

improving chances of success through time managment for specified categories of students with specific pressures

NARROWED TOPIC AREA
create immediate context

REFINE & CLARIFY THESIS
add specific qualifiers

First-year college students - social pressures, skills weaknesses, many distractions - need motivation to adopt effective method of time management - will create opportunities for academic success.

AUDIENCE
characteristics and interests

PURPOSE
relative to knowledge and specific needs

First-year college or university students who are having trouble achieving academic success because of weak skills, social pressures or outside responsibilities can benefit in several ways from adopting an effective time management system.

PATH STATEMENT

ONE BRANCH PER UNIT

A. handle deadlines and workloads
B. maintain psychological balance
C. have time for non-academic pursuits

PATH A - mini-thesis
Many students have trouble meeting deadlines and carrying workloads through inefficient use of time and energy - proper time management can fix.

PATH B - mini-thesis
Pressures arising from poor use of time create vicious circle of panic and anxiety - better time management can help one maintain perspective and reduce destructive anxiety.

PATH C - mini-thesis
Success requires healthy balance of study, family and personal relationships, and athletics or recreation - only possible through adoption of an effective time-management system.

Support Path 1 -details- ?

Support Path 2 -details- ?

Support Path 3 -details- ?

Support Path 1 -details- ?

Support Path 2 -details- ?

Support Path 3 -details- ?

Support Path 1 -details- ?

Support Path 2 -details- ?

Support Path 3 -details- ?

Thesis & Path Statement
Conceptual Layout
Stage Three

Benefits will apply not only in one's studies -- same principles apply to other areas, including business and industry. As pressure increases, benefits become more apparent and related skills more desirable.

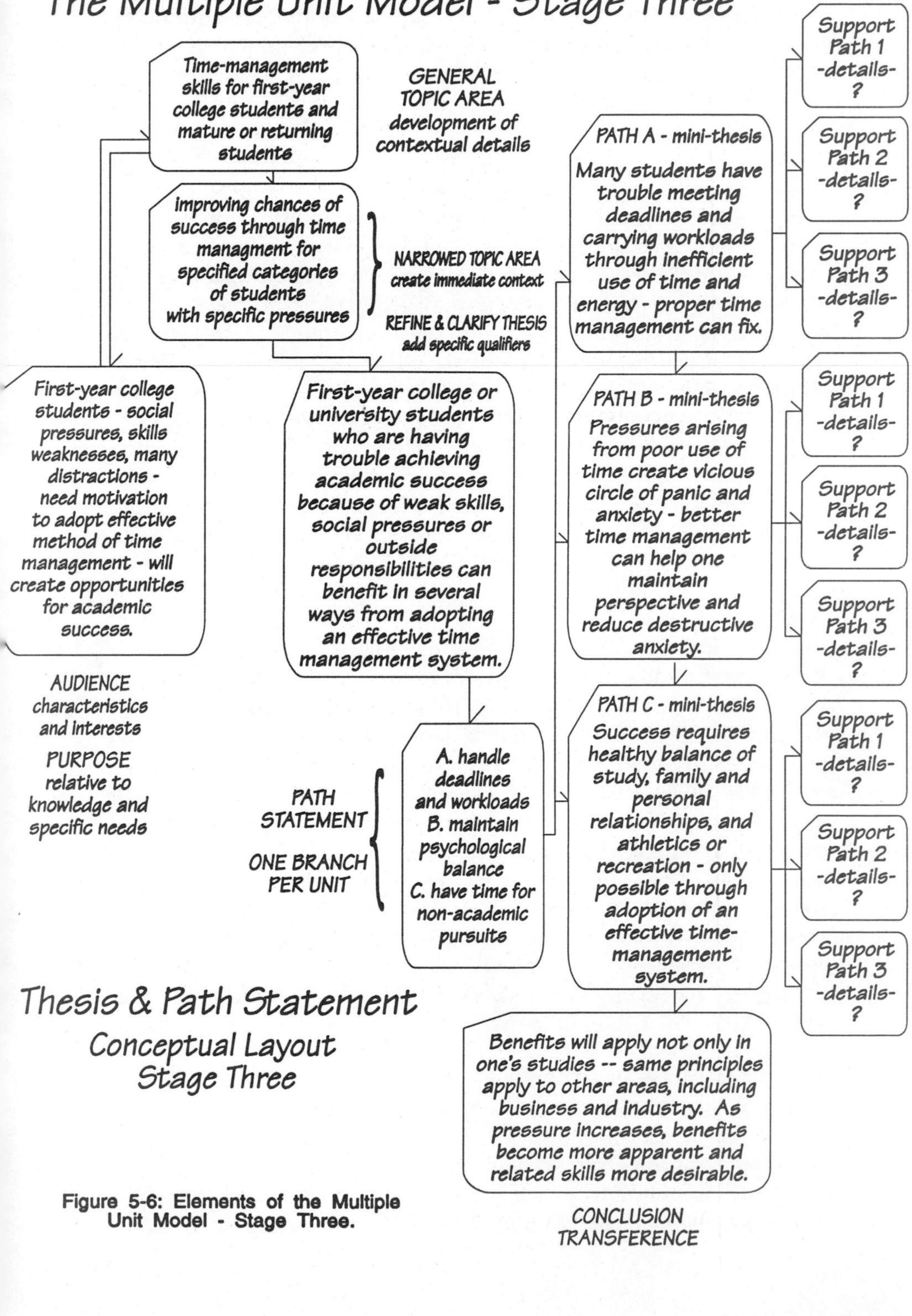

Figure 5-6: Elements of the Multiple Unit Model - Stage Three.

CONCLUSION
TRANSFERENCE

support-path components sufficiently. Thus, you could use the last stage in the development of the model as a kind of continuous self-testing process that would keep you on track.

Let's go back to our time-management example. The mini-thesis for path A—the second conceptual unit of the essay—focuses on the problems students typically have in meeting deadlines, carrying heavy workloads, and working with shifting priorities. This unit must explain effectively the specific nature of the problems students encounter in these areas. Then it must address the ways in which adoption of an effective time-management system can eliminate or reduce the magnitude of the problems. The thesis and path statement for the paper indicate that acquisition of effective time-management skills can benefit otherwise anxious and overstressed students in several ways, one of which relates to the handling of deadlines and workloads (path A). Within this branch of the path, you'll need to break the components of your argument or explanation into logically sequenced units. These are the support paths. When you create these additional components, you'll have to make an educated guess about how much material you'll generate in developing them. If you can give specific support and address specific problems in setting out the support paths—and you can do it without creating a unit that is as long by itself as the entire assignment is supposed to be—then you have narrowed enough. If you find that you can't do this, you'll need to back up through the process. Of course, if you grasped what we discussed in chapter 4—about the need for a clear context for your thesis and about the extent to which that context helps to define the scope of the task you set for yourself—then you shouldn't run into this problem . . . .

Figure 5-7 is a blow up of path A and its (nominal) three support paths in the time-management example. This time we've supplied some potential development information. You don't have to accept the validity of the arguments or explanations at this point. Instead, focus on the narrowness, clarity, and specificity of the points or details listed—maybe you can add useful information, see irrelevancies to be eliminated, or point to evidence of logical inconsistency or inadequate narrowing. You're seeking an understanding of the relationship between the components so that you can use the model appropriately to structure your own work. Examine the details provided: have we narrowed and clarified sufficiently for you to be able to make a reasonable attempt to write this unit of the paper?

Depending on the way you've been used to working in the past, this may seem to you to be more than sufficiently detailed for planning purposes. It's true that we've supplied some fairly specific information about content and about the relationship of the com-

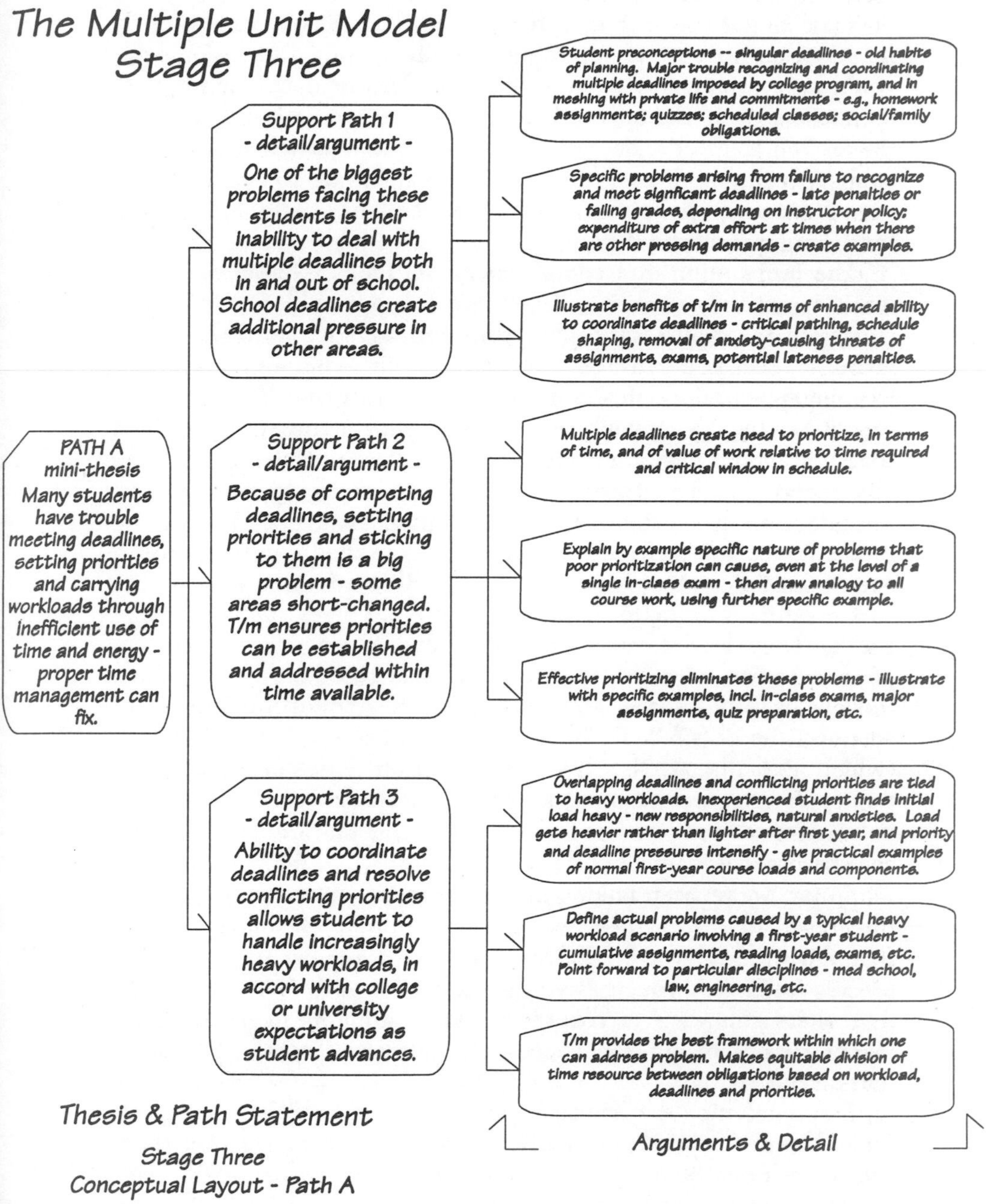

The Multiple Unit Model
Stage Three

Support Path 1
- detail/argument -

One of the biggest problems facing these students is their inability to deal with multiple deadlines both in and out of school. School deadlines create additional pressure in other areas.

Student preconceptions -- singular deadlines - old habits of planning. Major trouble recognizing and coordinating multiple deadlines imposed by college program, and in meshing with private life and commitments - e.g., homework assignments; quizzes; scheduled classes; social/family obligations.

Specific problems arising from failure to recognize and meet significant deadlines - late penalties or failing grades, depending on instructor policy; expenditure of extra effort at times when there are other pressing demands - create examples.

Illustrate benefits of t/m in terms of enhanced ability to coordinate deadlines - critical pathing, schedule shaping, removal of anxiety-causing threats of assignments, exams, potential lateness penalties.

PATH A
mini-thesis

Many students have trouble meeting deadlines, setting priorities and carrying workloads through inefficient use of time and energy - proper time management can fix.

Support Path 2
- detail/argument -

Because of competing deadlines, setting priorities and sticking to them is a big problem - some areas short-changed. T/m ensures priorities can be established and addressed within time available.

Multiple deadlines create need to prioritize, in terms of time, and of value of work relative to time required and critical window in schedule.

Explain by example specific nature of problems that poor prioritization can cause, even at the level of a single in-class exam - then draw analogy to all course work, using further specific example.

Effective prioritizing eliminates these problems - illustrate with specific examples, incl. in-class exams, major assignments, quiz preparation, etc.

Support Path 3
- detail/argument -

Ability to coordinate deadlines and resolve conflicting priorities allows student to handle increasingly heavy workloads, in accord with college or university expectations as student advances.

Overlapping deadlines and conflicting priorities are tied to heavy workloads. Inexperienced student finds initial load heavy - new responsibilities, natural anxieties. Load gets heavier rather than lighter after first year, and priority and deadline pressures intensify - give practical examples of normal first-year course loads and components.

Define actual problems caused by a typical heavy workload scenario involving a first-year student - cumulative assignments, reading loads, exams, etc. Point forward to particular disciplines - med school, law, engineering, etc.

T/m provides the best framework within which one can address problem. Makes equitable division of time resource between obligations based on workload, deadlines and priorities.

Thesis & Path Statement

Stage Three
Conceptual Layout - Path A

Arguments & Detail

Figure 5-7: Development of Path A - Time-Management Example

ponents in this stage of the model. However, as you look over the sample path A, the three sample support paths, and the information you might use within each, other ideas or examples or details might occur to you. If you were actually writing the assignment, you'd have to consider each of the new ideas or details in terms of its relationship to the appropriate support path, to path A, and to the thesis. You might decide to incorporate more material in additional support paths or discard some of our material in favor of the bits you've dreamed up. You might even see a better or more logical order for the arguments and details.

The preparation of a completed model looks like quite a bit of work. It certainly might be, depending on your subject. We've also suggested that you should have substantially completed the visual layout as best you can *before* you attempt to write your first draft. Despite appearances, this is not actually extra work. If you use the model correctly, you won't spend any more time on an assignment than you would have previously—after a bit of practice, you'll actually spend less. You'll have to get used to changing the way you allocate your time within the writing process. Proper use of the model forces you to front-load the process so that a higher percentage of the time you spend on the essay will be devoted to planning and organizing prior to drafting. There is a corresponding shrinkage of the time you might normally spend at the other end of the process. In fact, when you write the first draft based on the completed model, the process may seem much like a grammatical version of "connect the dots." You'll be able to concentrate on drafting issues (which we'll discuss shortly), rather than on issues of idea generation, planning, and organizing at the conceptual level. As a result, you may find that you need fewer drafts and that the drafting process becomes less uncomfortable.

So far, we've been talking about the model in terms of its components, and the pictures we've shown you of the model reflect that. Figure 5-8 is a bit different: this is a representation of the *process* you'll go through as you work with model. It is a flowchart that offers you ways to ensure that your attempts to use a visual layout for organization will meet with success, if you're persistent and careful.

If you examine the flowchart carefully, you'll be able to identify the components we've been discussing. You'll also see that there are some loops built in. These loops are designed to provide you with chances to narrow, review, or alter your material at key stages in the organizational process. For example, consider the loops involved in the steps leading to the presentation of your thesis statement. You'll see that you need to move back and forth between

The Multiple Unit Model
Flowchart of Process for Completing Multiple Unit Model

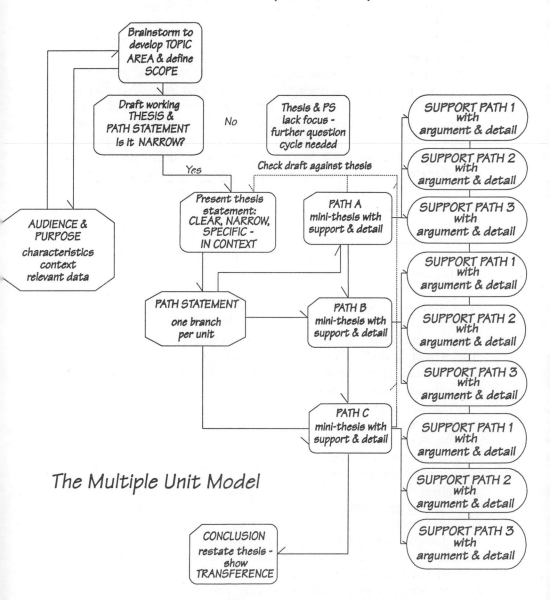

Figure 5-8: Flowchart - Generation of Multiple Unit Model

reviewing your information as to your audience and purpose, and brainstorming to develop and define the scope of your topic area. Your initial consideration of your audience and purpose will help you develop the platform from which you brainstorm and define. The results of your brainstorming ought to send you back to reconsider whether the way in which you are handling topic area and scope are still appropriate to your audience and purpose. When you're actually working on an assignment, you'll probably play this back-and-forth game quite a few times, until you begin to see your thesis and path statement emerging. Once that happens, you'll have to include in the loop the testing of the draft thesis and path statement for narrowness and clarity. Because narrowness and clarity depend to a great extent on your audience and purpose, you'll find yourself going back through the brainstorming stage in order to narrow further, and you'll be reconsidering your audience and purpose for the same reason. It may sound confusing, but the process actually leads to greater clarity.

A similar loop occurs after you've set out your path statement. You'll have to look at the mini-thesis in each branch of your path and determine whether its relationship with your thesis and path statement is clear and appropriate. Every time you make an adjustment, you're going to have to consider the impact of that adjustment on all the other components, in order to be sure that your logic is clear and that you haven't lost unity or coherence. The visual layout will help you prevent such loss, since you get to see all the components at once instead of having to juggle them in your head.

Some students feel an initial frustration with the model because they seem to be second-guessing themselves all the time. If you can make the process work effectively once, then you'll find the rewards far outweigh the discomfort caused by the change in your working pattern. Again, we don't want to suggest that you should reduce all your writing to a purely mechanistic activity; but most students seem to benefit from a structural approach to preparing their written assignments. So, we offer you the template contained in figure 5-9. The form of the template arises directly from the structure of the multiple unit model.

Again, you'll notice that all the components of the multiple unit model are present. However, when you use the template, it will be up to you to develop and include the appropriate information. If you try to follow the procedures we've recommended—and you're very fussy about having a narrow, clear thesis and path statement— then you can use this generic template to create consistency in your essay-writing process. You can (and should) also work with the form of the template, modifying it to suit your purpose on specific assignments.

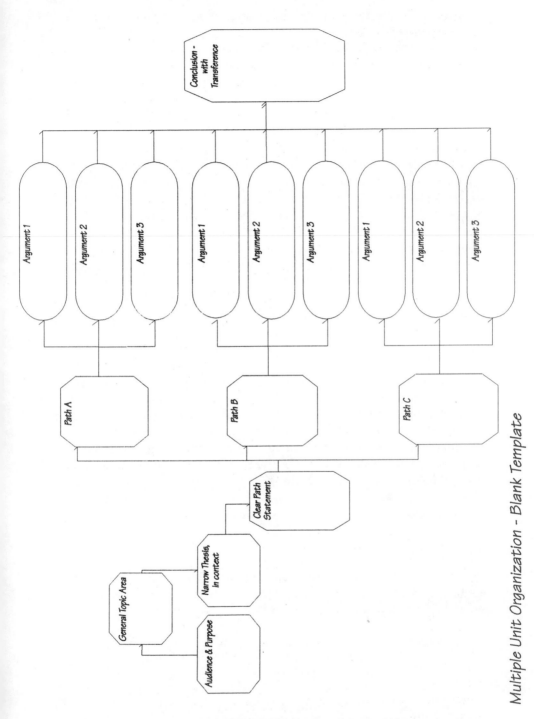

Multiple Unit Organization - Blank Template

Figure 5-9: Multiple Unit Model - Blank Template

You should copy the template and enlarge it so that you have ample room to work within it.

Please remember that the template form, of itself, is nothing. It's your understanding of the underlying operative principle expressed in the template that is crucial. We've had students take all kinds of liberties with the form of the template in order to make it work for them in the context of their own learning styles. One student obtained a huge roll of butcher paper; for every essay, she would tear off a strip about six feet long and four feet wide. Once she had a working thesis, she would tack her sheet of butcher paper on a wall and rough out a template on it. She would record the results of her brainstorming session in one corner. In the various boxes, she would include as much detailed, point-form information as she could think of. She'd go back and reconsider her thesis constantly, narrowing and refining as she went. When she was developing the support paths in each branch of her path statement, she'd use dozens of little sticky notes for her ideas. She'd juggle them from place to place on her template, and she'd use larger sticky notes for quotations or other source references. By the time she was through with the planning and organizing and felt ready to proceed with her first draft, her huge template contained, in point form, everything she wanted to say in the order she wanted to say it, right down to the specific supporting material she intended to use. From there, she had no trouble with her first draft and could turn her attention to proofreading and revision—always using the template's components as benchmarks for accuracy and organizational logic. Another student liked to work with a blackboard on which he had actually painted a permanent template. Still another used a corkboard with notes and pegs. Whatever you choose to do is fine—as long as you don't skip past the time- and labour-intensive planning and organizing stage in your eagerness to reach the "easy" drafting stage.

Exercises

We've thrown quite a bit of information at you in the last few pages. Now it's time to work with the model a little in order to see if you've understood the discussion and examples. So here's what we want you to do:

1. Earlier, we worked with path A of our time-management example—have another look at figure 5-7. Now, we want you to try to develop the stage-three parts of the model for paths B and C. Using figure 5-7 as your example, create a suitable mini-thesis for each path; then work out at least three support paths, with detail and argument for each. Remember: the time you spend doing this is not time "wasted on an exercise." It's time you are actually

using to experiment with the operative principle that will ensure your success on written assignments—if you understand the principle and can apply it properly. Of course, the material you create for this exercise should find its way into your note files.

2. Make a blank template like the one in figure 5-9. We want you to use this template in planning an essay around a topic of your own choosing. You don't have to write the essay; but we want you to complete the template to the point that you could actually write the essay without reference to any other material once you got to the drafting stage. In order to complete this exercise, you're going to have to go through some steps: consider your audience and purpose; develop and refine a topic area; narrow the scope to the point at which you can offer a narrow, clear thesis; devise a suitable path statement; and develop support paths for each branch of your path statement; develop arguments and details suitable to each support path. BIG HINT: we assume that, like us, you believe in "working smart," rather than merely in working hard. If you have an assignment coming due any time soon, consider working with your topic for that assignment in this exercise. Make the most of your investment of time and energy by making the exercise serve multiple purposes. If the multiple unit model, as we've set it out, seems to make sense to you, don't skip this exercise, and don't skimp on it either.

THE DRAFTING PROCESS

Unlike the writers of most other composition guides, we don't have alot to say about the initial drafting process. This is because your first draft—IF you've used the multiple unit model properly—will be little more than a game of grammatical "connect the dots," in which you work carefully from your detailed template and any resource materials. You should follow the template carefully, and focus on grammar and punctuation in linking the ideas set out there. Remember also that you will be engaging in intensive proofreading and revision later in the writing process. In chapter 8, this aspect of the process is discussed more thoroughly.

6
How to Work with
the Rhetorical Approaches

So far, we've been considering the essay in terms of a generic model for organization and layout. Within that model, you have at your disposal some well-established ways to handle the content of your essay. We call these ways of handling content "rhetorical approaches." They are really ways of structuring information to shape your reader's understanding. They are as much reflections of our culture, language, and nature as human beings, as they are strategies for approaching writing tasks. Included among these strategies are such things as <u>exposition</u>, <u>narration</u> and <u>description</u>. Within exposition, you are most likely to be working with <u>process</u>, <u>comparison and contrast</u>, <u>cause and effect</u>, and <u>classification</u>.

These approaches to the handling of ideas are intertwined in your head—you use all of them all the time, so much so that you don't usually think about what you're doing when you use them. For example, if you want to buy a sweater, you'll go through a *process* by which you define the kind of sweater you seek. In doing so, you'll identify *categories* or *classifications* of sweaters that you will consider, based on characteristics you have defined. You may decide to make a selection from the category of all sweaters that are fire-engine red and have long sleeves and crew necks. Within this group you might eliminate those sweaters costing more than $100 and less than $15. Based on your criteria, you'll ultimately decide between three or four sweaters presented to you by a salesperson. When you get to the point that your choice is between two specific sweaters, you'll be *comparing and contrasting*. If you make a choice based in part on how well each of the two sweaters is likely to wash up or how long each is likely to last, then you are incorporating *cause and effect* into your decision-making process.

There is often a gap between the way most of us work with the rhetorical approaches in our daily lives and the ways they are to be used in essay writing. When we're engaged in conversation or are thinking about something, we tend not to direct our attention to the way in which we are examining ideas. Our thoughts are fluid, our responses dictated by the context and by our reaction to the ideas of others. We may shift rapidly from examining a comparative statement to making a point about a result that might occur or about an appropriate way of doing something. As long as the parties to the conversation can see and hear each other and can seek clarification whenever necessary, the exchange of ideas will continue.

This is obviously not the case when you write an essay. The audience cannot see or question you when a problem or objection arises. The reader must depend on the logical premise you provide in your thesis and path statement, a premise that you must state clearly and explore thoroughly. Because of the separation between you and your audience, you must try to externalize the rhetorical approaches, to get them out of your head and onto the paper, so that you can make deliberate choices about using them for specific purposes in your essays. They are the tools at your disposal and the means by which you can address both form and content.

⇨ | *In any essay, you may have to use more than one of the approaches; but it is essential that you select and maintain throughout the paper a controlling approach that will dictate the logical structure of your discussion.* | ⇦

Your controlling approach is the particular rhetorical model on which your thesis and path statement are based. For example, if your thesis is that doing x will lead to results a, b and c, the controlling approach for the paper must be cause and effect, because your arguable assertion is that doing a particular action will cause particular results. The reader will then expect that the major body units of your paper will address the relationship between the causal event and each of the major consequences. Even though you might legitimately speculate in one unit about what would have happened if some other causal event had occurred, the comparison between the likely results of the two causal events is not the controlling model for the paper.

These approaches are sometimes discussed as if they had meaning or validity independent of context, subject, purpose, and audience. However, you should recognize that they are intellectual constructs—

devices you can use to present your ideas effectively from a specific perspective. Thus, they gain their apparent validity by way of application; they provide us with intellectual models for the examination and resolution of questions or issues. The rhetorical approaches also have something in common with the "rules" of grammar. Despite their acceptance as rules by generations of students and despite the centuries of practice and tradition associated with their use:

⇨ *We do not follow or adopt the rhetorical approaches because they are real, true, or correct; they are real, true, or correct because we follow them.* ⇦

They depend for their validity on their continuing effectiveness as devices for clear and effective communication. Because they have worked for us consistently and effectively for so long, we've given them the status of rules or firmly established principles.

In order to improve your understanding of these approaches as devices for presenting information or exploring ideas effectively, you must accept that the separation of the various approaches from each other, and from the purposes for which they are to be applied, is an artificial and arbitrary separation. It is intended (at least in part) to serve the requirements and expectations that govern the essay as a testing device. At the level of the undergraduate essay, you must learn to make each rhetorical approach work for you and to demonstrate your command of each as a tool for the analysis and synthesis of ideas, arguments and evidence.

EXPOSITION

Exposition is a global approach involving an explanation of something or an explanation of your viewpoint about something. You might also think of exposition as a kind of teaching in which you set material before your audience and explain it to them in such a way that by the time they have finished reading your work, they will have learned something useful. This means that when you write an expository essay, you're always dealing with one or more intelligent, meaningful questions that you are answering for the reader, or with issues or analyses that are narrowly focused and require explanation and elaboration through your discussion. In this sense, every essay you write is an expository essay, even though you may be using narration or description in the course of explaining something to your reader. We've already discussed the importance of narrowing; now we can see the connection between the nature of exposition (to teach or persuade), the need for specificity and meaningful information, and the knowledge and skills that the essay tests. Within the expository essay itself, you may be required to demonstrate your understanding of a particular rhetorical approach to the handling of ideas, or you may select a particular rhetorical approach because the content issues you're going to discuss seem to lend themselves to that approach. In presenting your explanations to your reader, you must support the points you make with meaningful examples and details—specific information intended to lead the reader to the conclusion that your explanations are correct.

PROCESS

Process, as an approach to essay writing, involves the presentation of a series of logically ordered, discrete steps in a predetermined sequence, in such a way that the reader is capable either of replicating the process or of teaching it to someone else based on the content of your essay. Think about this description of process for a moment, and compare it to your own sense of processes you use every day. You deal with process in some way, consciously or unconsciously, in every moment of your life. You depend on natural processes all the time: your autonomic nervous system operates, your heart beats, you breathe, your synapses fire. Each of these natural processes has a certain sequence to it. If the normal sequence is disturbed for any period of time, you can become ill. Similarly, we know that plants extract energy from sunlight through the process of photosynthesis; we know that the great tectonic plates beneath the earth move; we see the sequence of the seasons. In addition to natural process, you are also caught up with artificial or mechanical process on a daily basis. You impose some artificial processes on yourself: you wake up at an arbitrarily chosen time each day, shower, dress, eat breakfast, and head off for class. You have a routine, which is a self-imposed process. If it is disrupted, you can be off-balance for the rest of the day. You like your own artificial processes to function in the proper sequence. You deal with mechanical process when you use a toaster or a blender or a hair dryer, or when you drive a car. The machinery functions according to a series of principles that you may or may not understand, but you do know there is a sequence of logical steps that must occur before the machinery will function.

> *The examination in an essay of a natural process or an artificial or mechanical process addresses the question, "What happens, in what order?"*

A third aspect of process—one with which you, as a student, are familiar—is instructional process. Instructional process focuses on questions relating to how to do things. Again, you deal with this kind of process on a daily basis. You buy a new digital alarm clock, a camera, a stereo component, or some new computer hardware or software; you look through the manual for the installation instructions. These instructions are (or should be) a series of logically sequenced steps that show you how to install or work the item without blowing it (or yourself) sky-high. Most of us have had the experience of trying to do something according to written instructions and becoming frustrated because the instructions were inaccurate, incomplete, or out of sequence. We are driven crazy when we put something together according to instructions and there are two screws left over, or when we follow laundry directions and the new blue shirt turns out not to be colour-fast after all. Students who are living on their own for the first time may become familiar with the "how-to's" of frozen dinners and the culinary horrors that come from poorly written or badly followed instructional process. Even these problems pale into insignificance beside the devastation created by badly written computer software instructions.

What you do (or perhaps, what is done to you) when you attend college or university courses involves instructional process. Instructional process, on several levels, is used to increase your understanding and capabilities in a variety of areas involving, among other things, natural and artificial or mechanical processes. However, consideration of the sorts of instructional process we see in formal education raises a key issue in terms of how you use process in your own essays. When you're in class, your instructors are generally interested not only in having you see what happens or in showing you how to do something; they are also interested in the rationale behind the sequence of steps, the "why" of it all. In your writing, if you attempt to include the rationale behind the process, you may find yourself losing control of the model or approach that is supposed to govern your paper. The reason for this is simple: as soon as you get into "why," you've expanded from process into cause and effect. This may be appropriate—unless the assignment specifically requires you to use process as your controlling approach. You must make certain that your process essay focuses on what happens and in what order, rather than on why something happens the way it does.

The basic principles we discussed in earlier chapters apply equally to process essays. You must identify a suitable topic area; you must narrow appropriately, having in mind your purpose and the presumed need of your reader; and you must generate appropriately sequenced material that is calculated to fulfil those purposes fully, relative to the scope of your thesis and path statement. You must also remember that while the thesis is an arguable assertion, it need not be an argument. Thus, in a process paper, your arguable assertion might be a simple statement that members of a particular group with particular needs *should have* an understanding of a particular process in order to do something that is regularly required of them. That, in a process paper, is an arguable assertion. Similarly, the path statement won't necessarily look exactly like the conventional path statement in which there are x number of stops in different areas along a journey to a particular conclusion. Rather, the path statement may reflect very simply that the process which is the subject of your arguable assertion involves x steps, which you might or might not label separately. This alone will create an appropriate expectation in your audience: "The writer of this paper is going to tell me how to do something, or how something works; and this process which he or she is addressing in the rest of the essay will involve x steps." Process writing may therefore sometimes lack the fire and fluidity of some of the other approaches. However, it has its own intrinsic value because of the presumed importance of a particular process to the needs of a particular audience. The very nature of process and the extent to which it imposes order on your own organization and on the reader's understanding are very satisfying.

If you're told to write a process essay in which you have free choice of topics, you can follow the steps set out below (a process!) to get the job done.

1. <u>Be selective in your focus</u>. If your focus is too broad—for example, how to write a complex computer program—you won't be able to deal with it in 500 words. If your focus is trivial—for example, how to open a can of soup—it won't sustain a 500 word essay. You'll need to think of something that is both relevant to the course content and narrow enough to cover thoroughly. You'll also have to rethink our earlier comments about appropriateness: unless an instructor expressly gives you permission to do so, avoid writing process papers about how to give an ostrich a bubble bath.

2. <u>Formulate your thesis and path statement</u>. When you get to

step 3 below, you're going to have to give the reader a context. Be prepared to build in a characterization of the target audience for whom your process is relevant. Make certain that your thesis statement is an arguable assertion of the sort we described above. Make certain that your path statement is clear and indicates to the reader the number of steps in the process and the fact that there is an essential logical sequence involved.

3. Prepare the contextual material for the process in which you develop an appropriate context for your process thesis. You might choose to consider the nature of the audience and its needs, the requirements the process itself imposes (special equipment, required knowledge or training), and the importance of the application or result of the process as sources of material for context.

4. Make certain that your understanding of the principles governing the process is accurate. When you prepare your contextual information, you may have to explain a complex theory or series of principles to your reader. Thus, an essay which sets out a research process built on an understanding of Heisenberg's uncertainty principle will need this information, and you'll have to tailor it specifically for your immediate purpose and the level of entry knowledge you are assuming on the part of the reader. If you write a process essay on how to build a wooden box, you can probably omit any theoretical discussion.

5. Define the sequence of steps. You may or may not include the sequence as a list of discrete steps in the essay; but as the writer you must use it as your benchmark in ensuring that you are presenting an accurate, properly sequenced view of the process. Always assume that the reader is not acquainted with the steps in the process. If there is more than one acceptable ordering possible, then choose the one that makes most sense in your immediate situation—but let the reader know that there may be other possibilities.

6. Fit the sequence into the multiple unit model, giving key steps their own branches in the path statement, and grouping lesser steps appropriately. In the template, generate the detail you will need at the drafting stage. Warn the reader about pitfalls or difficulties in the process. Where appropriate, tell the reader how to avoid potential problems.

7. Prepare the conclusion. This is quite simple in a process essay: you need only summarize the process and its importance

to your reader's immediate need. If you can see a way in which the reader might take the process and apply it in a new or different context, you may even be able to effect transference—something which can be difficult when you are working with "pure" process.

Exercise

Although process sounds as if it should be the easiest of the approaches to understand, it can create some problems. The problems frequently stem from an improper formulation of the steps in the process (see step 5 in the process outlined above). If you try to write a process paper without being sure of what the steps are, how many there should be, or how logical your sequence is, your reader is likely to become confused. Therefore, in order to meet your obligations to the reader, you have to be able to outline the steps in the process *before* you write your first draft. In this exercise, you are to identify a process with which you personally are familiar; it doesn't matter whether the process is natural, mechanical or instructional in nature. The process you select must be simple enough to be explained or taught in five or six steps, yet it must be interesting to your presumed audience. For the purpose of this exercise, assume your audience is a generally well-informed and intelligent group of your peers. They have no specific knowledge of your process, but are interested and eager to learn—they will be relying on you for an accurate, logically sequenced explanation or instruction. Once you have clearly identified the process, outline the steps from first to last. Describe each step in one or two sentences, and make sure you've left out nothing your reader would need in order to complete the process on his or her own. In order to do this, you're going to have to look carefully at steps 1 to 4 above: you don't have to write them for this exercise, but you will have to think about them in order to get to the point of listing and ordering your own steps. For example, if you were outlining the process of writing a process essay, you might end up with something like this:

To write a proper process essay, one should:

1. Choose a topic carefully, making sure that the chosen process is narrow enough to cover.

2. Develop the thesis and path statement in which the number of steps is indicated and the importance of the process to the reader is emphasized.

3. Write a general introduction to the process, being careful to establish an appropriate context within which to introduce the process logically.

4. Identify the theory, if any, forming the basis of the process.

5. List and order the steps, keeping in mind the needs and current understanding of the reader.

6. Develop the steps, using sequencing and detail in order to ensure the reader's ability to understand or replicate the process.

7. Prepare the conclusion.

COMPARISON & CONTRAST

Comparison and contrast, as a rhetorical approach, focuses the reader's attention on the differences and/or similarities between items that share some characteristics, in order to help the reader determine the fitness of the items for a particular purpose. Contrast tends to focus on the differences between related items; comparison focuses on the similarities between related items.

> ➪ *"Comparison and contrast" might be described as a weighing of the relative advantages and/or disadvantages of the items being examined.* ⇦

In such a case, "relative" means relative to the purpose defined for the reader in the context, thesis and path statement. For example, if one is working with contrast, one might be looking at two single-lens reflex 35mm cameras. They share an obvious major attribute: they are both single-lens reflex 35mm cameras. However, if one is a very basic, manually controlled camera and the other is a fully automatic, autofocus camera with every option available, there will be ample points of contrast or difference for purposes of the assignment. Conversely, if one is looking at two cameras which are similar in all but one respect, it is feasible to compare by examining the most important ways in which the two are similar. Finally, if the audience consists of readers who want to select a camera that will give them professional results on a backpacking expedition in rough terrain where heat and dust are problems, then you would find yourself establishing a list of camera features and characteristics likely to be important to such a group. You would compare and contrast by examining the extent to which each camera fulfilled or failed to fulfil the readers' requirements.

Let's consider a template that you can use for the purpose of dealing with comparison and contrast. In figure 6-1, we've set out a grid which allows you to see the relationship between the items being

Modes and Approaches
Comparison & Contrast

	Item A	Item B	Mini-conclusion
Criterion 1			
Criterion 2			
Criterion 3			
Mini-conclusion			Global Conclusion

Figure 6-1: Comparison & Contrast Grid

compared or contrasted in terms of relevant features or criteria.

In the grid, you see column headings referring to the items being compared or contrasted. You also see row headings referring to the specific criteria—differing characteristics or shared characteristics of the items which would form the basis of the comparison and contrast. You also see row and column headings labelled "Mini-conclusion." These refer to the ways you deal with the issues in the paper and the reader's ability to absorb and remember crucial information over the length of the paper. Clearly, it's better for your reader if you present your information in a way that makes it easier for the reader to remember the main points you're making as he reads through to your conclusion. The grid provides you with two alternative ways to structure your work. Depending on the subject matter and the nature of your audience, you could choose to present your information horizontally or vertically.

First, you can work horizontally. That is, you can begin by discussing criterion 1 with reference to item *A* in your comparison; then you can discuss the same criterion with respect to item *B*. You would offer the reader a conclusion on the relative merits of the two items with respect to that criterion or characteristic only. This material would form the basis for the first branch of your path statement for the paper. Then you would go on to treat criteria 2 and 3 in the same way. Your treatment of criteria 2 and 3 would form the bases for the second and third branches of your path statement.

Alternatively, you can work vertically by focusing first on item *A* and discussing all three of the criteria in sequence, and then offering a mini-conclusion with respect to item *A*'s performance in all three areas. This would form the first branch of your path statement. Then you would move to item *B*, giving it the same treatment and creating the second branch of your path statement. When you work vertically, your path statement is likely to contain only two branches; but in either case, you would be obliged to offer your reader a global conclusion directly reflecting the premise in your thesis and path statement. Unless you're working with a comparison that requires you to use the vertical method, try to use the horizontal. Many readers find it easier to deal with what appears to be a single issue at a time and to keep in mind the individual mini-conclusions as they read through to the conclusion of your paper.

If we use our camera example, we can fill in the grid just enough to illustrate how the principle works. Figure 6-2 sets out the grid again, with some of the material you might need to proceed if you were going to write a comparison and contrast essay on the two cameras. As we noted, if you decide to work horizontally, the material you generate for each of the three criteria or important points of comparison would comprise one branch of your path statement in the multiple unit model we presented in the last chapter—see figure 6-3 below. If you choose to proceed vertically, you'll have to adjust the model to reflect two major branches rather than three, since you will be focusing on the two items (*A* and *B*) rather than on the three criteria for your structure. Note also that the number of support paths in each branch of the path statement may also change, as will the substance of your mini-conclusions.

If you're assigned an essay in which you are to use comparison and contrast as the controlling approach, you can try dealing with the assignment like this:

Modes and Approaches
Comparison & Contrast

	Camera 'A'	Camera 'B'	Mini-conclusion
Criterion 1 manual functions	?	?	A/B is better because...
Criterion 2 automatic functions	?	?	A/B is better because...
Criterion 3 lens quality & sharpness	?	?	A/B is better because...
Mini-conclusion	A/B is better because...	A/B is better because...	Global Conclusion

Figure 6-2: Comparison & Contrast Grid

1. <u>Choose an appropriate focus</u>. You must be sure that when you select the actual elements to compare, you can see a comparative basis that will have value to your reader in the context of the assignment. Moreover, it might be to your benefit to see that the comparison is not only valuable, but interesting as well.

2. <u>Establish a purpose for your reader</u>. The purpose you express in your paper is determined by your reason for writing and is shaped by the limits of time, space, and real or hypothetical audience characteristics. Remember: while it's true that proper narrowing in your thesis will usually help you address many of

The Multiple Unit Model - Basic Elements

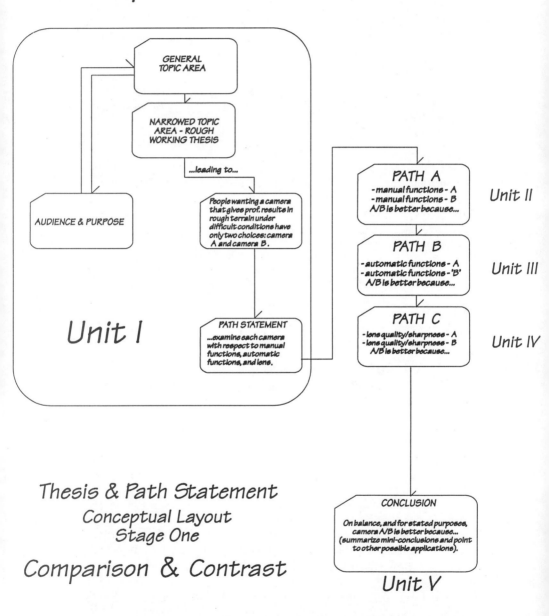

Figure 6-3: the Multiple Unit Model, Stage One - Comparison & Contrast

your concerns about the audience, you must look at the nature of the assignment as it has been presented to you in order to determine whether you must do some real targeting.

3. Limit the bases for your comparison to the most important points only in establishing a purpose for your reader. Depending on the things you're comparing or contrasting, you may find that there are literally dozens of points of similarity or difference. If you're dealing with a typical 500- to 1,000-word paper, you can't cover them all; don't even try. Instead, pick the criteria or points of comparison that seem most relevant to your purpose and the needs of the reader. If you're writing for an instructor who is expressly trying to test your knowledge, do your homework: confine your discussion to the criteria that are recognized as the most critical. You may decide to focus on similarities, differences, or similarities and differences, *relative to your reader's understanding of purpose*. You may have to rethink the issue as one of discussing the relative merits and disadvantages of the items being compared for a specific purpose.

4. Develop your thesis and path statement carefully. Remember to name or define the two items you will discuss, and state clearly the points of comparison that will form the branches of your path statement. You should reflect not only whether your paper will focus on similarities, differences, or both; you should also be clear about whether you will proceed by focusing on one criterion at a time or by focusing on one item at a time (horizontal or vertical).

5. Select your details and supporting components carefully. It isn't enough for you simply to state that a similarity or difference exists between the items you're comparing. You must show the reader, illustrating your points (relative to the reader's needs) by specific details and examples. For each point of comparison, list the details that occur to you so that you can pick the best for presentation in your discussion. You may find it useful to make a separate list for each item or criterion. At the proper stage, you can place the details you've generated into the grid.

6. Keep your discussion on track—don't allow yourself to be distracted by irrelevant details. For some reason, many students lose control of the comparison/contrast approach, especially if their supporting material involves the juxtaposing of cause/effect sequences. This happens when you are comparing, for example, two ways of doing something in terms of their results.

Remember what the controlling approach for the paper is supposed to be.

7. Form your conclusion. Try to summarize the critical differences and/or similarities and draw a clear and logical conclusion for your reader. Keep in mind that this is an expository essay when you frame your conclusion. Look for a way to create transference.

Exercise

In this exercise, you'll make a comparison-and-contrast grid like the one in figure 6-2. You'll need to identify a topic area and narrow it to a clear thesis and path statement, using the principles we discussed earlier. For example, if you're interested in stereo, you might think about the possibility of comparing analog recordings with compact discs, given a particular purpose or kind of music; or you might be considering a "closer" comparison between compact discs and digital audiotape. Start with a subject with which you are familiar, but remember that your audience may be new to the subject area. Proceed on the basis that your audience must make an important decision between two alternatives or choices before they can get more involved in the subject matter. Your job will be to explain the alternative choices and their implications, relative to the audience's needs. Once you've completed the grid, take the information and transfer it into the multiple unit model, placing it in the path-statement sections. Remember that sooner or later you'll be asked to write a comparison-and-contrast essay.

CAUSE & EFFECT

If you've ever conducted a scientific experiment, played a musical instrument, trained an animal, or changed your hairstyle, then you're familiar with cause/effect relationships. In its broadest sense, the principle of cause and effect rules the universe. There isn't anything that you can do that can't be seen as being part of a causal sequence, however remote the connections may seem. When you talk to your friends or dress yourself to achieve a certain look or forget to stop at the store on the way home to pick up some milk, there will be other events that occur in part because of what you did or didn't do. Legislators frame new laws to create particular changes within society; courts examine causal relationships in determining the guilt or innocence of accused persons. The planets move; the earth shakes. History unfolds itself before your eyes as a complex web of interrelationship, action and reaction. These things all reflect causal relationships. However, not all causal events and their effects would be suitable for discussion in an undergraduate cause-and-effect essay. Some may be irrelevant to your subject or discipline, while others may address trivialities. Some events may not be related in the way you think—you might mistake coincidence for cause/effect. Still other causal relationships may be too broad or profound to be discussed thoroughly in a short essay. Because things happen for a variety of reasons, you will usually want to focus on an event's principal or major causal factors, though there may be several indirect causes at work. Similarly, you'll want to focus on significant or immediate effects rather than more remote effects, unless a remote effect is the end-point of a causal sequence you are examining.

Cause and effect, as an approach, shares some characteristics with process, to the extent that both may involve explanations of a sequence of events. We've already described the difference between the two; but let us jog your memory.

⇨

Process concerns itself primarily with what happens and in what order, or with how to do something. Cause and effect may cover the same material, but will go beyond process to deal with the underlying rationale; the "why," "how," and "what if" of things.

⇦

As a result, if you're required to work with cause and effect (or you elect to use this approach) as your controlling approach in a paper, you'll have to be careful in identifying the components in your thesis and path statement and in making sure that as you write, you don't get side-tracked into process. Think of it this way:

Process: "This happens in this order," or, "Follow these instructions to get this result."

Cause and Effect: "Why does this happen in this order?" "What will happen if I do these things in this order, and how or why will results occur the way they do?"

When you deal with cause and effect, you aren't limited by time. That is, you aren't limited to an examination of causal relationships that developed in the past. Thus, you need not write only about past causes and their past effects, or sequences of events that started and finished in the past. You might be considering an event that occurred recently or is still in the process of occurring, and speculating about its most significant potential effects in the immediate future. You might be taking a current event as the beginning of a causal sequence and speculating as to the sequence of events likely to unfold from it over a specified period of time. As long as you can substantiate your position on the future existence of a causal relationship through evidence and argument, you can work with that relationship in an essay. Thus, you might speculate as to the impact on Maine's climate if global warming melts part of the polar ice-cap and the water level of the Atlantic rises by four inches. You could look at Portland college students' current problems in paying for housing and tuition in the face of recent reductions in federal or state student loan payments. You could work with a possible sequence of events that might occur in an environmentally sensitive area in which a certain animal species is threatened by a particular activity or type of pollution.

There are three forms of cause and effect that you can use in your essays. The first takes a causal event, defines it, and then focuses on a limited number of significant effects for a particular group or in particular circumstances. This first form requires you to create a thesis and path statement that focus on the x most immediate or most important specific effects arising from the causal event. For example, you might be considering consumption of alcohol by a woman during the second trimester of pregnancy as a cause, and the three most important, immediate and specific impacts on the unborn child as the effects. Figure 6-4 illustrates the relationship between the basic components; notice that it parallels the structure of the thesis and path statement.

The second form looks at an event as a result flowing from certain causes, and the thesis and path statement address the x most important, specific causal factors that made the event take place the way it did. For example, you might be considering a specific and violent incident in a labour dispute in terms of the three most significant and immediate (that is, directly related) contributing factors that led to the incident's occurrence. This form also lends itself to treatment within the basic multiple unit model (see figure 6-5). It is the opposite of the first form illustrated in figure 6-4.

If you look at figures 6-4 and 6-5, you'll see that, in terms of the kinds of content they would cover and the path the writer would pursue, they conform to the visual layout required for the thesis and path statement in the multiple unit model. The number of effects in figure 6-4 and the number of causal factors in figure 6-5 would determine the number of branches required in the path statement for each. Based on this information, it should be easy for you to apply either of these forms of cause/effect in terms of the basic template for the multiple unit model.

The third form, which many students initially seem to find much

Modes and Approaches
Cause & Effect

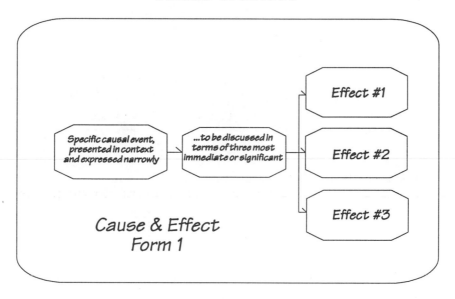

Figure 6-4: Cause & Effect - First Form

harder to handle than the first two, involves the examination of a cause/effect sequence. Your thesis will require you to explain the rationale behind the occurrence of a sequence of events over x period of time in chronological order. A cause/effect essay of this type might focus on an analysis of the causal sequence starting with the inhalation of a puff of cigarette smoke and culminating in the contraction of arteries in the smoker's body. This approach to cause and effect can be problematic because it may take some time before you see clearly the critical differences between the causal sequence and ordinary process. If you have trouble making the template work when you are dealing with a causal sequence, you may need to use a format that looks more like the one in figure 6-6.

In this illustration, we can see that the reader's need for a clear understanding of the sequential logic—the rationale by which the reader can justify moving from each step to the next in the sequence—is addressed expressly. If one step in the sequence is unclear or there appears to the reader to be no transitional logic between any two steps, the causal sequence breaks down at that point, just as would a process essay if you neglected to show the reader how to move from one step to the next. For example, if you

Modes and Approaches
Cause & Effect

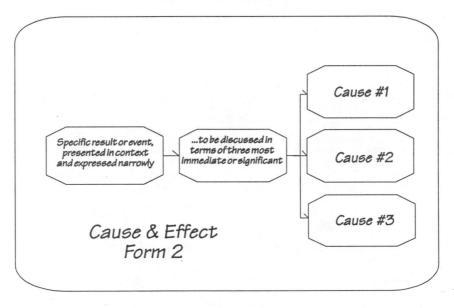

Specific result or event, presented in context and expressed narrowly

...to be discussed in terms of three most immediate or significant

Cause #1

Cause #2

Cause #3

Cause & Effect
Form 2

Figure 6-5: Cause & Effect - Second Form

are explaining a sequence of events that depends on the reader's understanding of a series of chemical reactions and you neglect to explain how the third reaction in the sequence triggers the fourth reaction, the reader has no way of moving from the step containing the third reaction to the step containing the fourth. As a result, the remainder of the sequence becomes unclear and open to challenge. When you work with a causal sequence, take pains to ensure that your reader does not have to struggle with or guess at the means by which each step in the sequence leads to the next.

If you are asked to write a paper with cause and effect as the controlling model, you might wish to review the following:

1. Given your subject matter, decide whether you will reason from cause to effects, from effect to causes, or from the beginning of an arbitrarily selected sequence to the end of the sequence.

2. In analyzing your material, avoid the temptation to generalize or oversimplify your focus. Particularly when you deal with complex causal relationships, you run the risk of losing the reader if he or she is unable to see the logical connections you

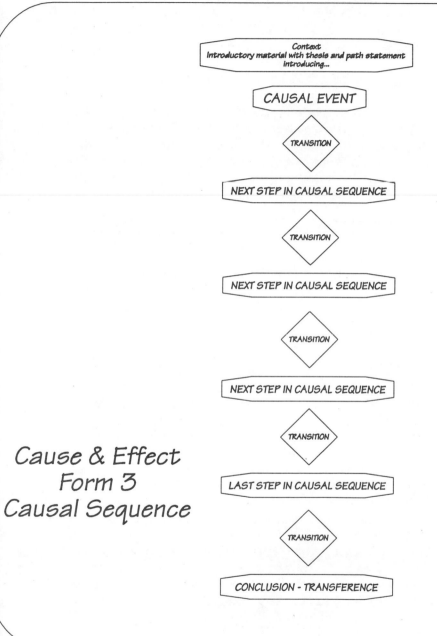

Cause & Effect
Form 3
Causal Sequence

Figure 6-6: Cause & Effect - Third Form

postulate between events. You'll have to provide detail as to both causal factors and effects. Avoid faulty or incomplete logic: "Canadian communities are declaring themselves as anglophone only; therefore, they are opposed to bilingualism." This is not necessarily true; such causal statements are easily challenged.

3. Recognize that the causal event you select is probably not the only causal factor related to your focus. Therefore, you should try to select the most directly related and significant cause(s) and effect(s) and anticipate arguments or objections that might be raised against your interpretation of the material. Is your cause really a cause or merely something that contributed to an effect? You may be forced to address other contributing factors if you are to meet your obligation to do a complete and thorough job.

4. Do a thorough investigation of the context in which the event occurred, so that you can assure both yourself and your reader that the relationship you see is causal rather than coincidental. Unrelated events may take on the appearance of causal connection because of coincidences of time, place or manner of occurrence. The fact that a cause and an effect may appear related does not make them related.

5. Make sure that the order of presentation you select for your material reflects the form of cause/effect with which you are working. If you are going to discuss the effects of an event, introduce the event in the first unit of your paper. Similarly, if you are focusing on a cause or causes of a particular effect, you should carefully present that effect to your reader in specific terms, so that your explanation of the causes and their relationship to the effect will be clear and meaningful. In either case, unless the material you use is ordered chronologically, select an effective order for presentation of the effects or causes you discuss. Should the most important come first, or last?

6. If you are dealing with a causal sequence, explain each factor in the sequence clearly and completely. Consider using the chronology of the sequence for your order of presentation, and use as much detail as necessary to establish the relevant reasons for the occurrence of the consecutive steps in the sequence.

Exercise

The purpose of this exercise is to get you to work with cause and effect, and to come to an appreciation of the differences between the three forms of cause and effect we've discussed: cause and effects; effect and causes; and causal sequence. Begin by identifying a subject area and a specific focus—you might want to select a current political, social or economic issue that affects a specific individual, group or institution in a number of ways. Then, approach the focus from the perspective of each of the three forms of cause and effect we've discussed. For example, if you were considering the 1991 beating of Rodney King by members of the Los Angeles Police Department, and you had read that in May of 1992, members of two major rival gangs in the area—the Bloods and the Crips—were trying to unite for the very first time, you might be able to look at their possible "unification" in terms of some specific causes. Alternatively, you could look at the unification as promoting certain specific effects with which police agencies might have to deal in the immediate future. You could, with a bit of reading, also make some forecasts about a possible scenario or sequence of events that might develop if there were another incident of alleged brutality involving the police on the turf of either of these gangs. Your goal in this exercise is to end up with three theses and matching path statements about the same topic— one for each of the forms of cause and effect.

CLASSIFICATION & DIVISION

Classification consists of identifying and categorizing items – concepts, fuel systems, fish, pieces of music, or almost anything else you might think of—into groups based on sets of shared characteristics or attributes.

Some categories or classifications of things depend on a few very basic shared characteristics, while other categories are defined by a large number of special attributes. For example, human beings, as a species, are divided into two gender classifications or groups: male and female. People qualify for membership in one or the other of these categories. Because the characteristics one must possess to be included in either group are few, and can be simply and clearly defined (despite the complexities of human beings as organisms), the groups tend to be enormous. None of the variations between individuals within either group—race, size, hair colour, national origin, linguistic background, and the like—has any impact on any individual's membership in either category. Conversely, if we consider the category of American males between the ages of eighteen and twenty-five who have been arrested for the first time for driving a car while intoxicated, it is not enough that potential members of the group be American or male. Age, past behavior, and present behavior under particular circumstances become defining characteristics of the class.

When we move from considering classes to individual items, we might wish to use division. Where classification is concerned with groups of items having shared attributes, division is concerned with single generic items that can be examined in terms of their defining parts. For example, one might classify stereo amplifiers into categories: class A power, class B power, solid state, tube, hybrid. One might apply division to the same subject: a stereo amplifier has a power source, an output stage, a cooling device, an AC power outlet, and the like. Like classification, division provides us with information we must have before we can engage in examinations of items, concepts and events.

Classification and division, as models for analytical thinking, will be important to you in several ways. For instance, it's possible to make educated predictions about particular classes in terms of behavior or causal relationships, provided one knows enough about the nature of the members in each class. Thus, if you can use division to clarify the components or nature of an economy car, you can reasonably predict that members of that class of automobile will probably be small, fuel-efficient and light. There would be other shared characteristics identifying the class: you might have grounds for believing that many members of the class are imported or at least partially assembled in a foreign country. You might also predict that they won't be luxurious in terms of interior appointments and that prices will be toward the lower end of the current price range. It might even be possible to create artificial subclassifications within the class in order to develop a particular thesis. If a member of the class doesn't meet one of the important criteria for membership in the class, then it may have been wrongly classified or misrepresented.

Classification and division are also essential to your understanding and application of comparison and contrast. If, as a writer, you lack an understanding of the means to group related items according to shared characteristics, you may find yourself trying to compare "apples and oranges." After all, if the audience for your comparison and contrast has particular needs you're attempting to meet by comparing two alternative answers or solutions, the items you're comparing must share enough clearly identified common characteristics to qualify each of them as a reasonable alternative in the perception of your reader. If one of the items has characteristics or attributes that would make it unsuitable for the reader's purpose, then your comparison can't be meaningful, and your paper won't be credible.

⇨

> *Before you can make a meaningful comparison or contrast, you must identify and characterize a single class and draw from within the class alternatives that you will present to your reader.*

⇦

Even if the items you're comparing are subclassifications, they will still share essential characteristics of a single larger group, and it will be those essential characteristics that make the subclassifications worthy of consideration for your reader's purpose. For example, you might be comparing domestic economy cars, and imported economy cars with respect to three or four characteristics that would be important to an audience of students looking to purchase their first automobile. Before you can provide examples of the members of either class of economy car, you would have to establish the requirements for membership in the larger class of economy cars, and the more specific requirements for membership in each of the subcategories.

Sometimes the process of classification can itself be your primary focus. You may be setting out to define categories or classifications that don't exist naturally, and your generalized purpose may be to expand your reader's understanding. For instance, you might be looking at federal bureaucrats and creating some artificial categories based on their responsibilities and behavior. Alternatively, you might be identifying and explaining natural categories that are already well researched and documented, in order to teach your reader something or (in the undergraduate essay) to demonstrate your own knowledge and understanding. Thus, if your audience is interested in botany, you might be classifying several species of plant life indigenous to an area where the ecology is being threatened by industrial expansion.

Whether you are creating your own categories or explaining existing categories, your purpose in engaging in the process of classification may be to provide the reader with sufficient information to make intelligent choices between classes or types of item. For example, suppose you are to write a paper for a hypothetical audience composed of males who weigh over 160 pounds and who are interested in fitness and sports, but are concerned about the risk of knee or back injury. You might decide that this group ought to know something about the shoes available to them for various sports or exercises. Your thesis and path statement for the classification essay might look like this:

> There are three basic categories of sport shoe available for men who weigh more than 160 pounds and who are concerned about minimizing the risk of knee and back injuries when they exercise. These categories are: aerobics shoes, jogging shoes,

and cross-trainers. An examination of each of these categories in terms of essential features should enable one to make an intelligent purchasing decision based on one's immediate needs and fitness interests.

We can see how the structure of this thesis and path statement would lend itself to the multiple unit model. The branches of the path statement would consist of the categories of sports shoes—one branch for each category. You'll also notice that this thesis expressly addresses the categories, rather than the shoes themselves, as the main focus. If you tried to write the paper and found yourself discussing two or three specific makes and models of shoes, instead of the categories, you would have moved from classification into a two- or three-way comparison and contrast. This would clearly be inappropriate if you had been assigned a classification paper. The point of the classification essay would be to inform the reader as to the essential features of the type of shoes in each category, with particular emphasis on features designed to minimize the risk of knee and back injury. You might provide examples of specific shoes within each category; you might provide price-range information; you might provide technical design information. You would do this for each category, being careful not to allow your controlling approach to shift to a comparison of the respective merits of the categories.

Below, we have offered some reminders for both classification and division. Read them carefully before going on with the exercises.

If you are asked to write a <u>division</u> essay, review the following points:

1. Division focuses on a single subject or type of item, one that you can reasonably discuss in terms of the components or parts that all items of that type would possess. Think of dividing *A* for the purpose of informing your reader; division will not work properly if you find yourself trying to discuss *A* and *B*.

2. If division is to be your controlling approach, then the division you propose must be sufficient by itself to fulfil your purpose in writing the paper. A division essay doesn't set out the division as part of a comparison and contrast or a cause/effect sequence.

3. The divisions you create must not only be reasonable in terms of the subject area; they must also be sufficient to support your ultimate aim in the paper. Thus, however you break up the discussion, the division you propose must reflect the whole item or subject you've set out—you can't do a partial division unless you expressly tell the reader that such is your intention.

4. You must look at the nature of the thing you are dividing and decide on the best order for presentation of the components. Is there an assembly sequence? Is there an order of importance? Are some of the components more common than others?

If you're asked to write a classification paper, review the following points:

1. Make sure the larger group you intend to break in to categories or classifications has enough members to make your classification meaningful to the reader. If you are looking at a group of seven members that you propose to break into three categories, you're likely to run into problems.

2. Make a decision about your reasons for presenting the classification to your reader. You must know in advance what you want the reader to take away from your paper. Are you pointing to the existence and significance of each category? Are you helping a specialized audience make intelligent decisions about something? Will the reader be able to engage in a cause/effect sequence of behaviors more efficiently or safely, based on his or her understanding of your classification?

3. Be certain to deliver on your obligation to completely and thoroughly discuss each category, relative to your reasons or purpose in presenting the classification.

4. Establish clearly for the reader the membership requirements for each category, and be sure that the categories don't overlap for the purposes of your immediate discussion. If you're unable to demonstrate that the categories you discuss do not overlap in this way, then maybe your own sense of the classification is faulty or incomplete or you need to rethink your purpose in dealing with the classification or the subject.

5. Where appropriate, be sure to provide the reader with examples of specific members of each category, together with the uses or applications of the items and information about other attributes that are relevant to your reader's purpose.

Exercises

Both classification and division lend themselves to use with the multiple unit model. Clearly, if one is writing a classification essay in which *x* classes will be discussed, then one might structure the paper based on the model, with *x* body units in which the discussion of each of the classes would be developed. Similarly, in a division essay, one might (if appropriate) allocate a unit to each of the components making up the subject item. In this exercise, we want you to create two completed templates or outlines based on the multiple unit model: one for a division paper and one for a classification paper. You should regard the task of identifying a subject area and narrowing to a workable thesis and path statement as part of the exercise. For example, in the division part of the exercise, you might be discussing the components of a specific type of 10-speed gear assembly for a bicycle; in the classification part, you might be examining three categories of women's mountain bikes—those for novices, those for intermediate riders, and those for expert competitors.

NARRATION

Narration consists of the recounting of a series of events, and the manner in which you present information in a narrative is governed by time. When you work in this mode, you must examine the events before you and determine the details that explain the events in terms of each of these questions: <u>who</u>, <u>what</u>, <u>where</u>, <u>when</u>, <u>why</u>, <u>how</u>? You narrate when you report to your reader what happened in chronological sequence, as you might if you were telling somebody about a car accident that you had witnessed. In your explanation of the accident, you would probably use descriptions of people, vehicles and spatial relationships in telling of the sequence of events that made up the incident. You would therefore use description, process and cause/effect. Because some narratives aren't detached, clinical reports of events, you might, in appropriate circumstances, include some of your subjective impressions of the events as you experienced them. You might even make a deliberate alteration to the order of presentation by using a flashback to stimulate the reader's interest, or by foreshadowing something that is to occur later. You also narrate when you tell a story, purely to entertain or to illustrate a point. Thus, your amusing anecdote about a silly action taken by a politician and your tale of the unpleasant experience of an intoxicated driver who spent the night in jail are narratives. Depending on the nature of the narrative you want to present, you may also have to convince the reader that you will be a credible narrator, one whose recounting of events will be accurate and meaningful in the context you've created. While all of us are familiar with narratives that entertain, in the writing of essays we are more concerned with narration that is limited to the reporting of events or that illustrates or introduces a position you're taking.

You can use narrative in an essay as your controlling model or as a supporting device. In either case, you will have to make several decisions in order to be certain that your use of narrative is appropriate in context. These decisions relate to clarification of your primary purpose in developing the narrative; the needs of your audience in terms of content and credibility; the selection of appropriate details in light of your purpose and the reader's requirements; the question of objectivity as opposed to subjectivity; and the natural coherence of the events making up the narrative. If your purpose is only to report a series of events, but to take no position and draw no conclusion respecting those events, then using narrative as your controlling model is a straightforward matter. You must narrow your focus to a specific sequence of events; the details you select and the order of presentation will depend on the actual occurrence, and your watchword will be accuracy in reporting. However, given the nature of the undergraduate expository essay as we've defined it, you'll rarely be given an opportunity to use objective narration as your controlling approach; nor is the situation likely to change when you use narration to illustrate a position. In the essay, it will be the position that must remain your focus; the narrative must serve to introduce, illuminate or clarify the position. It's therefore far more likely that you'll use narration as a supporting strategy in your essays.

Let's consider an example. Suppose you're asked to write a paper supporting the position that mandatory vehicle safety checks should be required on a semi-annual basis in your state. You might narrow this to a consideration of the need for such checks on commercial vehicles operating in the capitol region of the state. Whatever your specific thesis and path statement, you might introduce the subject by recounting a tragic and horrifying event that actually occurred:

> On February 12 of last year, John Smith was driving a 40,000-pound dump truck with a full load of gravel down from Bigtown to Smalltown. Several hundred yards ahead of Smith's truck, the members of the Jones family waited in their van at the end of a line-up of cars that was halted for road construction. At the appropriate time, Smith geared down and applied the truck's brakes. The brakes, which had been neither inspected recently nor maintained properly, failed. Smith's truck careened past frantic flagmen at increasing speed and smashed into the

Jones's van, killing the two children who were playing in the rear area. Two other family members were critically injured, but Smith himself was unhurt. Recently, the state Supreme Court found Smith guilty of criminal negligence causing death, and sentenced him to eighteen months' imprisonment. The state is currently appealing the sentence on the ground that it is insufficient. All parties to the tragic case have agreed that had Smith or his employer assumed the responsibility for seeing that the truck's brakes were inspected and properly maintained, the Jones family would have gone on to enjoy their outing without mishap. Cases such as this are compelling support for the view that regular inspection of commercial vehicles in [this region of the state] should be mandated and enforced vigorously, particularly with respect to the issues of . . . .

This example illustrates the use of narrative as an introductory device, leading the reader to a serious consideration of the thesis and its gravity. While you will probably not depend heavily on emotion or subjective impression in the body of the essay, the implied emotion and sense of horror contained in the introductory narrative do much to put your reader in an appropriate frame of mind. You'll notice that even before the reader gets to the beginning of the presumed thesis, the position to be supported is implied in the outcome of the narrative. You could similarly use such narratives in the body of the essay to exemplify the consequences of inattention to other mechanical problems. When you use narrative to bolster a position, whether as an introductory device or as support within the body of your essay, you must be sure that the implied message the reader should take from the narrative is consistent with the point to be supported. If you find that this is not the case, then you may have selected inappropriate narrative material for that particular position.

You might also need to include some narrative material in a paper because you can't address your thesis in the way you want without the narrative. For example, if you want to discuss the implications of a recent development in chemistry or to argue that handling an experiment differently would have produced a better or more valid result, you'll probably have to narrate the events and procedures that made up the original experiment. This narrative information will be the benchmark against which your reader will test the validity of the alternate view you support in your paper. For example, you may recall that several years ago some American scientists announced, on the basis of a reaction they created (apparently inadvertently) in their laboratory, that they had isolated a process called cold fusion. This was an important announcement: cold fusion, if it existed, could potentially provide a safe, clean, and virtually limitless supply of energy with little or no negative environmental impact. It was later suggested by other scientists that there was no proof of the actual nature of the reaction, which other researchers were unable to duplicate in their own laboratories. You might need to narrate an experiment of your own to support the statement that the original experiment could not be replicated, and to affirm your own qualification to take a position on the main issue. In the actual case, nobody could replicate the process by way of experiment using proper scientific methods. There was much criticism, which attacked the validity of the cold fusion results by examining the laboratory events and procedures leading to the original announcement. The narrative addressing the original experiments provided the critics with the point of attack they desired. Had the original experiment been conducted in a manner acceptable to these critics, no attack would have been possible on that basis.

If you engage in studies or activity in any field requiring you to present a series of events accurately, whether for the purpose of data recording, analysis, argument or emotional provocation, you'll have to become familiar with the use of narration, in conjunction with process and cause/effect particularly. If you must use narration in an essay, you must consider the following:

1. If you elect to present a narrative to your reader, whether as a controlling model or as a supporting device, the position you intend to take in the paper must be expressed or implied in the narrative. If you look at the example about the truck with the faulty brakes, you'll see that it is the expressed or implied viewpoint in the narrative that makes it relevant and credible for the writer's purpose.

2. Clarify your own purpose in presenting the narrative (relative to the needs of your audience), before you select the specific details you'll present to the reader. Not all details surrounding an event are relevant to all readers. If your purpose is to convey to an emotionally sensitive audience the horror of the terrible car crash, you might include details about the innocent, unknowing play of the children just before the crash occurred. On the other hand, if you're addressing a group of government inspectors, you might need to include specific information about the mechanical events that led to the failure of one vehicle's brakes.

3. Make sure that the length and the complexity of the narrative are consistent with the role the narrative is to play in your paper. If you use the narrative as an introductory hook in a paper that is

supposed to be only 500 words, then you can't afford to use a three-page narrative.

4. Carefully review the sequence in which you present the details of the narrative. The sequence will be governed by the chronology of the narrative itself *and* by the needs of the reader to get a clear sense of what happened. You might have to include in the sequence details that became apparent only after the fact, in order for the reader to see how events actually unfolded as they did. You might also find it advantageous to alter the sequence for greater effect, through flashbacks or foreshadowing.

5. When you review the details and the sequence of presentation, check to be sure that the information is both specific and concrete. If the details are vague, the reader may not see their relationship to the immediate subject in the essay.

6. Be sure that in presenting your narrative material, you either maintain a consistent point of view or let the reader know when and why you shift to a different point of view. This means, among other things, that you must select the appropriate tense and distance (degree of objectivity or subjectivity).

Exercise

This exercise consists of two parts. In the first part, we want you to use narration as an introductory device. Assume that you are working with the following thesis and path statement:

The Coast Guard plays a major role in overseeing marine rescue efforts in rough Atlantic coastal waters, but it can fulfil this role properly only when the senior levels of government properly fund Coast Guard training programs and activities. This is particularly true with respect to the Guard's obligation to commercial fishing vessels, pleasure boaters and local marine aviators.

Your introduction to this thesis should consist of a short narrative which establishes a meaningful and specific context within which the reader may consider the importance of the Coast Guard's activities. It should contain a readily discernible, implied position which is consistent with the thesis. If you aren't sure what this means, have another look at the example we gave earlier about the truck with the faulty brakes.

In the second part of the exercise, you are to focus on an event you can describe in three or four paragraphs. Assume that your purpose is to provide an objective report of the event; you aren't interested in making judgments about the event or in dealing with emotional reactions to it. Develop a thesis that directs the reader's attention appropriately and then foreshadow in your path statement the sequence you'll follow to reach the culmination of the narrative. Write the narrative. When you have completed what you think is a satisfactory draft, exchange your work with a writing partner. Each of you should approach the other's narrative with a willingness to be informed; but you should also insist on accuracy and sequential logic. When you have had an opportunity to read your colleague's narrative, discuss your work. It might be useful for each of you to begin by explaining to the other person what you learned about the sequence of events forming the basis of his or her narrative. You should also focus on the degree of objectivity achieved by the other person, as well as the appropriateness of material selected for the exercise.

DESCRIPTION

When you use description to develop an idea, you're attempting to paint a picture, recreate a scene, or perhaps even evoke a mood or emotional response. Description is a strategy that allows you to focus on an object or scene and expose it to the reader's scrutiny in such a way that the reader knows what it is and what it looks like in considerable detail. In addition, description may convey to the reader your emotional and intellectual responses to the object or scene before you. Thus, a sensitive description of a calm pastoral scene may convey or create a feeling of tranquillity in the reader, a feeling you might play upon if you can make the reader feel that the tranquillity of the scene is threatened by pollution. Because your perception and understanding of the physical world are tied to sensory input, you'll depend in your descriptive writing on the use of details discovered through your five senses and through the perception of spatial order and relationship that grows from your personal "translation" of sensory input.

As with narration, you can use description as either a supporting strategy or a controlling approach in your work; like narration, description may be primarily objective or primarily subjective.

⇨

Objective description consists of accurate, clinical and impersonal discussion of the details, observable facts and actual sensations one perceives. Subjective description is concerned with the personal, emotional and psychological impressions arising from observed facts and details.

⇦

Your descriptive writing will usually contain both objective and subjective elements. There will be verifiable factual details by which the reader will get a clear, accurate picture; and there will be details of "personal vision" expressed in carefully chosen words that make the objective information interesting and engaging. Except when you're working in a field like criminology, in which you must generate incident reports, or in one of the sciences in which you must produce technical or lab reports, you'll seldom use objective description as a controlling approach in a formal essay. Similarly, you'll seldom use subjective description as your controlling model in such an essay, except in work focusing on highly personal or emotional experiences.

In well-written descriptive material, the main point may be expressed or implied, but it will always be supported by sufficient concrete detail to make the point clear to the reader. Because we live in a culture where visual representation (as through television) is so important to our understanding of what goes on around us, you can use description very effectively in your essay work, as long as you're careful not to lose control of your material. Whenever you choose to use description, whether as a supporting device or as your primary strategy, you have an obligation to your reader to be certain that the descriptive details you include are accurate. This doesn't necessarily mean you have to be describing something real—you might be working with fiction. However, it does mean that your details must be both credible and capable of allowing the reader to recreate in her mind the complete image you're attempting to convey. If you use details or paint pictures that aren't familiar to the reader in her personal experience, then you shouldn't expect the reader to be able to reconstruct the image mentally—unless you provide the means for the reader to appreciate the unfamiliar image in terms she can understand. This requires you to be especially careful in your attempt to anticipate the reader's need for specific, carefully chosen details when she sets out to read the description you've created. For example, if you're a believer in astral travel or out-of-body experiences and you're trying to describe to a skeptical audience something you saw and felt during such an experience, you'll have to search for analogous experiences that they, as non-believers, might have had. Then you can use parallels and choose words based on those experiences to convey your sense of this alien experience.

In essays, the task before you is usually to demonstrate your familiarity with a subject and your ability to identify and work meaningfully with relevant issues from within that subject. Therefore, just as in the case of narration, it's far more likely that you'll use description as an introductory or supporting strategy than as a controlling approach. You might choose to use description as an introductory device because your thesis arises from an element within the description or because the entire description is an example or visual representation of the point contained in the thesis. In the former case, the description supplies both express and implied detail to create a context within which you can introduce the reader to the element giving rise to the thesis. For example, consider the following paragraph:

> The billboard advertisement showed a badly wrecked late-model car from the driver's side. The front end was crushed against a steel lamp standard so that the grill was bent inward into the hood in a sharp V toward the driver's seat. The hood itself had buckled upward and back, and the windshield was shattered and partially protruding from its frame so that it looked as if it were being held together by a myriad of crystalline spiderwebs running in all directions. The front tires were flat, the rims grossly distorted by the apparent force of the impact. The driver's door was open: one could see a sadly deflated airbag hanging off-center from the misshapen steering wheel, over the driver's seat, and onto the floor. There was a police cruiser in the background, and several feet from the wrecked car, a uniformed officer was helping the shaken driver limp away. At the bottom of the scene was a line of dialogue, in which the officer was saying to the victim: "If it hadn't been for the airbag, we'd be scraping you off the steering column about now . . . " Clearly, *the installation of driver-side airbags in all new automobiles should be mandatory, particularly in view of recent accident statistics concerning their effectiveness in minimizing head and thoracic injuries in accidents involving speeds of up to 60 mph.*

Now consider the use of a description which, as a whole, illustrates your main idea. The paragraph below is an example of a description in which the entire passage exemplifies the point to be expressed in the thesis:

> It is a quiet lunch-hour in the Williamson Middle School computer lab. The room is brightly lit, the full-spectrum neon light softening the polychromatic glare of the computer screens. There are twelve computers; there is a student before each, staring intently at lines of text, coruscating waves of colour, or gently flowing shapes. Three of the students are programming; several more are typing reports; another is laying out a poster for the upcoming Parents' Night. The rest of the students are playing educational games. The soft murmur of their voices blends with the even whisper of cooling fans and surge-protection devices, punctuated only by the occasional pleased exclamation or chuckle, or

by the voice of the lab monitor. The students, relaxed and comfortable, use the computer mice as extensions of their fingers; they extend themselves into the software, as they prepare themselves—all unknowingly—for life in a community where the model for business and behavior will soon be exclusively the information-processing model. *The students at Williamson School are getting ready to move ahead to secondary school, properly prepared to work comfortably with computer applications, particularly in the areas of programming, word processing and page design.*

In each of these examples, we can see how the descriptive introduction establishes an appropriate context, within which the writer can present the thesis and path statement to the reader. Of course, such descriptive material could also be used effectively within the body of the essay in any case where physical, objective descriptive material and/or subjective descriptive material would exemplify or create a meaningful context for a key point in the development of the path statement.

There may be rare occasions when you'll be required to use description as a controlling model in a paper. If you're to work with pure description, there may be no point or thesis other than to convey an appropriate sense of object or scene to your reader. If you must try to work through a thesis by using description, then the extent to which you must depend on the descriptive details to imply your position increases. You can't actually state your arguable assertion, but you can imply the point you want to make through the details you present and the subjective "charge" of the words you choose. You may also find that you need to struggle to maintain a balance between description and narration in such papers, since there is usually movement or change in the scene described. Therefore, you'll have to narrate to deal with the movement or change as an event or series of events. We suggest that you do not become overly concerned about this: in the undergraduate expository essay, you'll rarely be required to use description in this way, other than as an exercise to help you see how objective and subjective descriptions work, and how you can translate what you perceive into words that recreate a similar perception for your reader.

If you need to work with description, whether as an introductory device or as a controlling approach, you should review these reminders:

1. Determine the advisability of using description in the context of the given assignment. If there is material that lends itself to use with your intended thesis and path statement, that's fine; if there isn't any good material, or if your subject is completely unfamiliar to your proposed audience, re-examine your decision to use description—the need for care and attention to detail increases dramatically in such circumstances.

2. Make a decision about the size or scope of the description's focus in light of your proposed use of the descriptive material. You might select a simple scene or a single object to describe in the introduction or in a body unit of your essay. However, if a sufficiently detailed description would require 200 words in a paper that is supposed to be approximately 500 words long, the scope of the material is inappropriate for that assignment.

3. Always provide the reader with a way to establish the location or spatial orientation of the item or scene being described, regardless of your purpose in introducing descriptive material in your work. Remember that description depends on spatial relationships determined according to perception. The mind of the person perceiving a thing automatically tries to establish the boundaries within which he will examine the thing. When you write description, you must translate or establish these boundaries for your reader by using mere words.

4. Be selective, and be sure to sequence the presentation of details so that you paint the picture appropriately. The focus of your description, and the specific details and degree of objectivity or subjectivity you use, depend upon your immediate purpose, your reader's need, and the nature of the thing or things you are describing. Work from the middle outwards; work from the top down or from the bottom up; work from general to particular, or from background to foreground. DO NOT leap all over your imaginary canvas—the reader will be unable to recreate the image you want to convey.

5. Remember that your description must be accurate—it must create an unequivocal and unmistakable picture or mood. Therefore, you must provide sufficient concrete detail such that the reader can make a solid sensory reconstruction of the thing or scene you are describing.

Exercise

This exercise consists of several parts and requires you to use a variety of techniques that you may find helpful in preparing descriptive material for your essays. Keep in mind as you work through the exercise that each of the techniques may be used individually or in combination with the others to improve the quality of your descriptive writing.

1. Select a commonplace object to use as the focus of an objective description. Choose a particular location and set of lighting conditions from which to view the object. In a paragraph, describe the object in as much objective detail as you can, being careful to strive for accuracy. Consider all relevant spatial relationships, dimensions, sensory impressions, etc. Do not refer to the name of the object in your paragraph. If your description is clinical and sufficiently accurate, your reader should be able to identify the object based on your description. Test the effectiveness of your descriptive paragraph by working with a partner: have your partner read your paragraph and make a series of guesses as to the nature of the object you described. The more guesses it takes for your partner to identify your work, the more revision and detail you need to provide.

2. Using the same object that you used for the objective description, create a subjective description. Start from the premise that the object is like a dangerous animal or insect, poised to attack the reader viciously. Your description will have to include physical details; but you'll also need to work with simile and metaphor, as well as to create impressions that reinforce the reader's sense of danger.

3. Choose as the focus for another descriptive paragraph a scene in which there will be quite a bit of sensory information for your reader—for example, you might present a scene from the perspective of someone standing on a trail in the middle of a northwestern rain forest immediately after a rainfall. There will be information directed to each of the senses. Once you have determined your focus, you will write two descriptive paragraphs: the first will be a description of the scene as you would handle it if you were blindfolded; the second will be a description of the scene as you would handle it if you were deprived of your sense of touch.

4. Take the scene you described in part 3 of this exercise and describe it from a bird's-eye point of view.

The Multiple Unit Model - Basic Structure

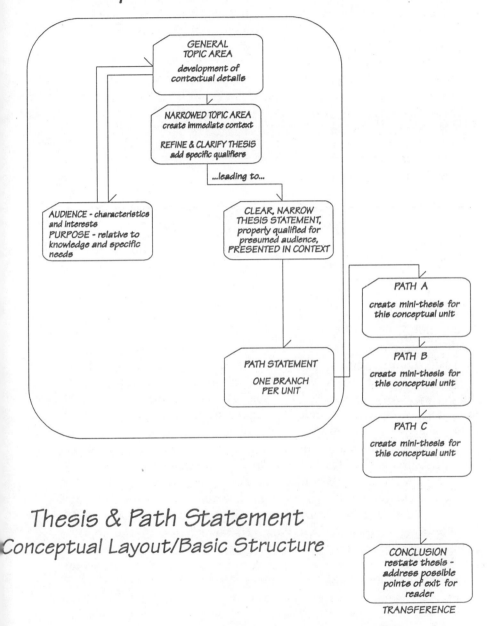

GENERAL TOPIC AREA
development of contextual details

NARROWED TOPIC AREA
create immediate context

REFINE & CLARIFY THESIS
add specific qualifiers

...leading to...

AUDIENCE - characteristics and interests
PURPOSE - relative to knowledge and specific needs

CLEAR, NARROW THESIS STATEMENT,
properly qualified for presumed audience,
PRESENTED IN CONTEXT

PATH A
create mini-thesis for this conceptual unit

PATH STATEMENT
ONE BRANCH PER UNIT

PATH B
create mini-thesis for this conceptual unit

PATH C
create mini-thesis for this conceptual unit

Thesis & Path Statement
Conceptual Layout/Basic Structure

CONCLUSION
restate thesis - address possible points of exit for reader

TRANSFERENCE

Figure 7-1: the Multiple Unit Model - Conceptual Layout/Basic Structure

7
How to Shape the Body Units

When we talk about the body units in an expository essay, we're talking about the units between the introduction and conclusion. They address the aspects of the thesis you've identified in the path statement. Generally, if the path statement sets out three issues or questions arising from the thesis, there will be three body units; if the path statement refers to seven important issues, then there will be seven body units. Remember that the term "unit" does not necessarily mean "paragraph." While it's possible that a body unit in a short essay might be only one paragraph long, the issues addressed in a single unit will often be too complex to be covered in a single paragraph.

Reconsider the layout of the basic structure for the multiple unit model, as shown in figure 7-1. You'll also recall the way in which the same structural breakdown occurs in each body unit of an essay. A unit representing one of the branches of the path statement has a mini-thesis and support paths, and each of those support paths will require discussion and detail. In chapter 5, we also saw the essay's components expressed in terms of this further structural breakdown (*see figure 7-2*). It would be possible, through research, to find enough material to fill several paragraphs under the "heading" of each support path. That is, each of the support paths might require one or more paragraphs of discussion. Consider our layout for one branch of the path in the time-management example we discussed in chapter 5 (*see figure 7-3*).

Figure 7-3 shows the content you might use in your discussion of one branch of the path statement. If you think about the argument and detail provided at the right of the diagram, it's easy to see that each of those areas of argument and detail might provide at least one paragraph of discussion. Thus, you could have three or

The Multiple Unit Model
Mini-theses & Support Paths

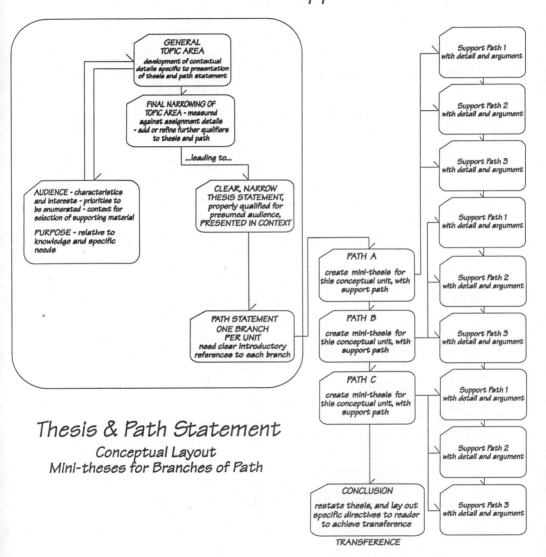

Figure 7-2: the Multiple Unit Model - Mini-theses & Support Paths

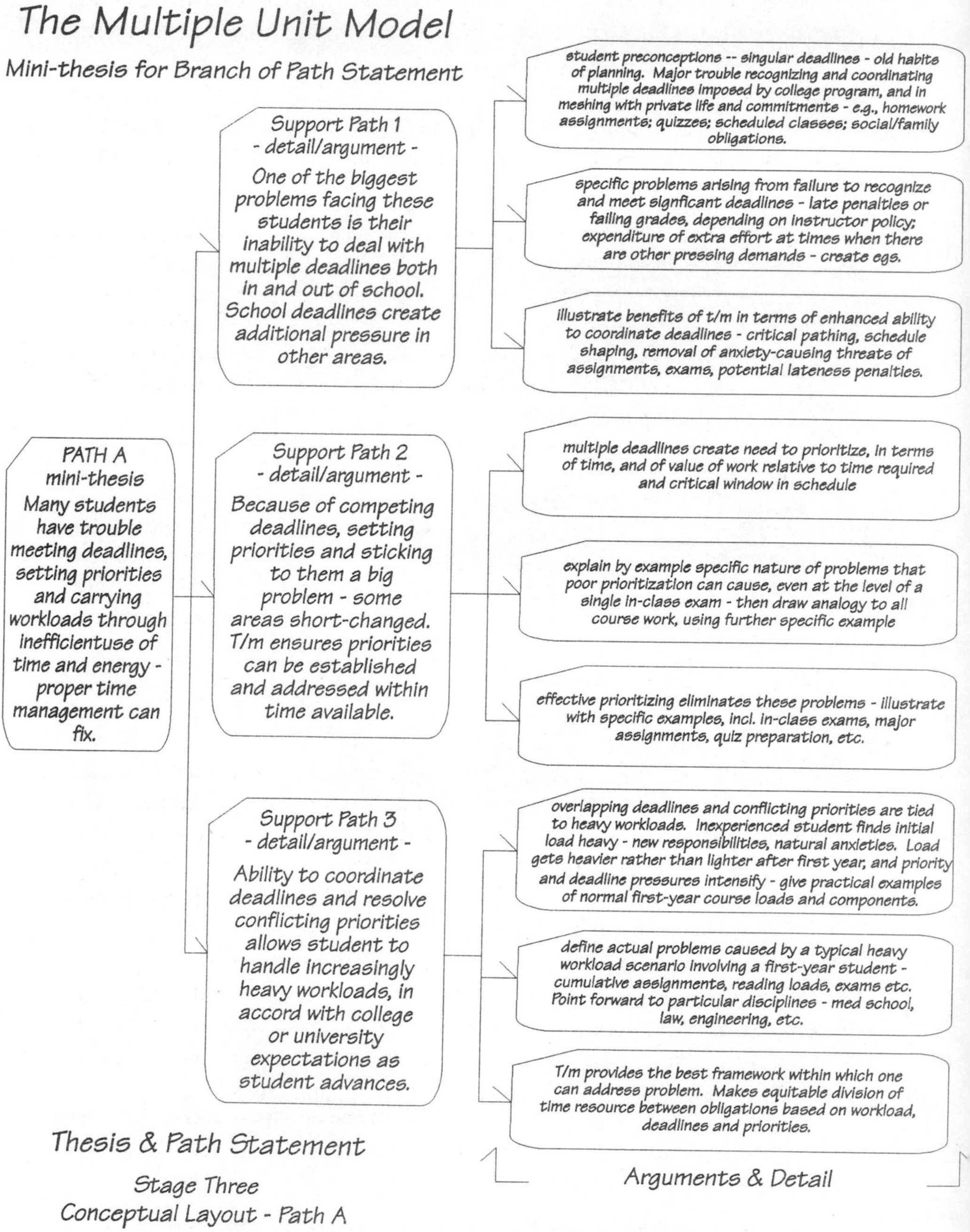

The Multiple Unit Model

Mini-thesis for Branch of Path Statement

Support Path 1
- detail/argument -

One of the biggest problems facing these students is their inability to deal with multiple deadlines both in and out of school. School deadlines create additional pressure in other areas.

student preconceptions -- singular deadlines - old habits of planning. Major trouble recognizing and coordinating multiple deadlines imposed by college program, and in meshing with private life and commitments - e.g., homework assignments; quizzes; scheduled classes; social/family obligations.

specific problems arising from failure to recognize and meet signficant deadlines - late penalties or failing grades, depending on instructor policy; expenditure of extra effort at times when there are other pressing demands - create egs.

illustrate benefits of t/m in terms of enhanced ability to coordinate deadlines - critical pathing, schedule shaping, removal of anxiety-causing threats of assignments, exams, potential lateness penalties.

PATH A
mini-thesis

Many students have trouble meeting deadlines, setting priorities and carrying workloads through inefficientuse of time and energy - proper time management can fix.

Support Path 2
- detail/argument -

Because of competing deadlines, setting priorities and sticking to them a big problem - some areas short-changed. T/m ensures priorities can be established and addressed within time available.

multiple deadlines create need to prioritize, in terms of time, and of value of work relative to time required and critical window in schedule

explain by example specific nature of problems that poor prioritization can cause, even at the level of a single in-class exam - then draw analogy to all course work, using further specific example

effective prioritizing eliminates these problems - illustrate with specific examples, incl. in-class exams, major assignments, quiz preparation, etc.

Support Path 3
- detail/argument -

Ability to coordinate deadlines and resolve conflicting priorities allows student to handle increasingly heavy workloads, in accord with college or university expectations as student advances.

overlapping deadlines and conflicting priorities are tied to heavy workloads. Inexperienced student finds initial load heavy - new responsibilities, natural anxieties. Load gets heavier rather than lighter after first year, and priority and deadline pressures intensify - give practical examples of normal first-year course loads and components.

define actual problems caused by a typical heavy workload scenario involving a first-year student - cumulative assignments, reading loads, exams etc. Point forward to particular disciplines - med school, law, engineering, etc.

T/m provides the best framework within which one can address problem. Makes equitable division of time resource between obligations based on workload, deadlines and priorities.

Thesis & Path Statement

Stage Three
Conceptual Layout - Path A

Arguments & Detail

Figure 7-3: the Multiple Unit Model - Mini-thesis for Path A (Time-Management Example)

more paragraphs of discussion for each support path—or you might have just one for each support path, if you could reasonably express the arguments and details in a single, well-written paragraph.

However, it's not enough merely to recognize that you can organize additional information within a unit into one or more paragraphs. The paragraphs within each unit, like the units themselves, must be logically sequenced. They must also be consistent with your rhetorical approach in the paper.

> *Each paragraph must relate directly to both the mini-thesis and support path for which it offers discussion, and to the main thesis of the paper. Each paragraph must raise a single key issue or subtopic related to the appropriate mini-thesis, and must present credible support, evidence or discussion that's likely to persuade the reader of the truth of the point raised.*

Each paragraph must also be sound in terms of coherence and transitions—the links between the ideas contained in the individual sentences and between the paragraphs within a unit. Both the order and the content of each paragraph within each body unit depend directly on the thesis and path statement, and on the rhetorical approach one adopts.

PARAGRAPH STRUCTURE

Early in their school careers, most students are introduced to some basic rules concerning paragraph structure and organization. The concept of the topic sentence is a familiar one, as is the requirement for explanation and development. Similarly, we can accept the general premise that any single paragraph should develop one key idea that's implied or stated in the topic sentence, whether that sentence occurs at the beginning, middle or end of the paragraph. We also know that a paragraph must have its own internal logic and must read smoothly from beginning to end, regardless of its length. The paragraph must also fit within a sequence of paragraphs to form the properly organized expository essay.

These are basic standards for paragraph structure. You can ensure that each paragraph you write satisfies these standards by applying the multiple unit model in developing a paragraph.

> *The paragraph's structure directly reflects the structure we see in the multiple unit model when we look at an entire essay.*

Document Development: Parallel Structures

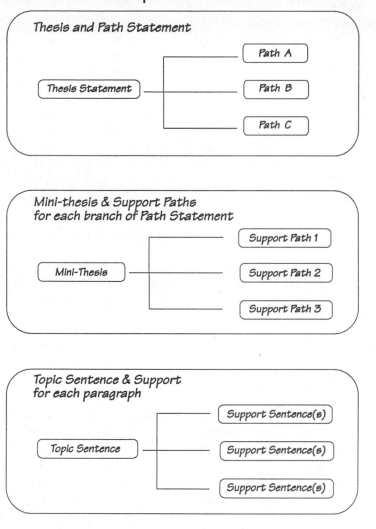

Figure 7-4: Essay Development - Paragraph Structures

If we think of the topic sentence of each paragraph as a kind of thesis itself, then the other sentences in the paragraph fulfill or develop the topic sentence. They parallel the support paths you use to develop each branch of the path statement and the branches of the path you use to develop the paper's thesis. Figures 7-1 through 7-3 demonstrated these structural relationships. The additional material you include in the paragraph is the means by which you convince the reader of the truth or accuracy of that paragraph's topic sentence. There will be one or more sentences in which you offer elaboration, examples or support for the topic sentence. Figure 7-4 shows the parallels between the controlling structures for the multiple unit model, the single branch of the path statement, and the individual paragraph.

We can work with this structure to assist us in constructing any single paragraph. Consider the following topic sentence:

> The food in the cafeteria is both overpriced and lacking in nutritional value.

This sentence sets out an assertion about some problems with food in the cafeteria. Perhaps it represents a mini-thesis for part of a path statement in an essay about problems at a particular school or place of business. It might be the opening of a support path within a unit. In either case, it provides clear information one might develop in a single paragraph. If we apply what we know about the multiple unit model to the task of writing the paragraph for this topic sentence, we might get something like figure 7-5.

In figure 7-5, the writer expressed two major areas of concern in the topic sentence: the price of the food and the food's nutritional value. We can view these areas the way we viewed the branches of a path statement. We can develop each of these two ideas by adding detail and support in the form of additional sentences. The model lets us juggle the ideas we're working with until we're satisfied that the paragraph is soundly structured and the relationship of the ideas within it is clear. Thus, when we write out the paragraph based on figure 7-5, we might get something like this:

> The food in the cafeteria is both overpriced and lacking in nutritional value. Most of our students are on a tight food budget, and forcing them to pay $3 for a hamburger, $1.50 for French fries, and $1.50 for a small juice does not help them keep to their budgets. In fact, according to a survey done last month by Student Services, some students are skipping lunch because they cannot afford the cafeteria's prices on a regular basis. As well, even those students who can pay the current prices complain that the items making up the daily menu lack any real food value. Even a cursory examination at any lunch-hour will reveal that the fries are undercooked and very greasy. The hamburger meat has high fat and cereal components, and the cooks appear to add monosodium glutamate (MSG) to almost everything. If students must pay exorbitant prices, then at the very least, they should expect to get adequate nourishment.

Paragraphs like this one resemble single-unit essays. The topic sentence contains two key ideas that are separated from each other and developed in the body of the paragraph. The sentences following

The Multiple Unit Model
Paragraph Structure

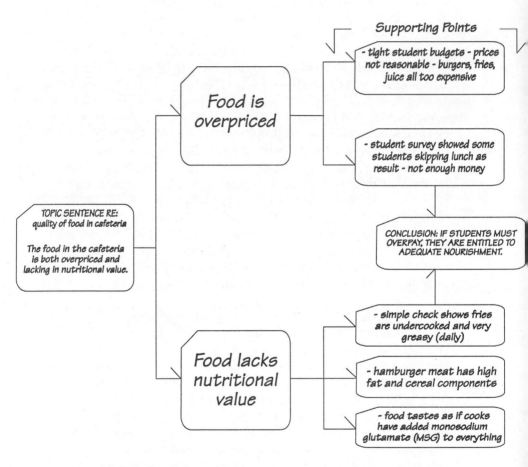

Paragraph Structure
Parallel to Thesis & Path Statement

Figure 7-5: the Multiple Unit Model - Paragraph Structure, Parallel to Thesis and Path Statement

the topic sentence incorporate evidence and examples or illustrations designed to support its accuracy. The last sentence summarizes the conclusion to be drawn from the ideas developed in the paragraph, and the reader may then either go on to the next paragraph (if there is one), or weigh the conclusion against his or her own experience. The sentences in the paragraph break down the ideas in the topic sentence into a logical sequence, with appropriate connecting words or phrases (transitions) between the sentences to make the paragraph flow.

Exercise

Below are three topic sentences. Using figure 7-5 as a model, construct paragraph layouts for each of the three. Try to develop some supporting material for each topic sentence and include this material in your layouts in point form. Then write out each paragraph in proper sentences. Later in this chapter, you can check the sort of supporting material you created against the kinds of support we will suggest to you.

Here are the three topic sentences:

1. Many college students discover that the process of applying for federal student aid money is frustrating and cumbersome.

2. Bungee jumping gives one an incredible adrenalin-filled thrill, as any experienced jumper can tell you.

3. Fibreglass snowboards offer beginners the best combination of safety, durability and price.

In the past, you may have been required to write stand-alone paragraphs—that is, paragraphs that are independent of other paragraphs or units of thought. Such experience is useful, since it forces you to focus on the components of the paragraph as a unit. The college or university essay requires more of you, simply because it consists of more than a single paragraph. You've already discovered, as a result of your work with the multiple unit model, that the central units in an expository essay must relate clearly to each other (and to the thesis of the paper) and must be presented to the reader in a logical sequence. The reader must be able to see the logical relationships that will allow her to move from one idea to the next, and from one paragraph to the next. You cannot truly isolate any one paragraph in your essay from the other components, even though each paragraph must be grammatically and conceptually complete in its own right.

Read the essay below. In it, we've highlighted the thesis and path statement, as well as the mini-thesis for each branch of the path statement and the topic sentences of each paragraph. Following the essay is a diagram (figure 7-6) setting out the relationship of these components in the multiple unit model. Notice, as you read the essay, the kinds of supporting ideas and details introduced in support of each topic sentence. Also consider the relationship of that support to the essay's thesis, and the transitions from idea to idea between paragraphs and within paragraphs. You will see that the number of support paths in figure 7-6 differs from the basic model; but the relationship of the components is still clear. As you read through the sample essay, consider how the writer moves you from the beginning of each paragraph to the end.

Young single women living today in any large American city have had to become more conscious of personal safety issues in their daily lives. The media are full of instances of crimes against women, including "date-rape" and other forms of sexual assault, battery, robbery, kidnapping and unlawful confinement, and other criminal offences. According to FBI statistics, incidence of such crimes is up, nation-wide, by x percent over three years ago. These offences no longer occur only at the hands of strangers or in locations where "trouble" is likely. In fact, they occur in private homes, in the workplace, and even in public in broad daylight. Women in the 18-25 age-group seem to be the most likely targets of violent attack and therefore are most in need of practical defensive strategies. Thus, we see more and more of these women seeking to take classes in one of the many martial arts now available in the west. Many of these women limit their choices for study to the two best known martial arts: judo and karate. This choice should not be a matter of uninformed personal preference. In fact, a woman in the 18-25 age-group who wishes to study one of these martial arts should make an informed choice based on an understanding of the essential nature of each of these arts. In particular, she should make a decision based on basic philosophy and approach, physical requirements, and practical application.

Although western understanding of judo and karate has greatly improved in recent years, there are still some popular myths (mostly derived from the movies) to be debunked before one can make an intelligent decision about which of these arts to study. The prospective student's first lesson is this: neither judo nor karate is magic, and no amount of training in either art can guarantee that one will emerge unscathed and victorious from an attack. In nature and approach, both of these arts depend on an understanding and mastery of technique and philosophy, combined with high levels of cardiovascular fitness, strength, and flexibility. Each approaches the question of self-defence by focusing on the student's mind as well as her physical skills. Both arts depend on basic principles of physics—and on constant practice, since they are made up of learned skills that can be applied in an infinite number of ways. They also depend on the student developing a willingness to endure some pain during the learning process: these are, after all, contact activities.

Judo, "the gentle way," depends on basic principles of physics for its effectiveness as an art and as a system of self-defence. It teaches respect for self and opponents and encourages non-aggression (including a willingness to walk or run away, if necessary) as a means of avoiding violence. In practical terms, the aim of judo is to use an opponent's weight and strength against him, breaking his balance and taking him to the ground by means of a throw or a tripping technique. The judo practitioner rarely delivers actual blows, though blows by an opponent can be effectively countered. One makes an opponent submit by applying a hold or lock to a joint or pressure point on the opponent's body, or by applying a stranglehold until the opponent submits or is choked into unconsciousness. From a woman's perspective, the size of an attacker is therefore irrelevant; in fact, a woman's comparatively small size may be an actual advantage in situations where a large attacker is close enough to grapple with her. However, since the male attacker will usually have a significant advantage in strength, a woman must develop a strong command of the techniques available to her and must condition herself to be unafraid to use them at a critical moment, if she is to overcome the attacker's strength advantage. Training is therefore rigorous: if one is not in shape initially, one becomes fit very quickly. Students regularly practice both limited and all-out sparring with classmates in the *dojo* or training hall.

Karate-do, the "way of the empty hand," also incorporates basic principles of physics and teaches respect for self and others. However, there are many styles of karate, and some have responded to the influence of western commercialism and professional athletics by focusing on the sensational aspects of the combat alone, moving away from the true spirit and philosophy of the art. Other styles have tried to achieve a middle-road between western lifestyles and traditionalism, while still others preserve traditional practices that seem out of place today. Each style tends to place a different emphasis on teaching defence skills, especially with newer students. However, most responsible instructors try to preserve karate's spirit of respect, courtesy, and determination, and all the styles operate on the same basic physical principles.

Unlike the judo practitioner, the karate student depends on a repertoire of blocks, kicks, punches and strikes with the elbow, knee, edge of the hand, or back of the fist. Each technique is delivered with proper form for maximum power, and students learn to master the required forms by practising kata or sets of movements against imaginary attackers. In karate, one is taught to use basic principles of movement to generate incredible striking power—power that is not dependent on the size of one's muscles. Thus, it is possible for a small woman to learn to strike an attacker with enough force to disable, or even to kill. What a woman may give away in strength against an attacker, she can more than make up for with speed and perfection of technique. Just as in judo, there are controlled exercises and sparring sessions with one or more opponents in the *dojo*, and there is rigorous training to prepare one physically to learn new techniques.

Each of these martial arts imposes physical requirements (and perhaps some limitations) on the female student. Some of these are relatively minor—for example, both judo and karate *sensei*s (teachers) will require students to cut their toenails and fingernails short. In judo, in which students grapple with each other by grasping and tugging on the heavy cotton *judogi* or uniform, one can have a long fingernail ripped out by a sudden movement. Long toenails will mean nasty cuts on the shins and feet of opponents when the student tries leg sweeps and other tripping techniques. In karate, the student cannot make a proper fist with long fingernails; and long fingernails and toenails will mean cuts to opponents when one is using slashing or kicking techniques.

On the other hand, there are some more serious physical considerations. The conditioning for both arts is rigorous. Students with existing medical or physical problems such as asthma, high blood pressure or other cardiovascular trouble, shin splints, disc or other back problems, or any kind of bone ailment must consult their physicians before attending even a single class in either judo or karate.

While the potential for injury exists in both arts, the risks are different. In judo, one learns to fall in such a way as to prevent injury and dissipate the force of an attack—but until one has mastered *ukemi* (breakfalls), bruises to the back, hips, and elbows are common. In the beginning stages of karate, there is no danger of falling or being thrown to the ground.

However, there are controlled sparring exercises involving application of basic techniques to an opponent. For example, the student may be countering a punch to the head with a rising block and a counter-punch. One does the technique repeatedly with increasing speed and power, stopping the instant before contact with the attacker's face or body occurs. Typically, beginners have plenty of power but little control: bruised ribs are common, and one may also get the occasional fat lip. There will be times when the female student must wear protective equipment over the chest area to avoid serious injury from improperly controlled blows. In both arts, one can pull muscles; in both, sloppy technique can produce broken toes, jammed knuckles and sprained fingers. Judo practitioners in particular seem to have bad luck with chronic knee injuries because of improperly executed twisting and sweeping techniques. However, as bad as these potential problems may seem to the beginner, one can avoid them through concentration and practice. The benefits to be derived from either judo or karate far outweigh the potential for injury.

The most important question for young female students has to do with the amount of study required before one is actually able to apply the respective techniques of judo and karate for practical self-defence. Experts in both these martial arts suggest that each is really a lifetime study. Indeed, if one subscribes to the philosophy of either art, one may well end up studying and practicing for many years, long after the demand for a practical means of defence is met. However, it should not be necessary to practice for a decade before one is capable of dealing effectively with an opponent. On the other hand, one occasionally sees advertised short courses (ten or twelve weeks) in judo or karate—or "self-defence." Such courses are likely to be of no assistance to the student, not because the techniques taught are valueless, but because there is not enough time for consistent and constant practice. As a result, the student is unable to master or even remember many important skills and techniques, and there is insufficient opportunity for developing appropriate attitudes or psychological readiness. The amount of time it will take a student to become ready to use her art for self-defence will therefore depend on the amount and quality of practice time, instructor emphasis on practical defence skills, the student's personal commitment of time and concentration, and the student's acceptance of what will eventually be a significant change in attitude and lifestyle. These, rather than the choice of martial art, will be the controlling factors in determining ease of application.

In recent years, we in the west have started to examine our

<u>own lifestyles more carefully, and many of us have concluded that our lifestyles and our sense of values as a society have made us vulnerable as individuals.</u> It might even be fair to say that in some cases, we have actually prepared ourselves to be victims. Martial arts such as judo and karate provide many women with the means to make positive changes in some key areas of vulnerability, provided that each student accepts the following truth. It is not your physical skills or your black belt that will keep you from being victimized; rather, it is the growth of confidence, coordination, readiness and respect for self and others that will mark you as someone who is no longer a victim. The growth of these qualities and attributes, as you practice your chosen art, will change not only your life, but the lives of those with whom you interact in your daily life. So, make your choice, and make the commitment—even if you never have to defend yourself, the rewards will be well worth the effort.

This essay is quite good, despite some flaws relating to the broadness of the thesis, wordiness, and some potential organization problems. It shows the way in which the components of individual paragraphs are combined to make each paragraph effective, so that it may itself become a component of the larger work. The central paragraphs incorporate supporting examples and details, together with generalized conclusions from experts in the field. There is also a clear awareness of the particular needs of the target audience, and the discussion is presented in an apparently logical order. When an essay is successful in making structure and organization serve thesis and content in this way, the reader tends not to notice structural components as things separate from content. The reader is taken by the force and clarity of the ideas themselves, instead of being distracted from the message by the form of presentation.

Exercise

From the sample essay above, select the paragraph you think is the most poorly written or organized. Rewrite it; feel free to change language, sentence structures, punctuation or presentation of support. Also consider carefully the organization of elements within the paragraph. The catch: make certain that your rewrite could be inserted in exactly the same position in the sample. The transitions between your rewrite and the paragraphs before and after it should be as seamless as possible.

The Multiple Unit Model
Breakdown of Sample Essay

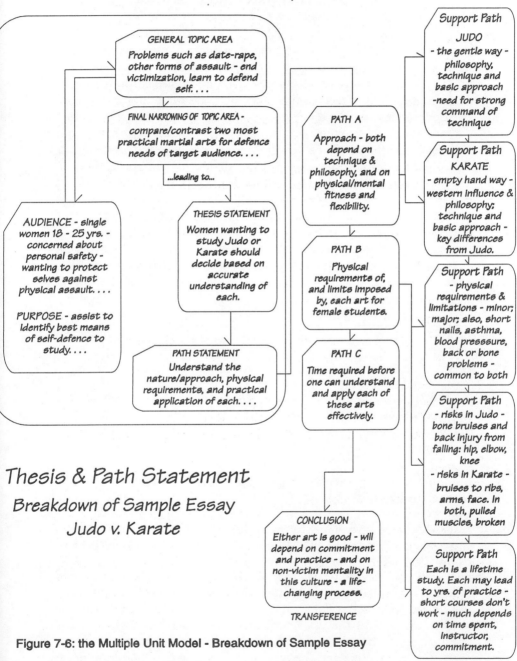

GENERAL TOPIC AREA
Problems such as date-rape, other forms of assault - end victimization, learn to defend self. . . .

FINAL NARROWING OF TOPIC AREA -
compare/contrast two most practical martial arts for defence needs of target audience. . . .

...leading to...

AUDIENCE - single women 18 - 25 yrs. - concerned about personal safety - wanting to protect selves against physical assault. . . .

PURPOSE - assist to identify best means of self-defence to study. . . .

THESIS STATEMENT
Women wanting to study Judo or Karate should decide based on accurate understanding of each.

PATH STATEMENT
Understand the nature/approach, physical requirements, and practical application of each. . . .

PATH A
Approach - both depend on technique & philosophy, and on physical/mental fitness and flexibility.

PATH B
Physical requirements of, and limits imposed by, each art for female students.

PATH C
Time required before one can understand and apply each of these arts effectively.

CONCLUSION
Either art is good - will depend on commitment and practice - and on non-victim mentality in this culture - a life-changing process.

TRANSFERENCE

Support Path
JUDO
- the gentle way -
philosophy, technique and basic approach
-need for strong command of technique

Support Path
KARATE
- empty hand way -
western influence & philosophy; technique and basic approach - key differences from Judo.

Support Path
- physical requirements & limitations - minor; major; also, short nails, asthma, blood pressure, back or bone problems - common to both

Support Path
- risks in Judo - bone bruises and back injury from falling: hip, elbow, knee
- risks in Karate - bruises to ribs, arms, face. In both, pulled muscles, broken

Support Path
Each is a lifetime study. Each may lead to yrs. of practice - short courses don't work - much depends on time spent, instructor, commitment.

Thesis & Path Statement
Breakdown of Sample Essay
Judo v. Karate

Figure 7-6: the Multiple Unit Model - Breakdown of Sample Essay

SUPPORTING MATERIALS

The body units in the essay use appropriately linked individual paragraphs to develop key ideas and to engage the reader's acceptance of the writer's views. A major part of this function involves the selection and orderly presentation of believable supporting materials. We may conveniently organize supporting materials into several generic categories: believable statements by knowledgeable persons or authorities; public positions taken, or statements made by bodies corporate; statistical information; direct factual evidence; meaningful examples or illustrations; and personal experience. These categories are arbitrary; we use them to provide you with a system for organizing your supporting material. Once you feel you have a sound understanding of their nature and applications, redefine or reorganize them in any way that makes sense to you, as long as you are consistent in using them.

Remember when you're looking for supporting material that there is a difference between quantity of support and quality of support. In an expository essay, a great volume of evidence isn't necessarily more effective than a small amount of well-chosen support. Lawyers have a pithy way of stating a rule you might adopt in selecting support for your essays:

> *The argument or position that succeeds is not the one based on the most evidence – rather, it is the one based on the best evidence.*

Except in situations where an assignment requires you to find and present all available support on an issue, try to follow this rule in making decisions about the support you present in your essay's body units.

Believable statements by knowledgeable persons or recognized authorities

Whenever you pick up a book, a newspaper or a magazine, you can find examples of writers quoting the words of other writers or experts as support for particular viewpoints. Most of us respond positively to convincing statements by persons who are supposed to know more than we do about a particular subject. If the supporting statement is believable in terms of what it actually says, and the person who made the statement is one a reader recognizes as a knowledgeable person or recognized authority, then the reader is more likely to consider the validity of the writer's argument. A good writer can manipulate evidence skilfully and can persuade a reader with supporting statements of doubtful credibility by presenting those statements as if they were truly authoritative. On the other hand, some readers will ignore important supporting statements for no other reason than their own failure to recognize the name or status of the person whose words are quoted as evidence.

Let's consider an example. Suppose that you've been assigned an essay by your physics instructor on some area of theoretical physics. It's been made clear to you that one of the purposes of the assignment is to do some research in a reasonably new area of physics so that you can see how new developments in the field occur. While preparing the material for your paper, you stumble across an interesting idea that you want to present as a tentative conclusion about some issue in the area you're discussing—but you're aware of the need for support for that conclusion. You begin to look around in your research materials for a source you can quote as support. It seems that there are some scientists, recognized authorities in the field, whose writings would support your position, though not one of these experts has actually done so directly. There is also a local scientist who is not well known, but who supports your conclusion in clear statements you could quote. This scientist has gone on to make a discovery of far-reaching implications that the scientific community has not yet recognized. Should you include all the support you've found? Would you use only the local scientist since his work is clearly the most advanced? Or, should you ignore the local scientist because very few of your readers will recognize his name or give any credibility to his theories and data? Is there some other alternative?

The local scientist is not yet an established or recognized authority, and therefore your readers might not recognize him as a believable source of support. This doesn't mean his work is no good; it means his name and reputation are not familiar to your audience the way Einstein's name and reputation are. However, his statements clearly would be the best evidence because they speak directly to the point you want to make. The other scientists whose statements you could use are certainly recognized authorities—and therefore your readers would regard them as believable sources— but there is no direct link between their statements and the new proposition you want to support. A possible solution is to introduce statements from your credible sources and establish a link between their work and the local scientist's research. In this way, you borrow their credibility and apply it to the new material. Alternatively, you could focus on the local scientist's work, starting from the point at which he was working with established and recognized scientific principles. Thus, you would show that he had been working in a credible way, and you would then try to show a logical development toward the new theory and the statements you want to use in your paper. These statements would then derive believability from your logical presentation. This is a way in which you can qualify your otherwise unknown source.

How should you integrate believable statements by authorities into the body units of your essay? You can sometimes use such a statement as the opening sentence in a paragraph. For example:

> Dr. Donald L. Currie, a noted genetic research scientist with ABC Foundation, recently stated that based on current research and developments in the medical genetics field, "Within five years, it will be possible to select, not only the sex of an unborn child, but also to determine other characteristics such as hair and eye colour, muscular potential, and various intelligence-related attributes" (Currie 107). If Dr. Currie is correct in his assessment, the ordinary family will have several important moral and ethical questions thrust upon it in the area of family planning. The most significant of these relates to the extent to which parents ought to tamper with the force of natural selection in ordering their unborn child's characteristics.

If the scientist is one whose name is known to the audience—or if the writer has previously qualified him as an expert for the audience—then the statement provides a platform on which part of the writer's discussion can now be based. One might use believable statements in this way at any stage during an expository paper, even in the introduction.

You're also likely to present believable statements by way of proof (rather than introduction) within the central paragraphs or units of your paper. The idea is to rely on persuasive conclusions developed by believable authorities as proof for related propositions of your own. So if you're writing about the dangers of abusing anabolic steroids and have already introduced the reader to a level of credible support in the paper, you might do something like this:

> Young male users of anabolic steroids are particularly vulnerable to potentially lethal side-effects if they abuse drugs "A" or "B" over prolonged time periods. It is quite true that both these chemicals stimulate muscle growth by causing abnormal balances of testosterone and various other growth-related substances in the body; but recent research at City University confirmed that:

Drug "A," when used by young male bodybuilders for periods in excess of six months, is clearly related to the occurrence of violent mood swings, high blood pressure and cardiac problems, and tumours of the liver and kidneys. As a result of continuing abuse, more of these problems become life-threatening in the subject group than in the normal population. (Williamson, Journal 43)

Moreover, users of drug "B" were said to face the potential for skin cancers, including malignant melanoma, as a direct result of extended abuse: "drug "B" is a pernicious, habituating drug which causes permanent cellular damage and has been repeatedly linked to abnormally high incidence of malignant melanoma in young male abusers. (Peters, 21)

In this example, we see both longer and shorter statements used as support for the initial proposition in the topic sentence. They are integrated in such a way that they illustrate and support the truth of the assertion in the writer's topic sentence. They work because they directly support the topic sentence and because the reader has been led to view the level of support the writer provides as academically credible or believable.

When you want to use quotations from believable sources or recognized authorities as support in your essays, be sure you can answer the following questions appropriately:

1. Is your source believable? Is the person whom you intend to quote a recognized authority in the field? Remember that in this context "recognized" means "recognized by your audience." Is there any doubt about the source's professional credentials or reputation? If the source isn't well known, is there any way that you can qualify him or her as a believable source, given your thesis and the other materials you'll be presenting?

2. If the source is believable in terms of personal or professional reputation, is the statement (or statements) you wish to use also believable? It's possible for a believable or recognized source to be in error or to make a claim that's too broad or sweeping to be useful to you. Are there any obvious problems with the wording of the statements that would make them inappropriate or open to challenge, given the point you're trying to support?

3. If the source and the statements to be used are acceptable, are the statements the *best* statements available as support for your particular point? Could the statements be interpreted as

support for some proposition other than the one you're trying to support? Is there a likelihood that the reader will either mis-interpret or not understand the significance of the statements?

4. <u>Can you present the statements without having to take them out of context to get the meaning you want?</u> That is, will the general import or meaning of the statements change dramati-cally when you use them in your essay, in such a way that the reader will be misled as to the source's meaning and intent?

Remember in addressing these questions that your reader can at-tack the validity of your argument by attacking the strength of supporting statements and their sources. If one of your supporting statements is attacked successfully, your whole essay will suffer as a result. Finally, be aware that you can also take statements by authorities for the viewpoint opposed to yours and attack them in your paper. If you can prove an opposing view to be inaccurate or illogical, that may lead the reader to conclude that your view is correct—even though you've offered no believable statements in affirmative support yourself.

Exercise

In this exercise, we want you to locate a believable statement from a recognized authority that will support each of the propositions below. In gathering your material, be certain that you can answer appropriately each of the four questions set out above. Once you've identified suitable material, put each of the propositions into a para-graph in which you can present the support you've found so that each paragraph reads smoothly. Try to use a layout similar to the para-graph layouts you used earlier in this chapter.

1. Given the speed at which Brazilian rain forests are currently being destroyed, we can expect that numerous medically significant species of plant and animal life will be lost to us within five years.

2. Liquor advertisements on television affect teenage viewers negatively because they mislead young people about the lifestyle associated with regular drinking, particularly with respect to at-tractiveness to members of the opposite sex.

Public positions taken, or statements made by bodies corporate

We find ourselves surrounded by a proliferation of public and private agencies and corporations. Our municipal, state (or provincial), and federal governments are often viewed as single entities, as are political parties. In this sense, they are "bodies corporate" and are capable of making public statements or taking positions on a variety of issues and subjects. Similarly, actual corporations (business organizations formally incorporated under prevailing legislation) can be viewed as individual beings in terms of the policies they adopt or the positions they take on particular issues. Obviously, both public and private corporate entities are also made up of individual human beings, subgroups, branches, departments, and the like. When one of these agencies or bodies, through a recognized spokesperson, makes public pronouncements about something, you can often incorporate those pronouncements into a paper by means of support. However, we must make a distinction between believable statements made by recognized authorities and the kinds of statements corporate bodies are likely to make.

It's true that believable statements by recognized authorities can be used to introduce a point or provide a basis for attack or disagreement. Generally, one uses such statements because the research of the authorities cited supports the point to be made. The writer invites the reader to accept the truth of the statements and the point they support because of the aura of credibility surrounding the source. Statements by bodies corporate might be used in this way also, but there can be a great difference in the reader's sense of the source and its credibility, especially where political bodies or huge corporations are concerned. Consider: when a writer presents scientific research to prove a point, does the reader immediately attack the truthfulness of the researcher whose work is cited? Even critical, knowledgeable readers tend not to do this, unless they have some special knowledge about the research the writer is using. On the other hand, how will a reader react to a statement from a huge chemical company about its publicly held view that there is no conclusive evidence of damage to the ozone layer from chlorofluorocarbons (CFCs)? Because the reader is sensitized to the latter issue, she may immediately challenge the integrity of the chemical company for its public stand on the matter.

Frequently, a writer will quote corporate policy or position statements as evidence for an interpretation of the source's position on an issue or of a course of action the corporate body intends to take. How you might use such statements will depend upon the importance or notoriety of the source and the extent to which your reader will regard the source's pronouncements as statements of fact. This type of supporting material is an excellent source of ideas, especially because people are often led to believe that they ought to rely on public statements by various organizations and groups.

Let's look at some examples. If you were writing an essay for an economics assignment requiring you to show whether a recently imposed tax would create a significant additional burden on taxpayers, you would want to look for government or tax department policy or news statements that dealt with the purpose and consequences of the tax. Suppose you found the following official statement, as reproduced in a daily newspaper:

> At a news conference held last night, Mr. William A., secretary of the state treasury, stated that the recently passed tax on wide categories of consumer items would be a "revenue-neutral" tax. When questioned by reporters as to the meaning of this term, Mr. A. set out the government's position: "We are of the view that this tax is a fair one, since it will redistribute portions of the tax burden across a wider tax base, creating a fairer apportioning of the burden than presently exists. However, this tax will have little or no effect on total tax revenues, and in that sense we believe the tax to be revenue-neutral."

In this example, we have a designated spokesperson outlining the position of a hypothetical government on an issue in response to a direct question. Clearly, the statement need not be accurate in order for you to use it—it does set out a government's publicly held position, right or wrong. In fact, the statement need not even be truthful, since your reader is going to weigh its truthfulness in light of your reason for offering the statement. If your thesis in the paper is that the tax is indeed revenue-neutral, then you might be using the statement to make clear the government's position, the fairness or truthfulness of which you would then demonstrate in the rest of the paper. Alternatively, you might be trying to show that the government had misled the public as to the impact of the tax. If so, you might offer the statement to show the government taking a position that it knew, or ought to have known, was incorrect (as you must then prove in your paper). You could integrate the statement in the same way you would integrate a believable statement from a recognized authority, but your purpose in doing so would be different.

Consider another example. If you were going to write a paper on the role of militant environmental groups in a particular region, you might be able to find an official statement or policy of one of the groups that you could turn into support for your interpretation of the group's status or conduct. Suppose you come across this statement:

> The Friends of Nature is a group committed to the preservation and enhancement of the state's wilderness areas at all costs. We believe that the ecological condition of this state is critical; and

we further believe that the conflict between the Friends and the forces of those who wish to exploit our resources to the point of depletion is no longer merely an economic and political struggle. It is now, in fact, a struggle for survival—not only for the plant, marine and wildlife species in the state, but for ourselves and our children. Accordingly, it is the policy of the Friends of Nature to regard the entire state as a preserve to be defended vigorously on all fronts by all means necessary, including political, social and economic measures, and where necessary or unavoidable, civil disobedience and even violence. This is no longer a debate. This is a war.

This radical statement addresses a position this fictional group will publicly adopt. You could therefore use it to create support for the contention that this level of radicalism exists and that violence is possible. Alternatively, if you thought the group was merely trying to intimidate people but did not really intend to use violence, you might use the statement as support for the proposition that some of these groups use a certain kind of propaganda to achieve their goals. You might present the former view like this:

The Friends of Nature is a group that exemplifies a growing commitment on the part of many environmentalists and groups to take an increasingly militant and potentially violent posture toward resource exploitation and its environmental consequences in our state. Their own publicly stated policy statement makes clear the potential for environmental war:

> ... We further believe that the conflict between the Friends and the forces of those who wish to exploit our resources to the point of depletion is no longer merely an economic and political struggle. It is now, in fact, a struggle for survival—not only for the plant, marine, and wildlife species in the province, but for ourselves and our children. Accordingly, it is the policy of the Friends of Nature to regard the entire province as a preserve to be defended vigorously on all fronts by all means necessary, including political, social and economic measures, and where necessary or unavoidable, civil disobedience and even violence. This is no longer a debate. This is a war.
>
> (Friends, 2)

If you're going to use public statements by corporate entities as support in your essays, make sure that you address the following questions about the material you intend to use:

1. Have you made absolutely certain that the statement you want to present is accurate in form and content? That is, are you sure that you're accurately and fairly stating the source's publicly held position on the issue in question? It's academically (and even legally) risky to tell your reader that a corporate source has publicly stated something if you're unable to quote the source specifically and accurately.

2. In presenting the material you've found, have you been careful to provide an appropriate context? If your source's statements show a particular bias, interpretation or perspective concerning the subject matter, then you're obliged to make sure they retain that meaning in the form in which you present them to your reader. In other words, you must not, by omission of essential information, allow your reader to misinterpret what your source is talking about in the statement.

3. Have you made clear to your reader your sense of the statement's accuracy or truthfulness, and have you been clear about the purpose for which you are presenting the statement? Because these statements are not proof in the same sense as believable statements by recognized authorities, you should take care to let the reader know the extent to which he or she can rely on the statement for a particular purpose.

Exercise

This exercise requires you to examine the daily newspaper or a current periodical and to identify two examples of public positions taken or statements made by bodies corporate on a specific issue of your choice. For each example you find, try to write a paragraph that incorporates the position or statement as support for a position you will take on the key issue. In other words, present the statement as a platform from which you'll make an assertion that you either agree or disagree. Base your assertion on at least two or three important considerations. If you do the exercise properly, you'll end up with two paragraphs, each of which could be turned into an introduction for an essay, complete with its own thesis and path statement.

Statistical information

Statistics can provide a valuable means of support for assertions you make in your essays. In fact, statistics are so persuasive that commercial advertisers use them regularly, as do public pollsters, to alter or measure the responses of a segment of the public about something. While statistics can be presented simply and informally (or technically and formally), it's important to remember what statistics represent. They set out in numeric form a conclusion or series of conclusions about matters of apparent fact, according to recognized principles of research and mathematics. Because statistics are supposed to address factual matters, they create an aura of credibility about your assertions, particularly where one's audience is acquainted with the means by which the statistics were obtained. However, many readers have learned to be suspicious of statistical information that is overly generalized or not prepared according to recognized methods.

You should not hesitate to use statistical support, subject to a few conditions. First, the statistics you want to present must be relevant to the specific point you are trying to make. There is little merit in statistical evidence that refers only to a related point or to a point that is much broader in scope than yours. The conclusion you wish to support must accurately state the results of the research from which the statistics are drawn, and your conclusion's relationship to the statistics must be logical. The statistical information must also be integrated smoothly into your paragraph. For example, it would be inappropriate to use statistics like this:

> Last year, 63 percent of all crimes committed in North America involved firearms. This demonstrates that if Washington State tightens its gun control legislation, fewer crimes will be committed there.

Here, there's no indication that the statistic cited was developed by a reliable source. There's no way of knowing how many of the crimes that were sampled actually occurred in Washington State, nor is there any indicator of the type of crime or the sort of firearm used. We don't even know how many of the crimes involved actual gunfire. There's no clear link between the notion expressed in the conclusion (that tightening Washington's gun control laws would reduce crime) and the information embodied in the statistic. The writer has thus created a serious logical fallacy. Consider an alternative:

> According to figures released for 1991 by the Washington State Department of Criminal Justice, 63 percent of all violent crimes committed in the state in that year involved a handgun that was actually discharged during the commission of the crime. In addition, of these crimes, 76 percent were found to have been premeditated, and the criminals' access to firearms was said to have contributed to the decision to commit the crime in at least

half of these cases. Therefore, we may reasonably conclude that if the state were to tighten its gun control legislation, particularly where legal means of access to handguns is concerned, we would expect to see a sharp decrease in the commission of violent crimes involving such weapons in the state.

Here, we're given a source that is a government agency; we have more details about the kinds of crime and the region sampled. We also have information that will allow us to see a logical relationship between the writer's conclusion and the statistical evidence presented in support of that conclusion. There are few gaps in detail or logic, and the whole paragraph reads smoothly—the writer integrated the statistical information properly.

If you decide to use statistics as support, make sure you address the following questions about the material you intend to use:

1. Is the statistic you intend to use specific to the circumstance(s) and the point(s) you are trying to support? Remember to avoid statistics that are too broadly stated for your specific purpose, or that address a sample or population substantially different in size and nature from the one you are considering.

2. Have you ensured that your source is clearly identified or cited, and is recognizable to your reader as a believable or reliable source for statistical information? This is the only way in which you can demonstrate to the reader that you're working with actual data and accurate interpretations of that data. This is essential if you are to rely on the statistics as meaningful support. In the example above, readers are referred to the state agency responsible for the administration of criminal justice as the source for the statistics. This agency would be the primary source for fact summaries pertaining to the incidence of crime in the region. The reader could, if she wanted, verify the figures by contacting the agency independently. That potential for verification itself lends credibility to the source.

3. Are your statistics consistent with any conclusion other than the one you are trying to support? Remember: it's not sufficient that the statistics you decide to use are from a believable source and are appropriate to the point you're making. They must also be inconsistent with other conclusions that are opposed to your point. In other words, if a reader could cite your statistics for a different, related, or opposing proposition with equal validity, then you must abandon or qualify those statistics.

It's useful to remember that statistics represent fact summaries, which writers and readers will interpret according to their understanding of the issue at hand and their own biases. Sometimes statistical information can be ambiguous or misleading in that it may support more than one conclusion. In such cases, you must explain your interpretation of the supporting material to rule out interpretations that are inconsistent with the one you want your reader to adopt.

Exercise

In this exercise, you're to refer again to local newspapers and current periodicals in locating at least two instances in which statistical information is used to support a limited point or proposition. Read the piece in which the statistics are used, and determine whether the writer has accurately and fairly reported enough detail for the reader to be convinced of the point based on the statistical evidence. Be critical—try to find as many weaknesses as you can. This exercise is a simple one and is designed to help you become sensitized to the overuse and misuse of statistics in writing. The more sensitive you are to the problems, the less likely you are to make the same errors in your own use of statistical material.

Direct facts

Direct facts consist of matters like objective eyewitness observations, acknowledged true events or occurrences, clinical scientific data (excluding statistics of the sort described above), empirical measurements, and the like. Putting it another way, facts are statements about things that your reader will accept as true without challenge AND that may be verified independently. They are useful as support only so long as you are able to show how the idea you're supporting is based directly, logically and accurately on the facts you offer in support. So, you might rely on a verified eyewitness account of a particular event—factual information—to support an argument that the event could have been prevented. If you're able to make a logical argument based on the facts, the reader may agree with your recommendations about preventive measures.

Consider an example. Suppose you're writing an essay on whether large rock concerts should be allowed to take place in a particular region where there's resistance to the idea. Recently, a famous rock band was to perform a concert in a large indoor arena, somewhere in southwestern California. There were to be several backup acts, and all the details pertaining to stage, lighting, electronics and admissions were to be handled by a local crew. On the night of the concert, twenty minutes into their set, the members of the famous band threw down their instruments, screamed some insults into the microphones, and walked off the stage. Pandemonium ensued: the fans rioted, people were injured, equipment was damaged. Local authorities wanted to blame the problem on the band; some critics blamed it on rock music and the sorts of people who like it. As a devoted rock fan, you don't want to see large concerts banned in the area, and you're sure that there must have been some reason for what occurred. You do a little research and find that, according to eyewitnesses, band representatives, and local police and emergency personnel, the local crew failed to do its job properly in setting up for the concert. The problems have been corroborated by several sources. It was raining that night; there was a roof leak that hadn't been repaired on time. As a result, there was water on the stage near the equipment (a major safety hazard), and there were various problems with lighting that were attributed to inadequately checked connections. The sound equipment that the band had ordered was not what they actually got. The local organizers were to have had fifty security people between the front row and the stage. Instead, there were only eight security officers, and people in the first two rows threw several objects at band members prior to the walk-off. Clearly, the problems could have been avoided, had the local organizers fulfilled their obligations to the band.

Given your particular interest in the subject, you're able to use this information in creating the following paragraph:

> The riot that occurred last week at the large rock concert in Midtown, California has been blamed variously on the headliner band, some unruly fans, the concert organizers, the local authorities, or the nature of rock music, depending on the personal biases of those trying to affix blame for the damage caused that night. However, careful investigation has revealed that the band members, however inappropriate their attitudes may have been, were not to blame for the events that occurred. In fact, according to eyewitness accounts which have been corroborated by local police and safety authorities, there would have been no trouble at the concert if the organizers had fulfilled their contractual obligations to the band and acted according to local safety regulations. The organizers neglected to see to various hall repairs before the concert, thereby creating electrical and fire hazards which threatened the safety of performers and fans. The organizers also failed to supply equipment they had promised to deliver, and their security arrangements were totally inadequate for the size of the hall and the number of fans, according to both police and fire officials. Under the circumstances, it would be unjust

to blame the band, the nature of the music, or even the unruly fans. Nor would it be fair to ban all further concerts in the area. Instead, organizers of future concerts should be made to adhere to much more stringent licensing requirements and to obtain written approval for all electrical, safety and security measures they must take before any performance.

You can see that all the facts are either summarized or repeated. There is enough information for the writer to use this material as a basis for the contention that not all concerts should be banned because this one was a disaster. The weight of factual evidence, confirmed by local officials, does point to the failure of the organizers, rather than to any cause that would require the banning of all future performances.

If you intend to rely on direct factual material in an essay, make sure you address the following questions about the material you use:

1. Have you examined the facts to see if they're independently verified—or are they merely statements of opinion dressed up as factual statements? People will often state their beliefs about something as if those beliefs were independently verified facts. Similarly, you may see conclusions based on fact stated as if the conclusions themselves were factual. The conclusions might be right or wrong, depending on the logic (and the facts) on which the conclusions were based.

2. If the facts you want to use are verifiable or generally accepted as true, are they appropriate in the context of your discussion? Even factual statements can take on alternative meanings if you present them in different situations or circumstances. Think of a fact as if it were something a person said in a conversation. There's no doubt that the person said it; but if you repeat it to someone without telling that person about the rest of the conversation, he or she may misunderstand or jump to a wrong conclusion. Thus, if you present facts as evidence, you must be careful not to deliberately mislead your reader as to the meaning of the facts in the context of your essay.

3. Have you been careful to offer enough facts to create a basis for the point you want to make, and have you made clear the logic that should lead the reader to your conclusion based on those facts? Factual evidence is like any other kind of supporting material: you can determine how much is enough by putting yourself in the reader's position. How much factual information would it take before you would accept the factual basis for a

conclusion? Similarly, you must ask yourself whether the logic relating the facts to the conclusion is clear and complete.

Meaningful examples and illustrations

Examples and illustrations are probably the most familiar kinds of supporting material. Writers (and speakers) use them to offer particular instances that demonstrate the truth of a statement or show how something works or how something might happen based on a prior event. If we were having a conversation now with you, the student, about using the computer, we might say, "You have to be careful—you can lose all the data in your computer if you type in a wrong command." You question us as to how that could happen. We answer: "Well, for example, if you type the "format" command without adding the drive letter, the computer will wipe all the data from its hard disk drive." Here, we would have offered you an example that shows how the prior event (typing the wrong command) leads to a particular unpleasant result (the loss of all your data). Moreover, this little scenario that we've just described is itself an example of how you can use examples to illustrate how something might happen based on a prior event!

When you're writing, there will be many occasions when you can offer your reader an example to illustrate a truth you want the reader to accept. For almost any claim you might make, it would be possible to offer an illustration that takes the reader from the generality of the claim ("It is true that x is so") to specific verification ("For example, if a and b are put together under specific circumstances and conditions, they result in x"). However, when you try to develop examples and illustrations for your essays, you must remember the following rules:

1. The examples and illustrations you choose must be the best and most relevant examples available for the thesis you are developing and the specific points you want to make.

2. Your examples and illustrations should be specific and practical, rather than generalized or fanciful.

3. The examples you choose must also be the most appropriate ones available, in terms of your audience's ability to understand and relate to them.

You may recall what we said earlier about using the best evidence available to support your points, given your context, thesis and path statement. The general rule applies to your choice of examples and illustrations. While you may occasionally want to present many examples to illustrate a single point, most of the time you're likely to impress the reader much more by offering a few very clear, well-chosen and relevant examples that relate directly to your thesis and your particular points—the best support, rather than the most support. If you can see several ways to exemplify a point, but one of those ways is much clearer than the others, then you should use that example and exclude the others. If one example is more directly relevant to or supportive of your point, choose that example. Similarly, the examples you choose should be specific and practical, rather than overly general or unrealistic. That is, unless your subject matter requires otherwise, you should opt for more specific over less specific, actual over hypothetical, familiar over bizarre or unfamiliar. Readers are more likely to be convinced by examples that are somehow connected to reality—such examples help your reader to understand the point you're making as something practical, rather than something theoretical.

In a given essay, you might use examples that are clear, specific, and appropriate to your thesis and the point you are making, but your reader may still miss your message. Your examples must also be appropriate in terms of the understanding and experience of your audience. If you select materials that support your point well but that are completely alien to your audience's experience or understanding, then your audience is likely to reject those examples. Suppose, for instance, you've been assigned a paper on trends in popular music in the last two years, and your readers will be conservative, educated individuals who are over the age of sixty. These people may pay attention, even if you're talking about rock music and the changes it has created. However, you select, as examples to illustrate your points about musicians and songs, such titles as "I Like Choking My Cocker Spaniel" and "Bleed On The Earth, You Filthy Swine." You refer to groups like The Barfing Eels, Killing Machine, and The Oozing Toads. Even if these examples illustrate your points accurately and specifically, and even if they are appropriate to your thesis and the points you're making, they may be so alien to the experience of your audience that your readers may reject your points. In fact, the readers might become so offended that they refuse to read beyond the examples.

If you intend to present a sequence of examples and illustrations in an essay, make sure you address the following questions about the material you use:

1. Have you identified several examples or illustrations for a particular point and then evaluated those examples based on clarity and relevance to your point?

2. Have you done all you could to see that your examples are specific and practical, as opposed to general or unrealistic?

3. Have you chosen examples that will be meaningful to your particular audience without being alien or offensive?

Exercise

In this exercise, you're to develop three positive statements or assertions that you will support by example. Treat each of your three statements as a topic sentence for a paragraph; the examples will form the basis for the rest of the paragraph in each case. For instance, if you play soccer, you might use this statement:

> Soccer boots with traditional wooden cleats will not perform as well in bad field conditions as newer boots with synthetic cleats.

If this is one of your statements, you'll have to develop some examples—relating perhaps to two or three different field conditions or playing situations—that you could offer as support in the rest of the paragraph. Once you've developed your statements and the supporting examples, write the paragraphs.

Personal experience

Most people, if asked a question about something, will answer based on their personal experience, their background and their individual understanding. If they must defend or prove a point in a conversation, again they're likely to resort first to things they know or believe based on their personal experience. If that experience includes a particular level of education or work with a relevant subject area, they may be able to use their own experience convincingly in supporting or defending the point in question. Thus, if one is discussing the right way to train a pet and can say, based on five year's experience as an animal trainer, that a certain technique does or doesn't work, then that relevant experience will be viewed as strong support.

Using personal experience as support in an expository essay is more problematic. If you're writing a formal essay, then personal experience (however relevant and appropriate it might otherwise seem) is probably not a good source of supporting material to be set out directly in your paper. The formal expository essay, as a testing device, requires you to adhere to certain conventions and expectations. One of these is that you take an objective posture and deal with the thesis by means of research, analysis and evaluation, rather than through subjective experience. Another is that you will not speak personally and directly to the reader, but will maintain a certain formality and distance. When you recount personal experiences, there's a natural tendency to speak in the first person, as "I," and to address the reader as "you." It's not technically wrong to do this; in fact, it can make your message clearer. However, in the academic world, it's sometimes viewed as informal, clumsy and amateurish—and is therefore to be avoided in the formal essay. On the other hand, if one is writing narration or subjective description, or is working with the personal essay, then personal experience becomes the critical source of information, and the personal and less-formal mode of addressing the reader becomes appropriate.

There's a way you can make personal experience work for you in finding supporting materials. If you have experience in an area and have gained some knowledge as a result of that experience, you can direct your research more efficiently by looking for materials that corroborate what you already know or believe about your subject. You would use the knowledge to save you from having to start from scratch in your research, and to avoid potential dead ends. Thus, if you were an expert mountain biker and were writing about which frame design was best for the novice rider, you might already have decided, based on your experience, that a tubular aluminum frame would be best for beginners. You would also know what the practical advantages of that frame type would be, and you could search directly for materials that supported your viewpoint without having to do more basic research into the various types of frames that exist. You would use your experience to find an independent source confirming your understanding, and you would use that independent source as the support in your essay.

TRANSITIONS

Have you ever read an essay or article that left you confused or made you feel that the writer was jumping from idea to idea without really telling you how to follow? Did it seem as if there were gaps between sentences in a paragraph, or did the paragraphs seem to deal with unrelated issues? If the writer offered a clear thesis, then he or she was having problems with transitions and coherence. A transition is a change from one place or subject or state of being to another. The transitions that occur in an essay are the linking words and phrases by which the ideas expressed in sentences and paragraphs are linked in a logical sequence to each other and to the thesis. If a writer doesn't provide clear transitions, the reader may be unable to follow the chain of logic leading to the writer's conclusion. If the problem is severe, the reader may not be able to finish reading the paper—it will seem to be nonsense, even if the material is actually good and even if the logical connections were clear in the writer's mind at the time of writing. A lack of coherence—orderly, logical connections and flow between the parts of the paper—arises as a result of problems with transitions.

To create proper transitions, you must remember:

⇨
> *When you write, the reader is not there with you in your head and may not see connections you think are clear or obvious. The reader is not you.*
⇦

Accordingly, you should not take for granted that the reader will automatically be able to draw the same conclusions you did when you were considering the same material. You must provide words that allow the reader to move from idea to idea and show the relationship between ideas. If you're presenting several examples or pieces of evidence for a single point in a paragraph, then you must include words that reflect the building weight of evidence:

There are several fine local guitar builders. <u>First</u>, there is Juan Pascal, who was trained in Malaga, Spain, and who builds fine flamenco and classical guitars. He uses only the finest rosewood, ebony, spruce and yellow cypress. <u>Then</u>, there is Michael Tremain, an Englishman who specializes in classical instruments, including lutes. His instruments fetch high prices both locally and abroad. <u>Finally</u>, Peter Cameron builds acoustic-electric guitars for performers who want an amplified acoustic sound. He has experimented successfully with synthetic materials and has earned a good reputation among professional musicians and singers.

Consider another example:

The process of obtaining student financial aid is relatively simple. <u>Initially</u>, one meets with the institution's financial aid officer to have a preliminary interview. <u>During the interview</u>, the student will be questioned about personal assets, income level, family status and amounts required. The information the student provides must be accurate, or criminal liability may arise. <u>On completion of the interview</u>, students who meet the basic requirements will receive a series of forms to be filled out. These forms must be completed accurately, and in the case of students under nineteen years of age, must be co-signed by a parent, family physician, or other responsible adult who is personally acquainted with the aid applicant. <u>Once the student has completed the forms</u>, he or she must arrange another meeting with the financial aid officer, at which time the forms are submitted for processing and the student receives a card indicating his or her present status. The processing of the forms takes about three weeks. <u>After that time</u>, the student will be advised in writing as to the final status of his or her application for funds.

In these examples, the relationship between the ideas within the paragraphs is relatively clear. The underlined words simply confirm the writer's meaning and the sense of sequence she has chosen. In the first example, the writer refers to three instances or examples of local guitar builders, numbering and presenting them according to an arbitrary priority. In the second example, the writer deals with a process that *must* happen in a certain sequence, and the transitional words and phrases used clarify the relationship between the steps in the process. Thus, students applying for aid will only receive the application forms "on completion of the interview"; a second interview is only possible "once the student has completed the forms." Processing takes three weeks, and the student will be advised of the result only "after that time." If these transitional links were omitted from the paragraph, the meaning might still be clear to the reader, but the resulting paragraph would not read smoothly. In the example, nothing is left to chance, and there is much less room for misinterpretation on the reader's part. Similarly, if you're working with cause/effect, you'll need to develop transitions that remind the reader of your controlling model in the paper and that help the reader see the causal relationship between the ideas in successive paragraphs. Transitional words and phrases such as "as a result" and "consequently" indicate a causal relationship. If you're working with comparison and contrast, you might be using expressions like "similarly," "conversely," and "on the other hand." For each of the rhetorical approaches, you'll find that there are stock transitions available to indicate the appropriate relationship between sentences and paragraphs.

While it's important that the transitional words you use within each paragraph accurately reflect the relationship between the ideas with which you are working in that paragraph, it's just as important that the transitions *between* paragraphs be equally clear. These transitions depend largely on the relationship between your thesis and the ideas you set out in the branches of your path statement. You might choose to use phrases that reflect your rhetorical approach in a given essay, just as described above. Alternatively, you might follow the practice of including in the opening sentence of each new paragraph some key word, phrase or idea from the body or conclusion of the preceding paragraph:

> ... and the net effect is an <u>effective doubling of the power from the amplifier to the speakers</u> in the normal listening situation.
>   The use of low, impedance speakers, <u>in addition to effectively doubling the power from the amplifier to the speakers, also increases the amplifier's dynamic range as measured in decibels of "headroom"</u> ....

In this example, you'll notice that the idea from the preceding paragraph is repeated, and the material to be presented in the second paragraph is "in addition" to the earlier information. Thus, the writer builds emphasis on the cumulative weight of the points he is making, rather than separating each argument or point from the others. This simple practice will ensure sound transitions between paragraphs in the body units of your papers much of the time. When you're making a transition between the end of the discussion of one branch of your path statement and the next, you might find it equally useful to return to the actual language you used in the path statement. By mentioning the branch you've just discussed and relating it to the branch you're about to discuss, you remind the reader of your purpose in the paper. You help to keep the reader following the development of your thesis, and you also provide yourself with a reminder about what you're supposed to be doing. Suppose this is your thesis and path statement:

> Round trampolines are much more suitable to home and family use than are square or rectangular ones, especially with regard to <u>the ability to absorb stress from constant jumping, the product longevity, and many key safety factors.</u>

Here the underlined terms represent the branches of the path statement the writer intends to address. The writer will present his or her introduction with the thesis and path statement (the first unit of the paper), and will then go on to the second unit (the discussion of the relative ability of each type to absorb stress). The second unit may take up several paragraphs, especially if the writer intends to introduce technical information. At the conclusion of the second unit, the writer might make the following transition to the third unit (product longevity):

It is clear that a circular frame, because of its ability to distribute force around its perimeter evenly, according to basic principles of physics, is superior to square or rectangular designs in its ability to absorb the stress of constant jumping. Because no single part of the frame can be "overloaded," it follows that a round trampoline frame is likely to last longer than a square or rectangular frame made of the same material.

Product longevity is also an important consideration for home users, principally because of initial cost and continuing interest among family members . . .

Here we see how the same rule we used above applies between branches or units. The message of the preceding unit is summarized nicely and then used as a basis to set up the discussion in the next unit. This is an effective way of making the shift to the next part of the discussion. Once you're able to handle transitions consistently in this way, you need only police yourself to see that you've expressed the transitions clearly to your reader to minimize the possibility of confusion or misinterpretation.

Exercise

We've set out, below, the essay you read earlier in this chapter. Read it again; but this time, identify and list or mark the transitions between the paragraphs, making special note when a transition also addresses the shift between branches of the path statement. Once you've listed or marked all the major transitions, re-examine the thesis and path statement in order to see how the transitions reaffirm or clarify the relationship between the assertions made. Are there any you would have omitted or phrased differently?

Young single women living today in any large American city have had to become more conscious of personal safety issues in their daily lives. The media are full of instances of crimes against women, including date-rape and other forms of sexual assault, battery, robbery, kidnapping and unlawful confinement, and other criminal offences. According to FBI statistics, incidence of such crimes is up, nationwide, by x percent over three years ago. These offences no longer occur only at the hands of strangers or in locations where "trouble" is likely. In fact, they occur in private homes, in the workplace, and even in public in broad daylight. Women in the 18-25 age group seem to be the most likely targets of violent attack and therefore are most in need of practical defensive strategies. Thus, we see more and more of these women seeking to take classes in one of the many martial arts now available in the West. Many of these women limit their choices for study to the two best known martial arts: judo and karate. This choice should not be a matter of uninformed personal preference. In fact, a woman in the 18-25 age group who wishes to study one of these martial arts should make an informed choice based on an understanding of the essential nature of each of these arts. In particular, she should make a decision based on basic philosophy and approach, physical requirements and practical application.

Although Western understanding of judo and karate has greatly improved in recent years, there are still some popular myths (mostly derived from the movies) to be debunked before one can make an intelligent decision about which of these arts to study. The prospective student's first lesson is this: neither judo nor karate is magic, and no amount of training in either art can guarantee that one will emerge unscathed and victorious from an attack. In nature and approach, both of these arts depend on an understanding and mastery of technique and philosophy, combined with high levels of cardiovascular fitness, strength and flexibility. Each approaches the question of self-defence by focusing on the student's mind as well as her physical skills. Both arts depend on basic principles of physics—and on constant practice, since they are made up of learned skills that can be applied in an infinite number of ways. They also depend on the student developing a willingness to endure some pain during the learning process: these are, after all, contact activities.

Judo, "the gentle way," depends on basic principles of physics for its effectiveness as an art and as a system of self-defence. It teaches respect for self and opponents and encourages non-aggression (including a willingness to walk or run away, if necessary) as a means of avoiding violence. In practical terms, the aim of judo is to use an opponent's weight and strength against him, breaking his balance and taking him to the ground by means of a throw or a tripping technique. The judo practitioner rarely delivers actual blows, though blows by an opponent can be effectively countered. One makes an opponent submit by applying a hold or lock to a joint or pressure point on the opponent's body, or by applying a stranglehold until the opponent submits or is choked into unconsciousness. From a woman's perspective, the size of an attacker is therefore irrelevant; in fact, a woman's comparatively small size may be an actual advantage in situations where a large attacker is close enough to grapple with her. However, since the male attacker will usually have a significant advantage in strength, a woman must develop a strong command of the techniques available to her and must condition herself to be unafraid to use them at a critical moment if she is to overcome the attacker's strength advantage. Training is therefore rigorous: if one is not in shape initially, one becomes fit very quickly. Students regularly practice both limited and all-out sparring with classmates in the *dojo* or training hall.

Karate-do, the "way of the empty hand," also incorporates basic principles of physics and teaches respect for self and others. However, there are many styles of karate, and some have responded to the influence of Western commercialism and professional athletics by focusing on the sensational aspects of the combat alone, moving away from the true spirit and philosophy of the art. Other styles have tried to achieve a middle road between Western lifestyles and traditionalism, while still others preserve traditional practices that seem out of place today. Each style tends to place a different emphasis on teaching defence skills, especially with newer students. However, most responsible instructors try to preserve karate's spirit of respect, courtesy and determination, and all the styles operate on the same basic physical principles.

Unlike the judo practitioner, the karate student depends on a repertoire of blocks, kicks, punches and strikes with the elbow, knee, edge of the hand, or back of the fist. Each technique is delivered with proper form for maximum power, and students learn to master the required forms by practicing *kata* or sets of movements against imaginary attackers. In karate, one is taught to use basic principles of movement to generate incredible striking power—power that is not dependent on the size of one's muscles. Thus, it is possible for a small woman to learn to strike an attacker with enough force to disable, or even to kill. What a woman may give away in strength against an attacker, she can more than make up for with speed and perfection of technique. Just as in judo, there are controlled exercises and sparring sessions with one or more opponents in the *dojo*, and there is rigorous training to prepare one physically to learn new techniques.

Each of these martial arts imposes physical requirements (and perhaps some limitations) on the female student. Some of these are relatively minor—for example, both judo and karate *senseis* (teachers) will require students to cut their toenails and fingernails short. In judo, in which students grapple with each other by grasping and tugging on the heavy cotton *judogi* or uniform, one can have a long fingernail ripped out by a sudden movement. Long toenails will mean nasty cuts on the shins and feet of opponents when the student tries leg sweeps and other tripping techniques. In karate, the student cannot make a proper fist with long fingernails; and long fingernails and toenails will mean cuts to opponents when one is using slashing or kicking techniques.

On the other hand, there are some more serious physical considerations. The conditioning for both arts is rigorous. Students with existing medical or physical problems such as asthma, high blood pressure or other cardiovascular trouble, shin splints, disc or other back problems, or any kind of bone ailment must consult their physicians before attending even a single class in either judo or karate.

While the potential for injury exists in both arts, the risks are different. In judo, one learns to fall in such a way as to prevent injury and dissipate the force of an attack—but until one has mastered *ukemi* (breakfalls), bruises to the back, hips and elbows are common. In the beginning stages of karate, there is no danger of falling or being thrown to the ground. However, there are controlled sparring exercises involving application of basic techniques to an opponent. For example, the student may be countering a punch to the head with a rising block and a counter-punch. One does the technique repeatedly with increasing speed and power, stopping the instant before contact with the attacker's face or body occurs. Typically, beginners have plenty of power but little control: bruised ribs are common, and one may also get the occasional fat lip. There will be times when the female student must wear protective equipment over the chest area to avoid serious injury from improperly controlled blows. In both arts, one can pull muscles; in both, sloppy technique can produce broken toes, jammed knuckles, and sprained fingers. Judo practitioners in particular seem to have bad luck with chronic knee injuries because of improperly executed twisting and sweeping techniques. However, as bad as these potential problems may seem to the beginner, one can avoid them through concentration and practice. The benefits to be derived from either judo or karate far outweigh the potential for injury.

The most important question for young female students has to do with the amount of study required before one is actually able to apply the respective techniques of judo and karate for practical self-defence. Experts in both these martial arts suggest that each is really a lifetime study. Indeed, if one subscribes to the philosophy of either art, one may well end up studying and practicing for many years, long after the demand for a practical means of defence is met. However, it should not be necessary to practice for a decade before one is capable of dealing effectively with an opponent. On the other hand, one occasionally sees advertised short courses (ten or twelve weeks) in judo or karate—or "self-defence." Such courses are likely to be of no assistance to the student, not because the techniques taught are valueless, but because there is not enough time for consistent and constant practice. As a result, the student is unable to master or even remember many important skills and techniques, and there is insufficient opportunity for developing appropriate attitudes or psychological readiness. The amount of time it will take a student to become ready to use her art for self-defence will therefore depend on the amount and quality of practice time, instructor emphasis on practical defence skills, the student's personal commitment of time and concentration, and the student's acceptance of what will eventually be a significant change in attitude and lifestyle. These, rather than the choice of martial art, will be the controlling factors in determining ease of application.

In recent years, we in the West have started to examine our own lifestyles more carefully, and many of us have concluded that our lifestyles and our sense of values as a society have made us vulnerable as individuals. It might even be fair to say that in some cases, we have actually prepared ourselves to be victims. Martial arts such as judo and karate provide many women with the means to make positive changes in some key areas of vulnerability, provided that each student accepts the following truth. It is not your physical skills or your black belt that will keep you from being victimized; rather, it is the growth of confidence, coordination, readiness and respect for self and others that will mark you as someone who is no longer a victim. The growth of these qualities and attributes, as you practice your chosen art, will change not only your life, but the lives of those with whom you interact in your daily life. So, make your choice, and make the commitment—even if you never have to defend yourself, the rewards will be well worth the effort.

8
Writing the Research Paper

RESEARCH– "THE GAME'S AFOOT"

Most of the papers you'll write in college or university will require some research. The process may be as simple as going through your class notes and finding important points your instructor made; or it may be quite complicated, involving weeks of library work. The chances that you'll be able to sit down and write a convincing, effective essay off the top of your head are not very good. Although many people only think of research when they consider writing a "term paper," you should be prepared to apply proper research techniques to most of your essay assignments. Once you have a reliable system in place, you can expand or compress it as the simplicity or complexity of the subject and length of the essay require. However, there are some skills that you must master regardless of the scope of a given assignment. You must be able to use the library effectively, and you must be able to cite properly the origins of your sources. These skills are necessary whether you write a two-page paper in which you make reference to a single resource work, or a doctoral dissertation requiring a large number of resources. As well, it's useful to have a reliable system for conducting your research and recording the results.

Most research begins with a question. The question may be posed by an instructor: "What is the most important archetypal theme present in Robert Pirsig's *Zen and the Art of Motorcycle Maintenance*?" The question may arise out of your own need to find more information on a subject: "What is an archetypal theme?" Most often, the question will derive from the preliminary thesis that you develop for your essay. You'll form a hypothesis: "The quest is the primary archetype used in Pirsig's novel." The question you must answer is: "Is this an appropriate, defensible position?" Your hypothesis, and your need to prove its validity, initiate one of the most interesting and productive processes that you'll engage in as a student—conducting research. In the words of Sherlock Holmes, "The game's afoot!"

DEVELOPING A PLAN OF ACTION

Let's assume that you have been asked to write an essay analysing Arthur Miller's play *Death of a Salesman*. You have no further instructions. How do you begin? You've read the play, and you have some ideas about why it is an important dramatic work. Should you start by going to the library? Should you first try to formulate a thesis statement? Often, an open-ended assignment like this can cause you to blank out just as you're starting. Even when you've carefully read the work and feel comfortable with it, you can be intimidated by the scope of the problem posed for you.

The easiest way to break the intellectual log jam is to list what you know—to brainstorm, as we discussed earlier. The assignment asks you to analyse Miller's play. Think about literary analysis. What do you know about the process of analysing a literary work? Before you delve into the play, you should consider what tools are available to you. This will help to narrow the scope of your problem and to direct your library work once it begins. Some key words relating to a literary analysis of *Death of a Salesman* might be: character, tragedy, conflict, theme, etc. From your initial list, you can pick ideas that you feel show promise and use them to construct more narrowed lists (*see figure 8-1*).

As you can see from figure 8-1, you can narrow quite a bit just by brainstorming. This reduced list allows you to make the final preparations for your first trip to the library. If you wish, you can construct a working thesis from what you've done. It might take the following form:

> Any analysis of Arthur Miller's *Death of a Salesman* must deal in detail with the climactic scene at the end of act 2 between Willy Loman and his son Biff. This scene is the pivotal point in the play. It discloses the nature of Willy's tragic flaw, it brings to a climax the breakdown of the Loman family, and it poses the question: "Is this Willy's or Biff's play?"

Alternatively, you could make a list of key terms you feel need to be researched before you can formulate a working thesis. In either

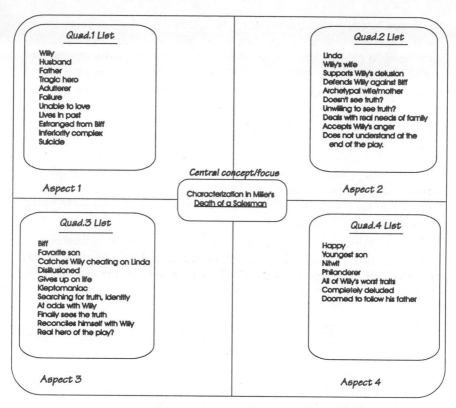

Figure 8-1: Using Brainstorming Lists with <u>Death of a Salesman</u>

case, you must keep in mind that you've merely created an entry point. Your research may show that you're on the wrong track; it may lead to a more interesting approach; it may reinforce your initial sense of the play but show that you need to do a lot more narrowing; or it may lead you to believe that your first analysis was off the mark and requires more thought. Ideally, your initial research will confirm your intuitive analysis and all you'll have to do is fill in the grey areas in your work, find support for your position, and document your sources.

It is a good idea to begin your research simply. You will need specific, clear ideas to research. If you cannot express an idea as a single word or phrase, you cannot use it as a search key. In the beginning, your efforts will be spent trying to generate terms and ideas that can be used in the library. The working thesis provides a few obvious leads: Arthur Miller, tragedy, *Death of a Salesman* and American drama. If you begin the research using general reference sources (encyclopedias, dictionaries, bibliographic listings, etc.), you'll be able to generate a list of authors, publications and concepts that will help you when you do more detailed searches of the library catalogue.

If you begin by simply looking up "Arthur Miller" in an encyclopedia, you'll discover a number of things you can use to direct your primary research. For example, Miller was politically active, and the themes that recur in his plays are "family relationships" and "social responsibility." His plays include *All My Sons* (1947), *Death of a Salesman* (1947), *The Crucible* (1953), *A View from the Bridge* (1955), *After the Fall* (1964), and the screenplay for *The Misfits* (1961). He won the Pulitzer Prize for *Death of a Salesman*, which premiered on February 10, 1949, in New York. In an interview given in 1949, Miller argued that the common man was as good a subject for modern tragedy as royalty was in classical tragedy. Miller was heavily influenced by Henrik Ibsen and wrote an adaptation of Ibsen's play, *An Enemy of the People*.

This simple trip to the encyclopedia has provided a number of new ideas you can add to your list of research keys. As well, it has provided an important date—1949. Any searches for information relating to *Death of A Salesman* in indices that are organized by date should begin with catalogues dated 1949 or later.

THE LIBRARY

The library is at the heart of everything you do as a researcher. For that reason, you must be familiar with the resources it offers you, in terms of both holdings and research assistance. If you're attending a large university such as the University of Toronto or the University of California at Berkeley, you have access to libraries with extensive holdings. However, if you're attending a small community college, you'll find that the range of titles available to you is limited, as is the number of extra copies of "in demand" individual titles. This may seem to be a basic consideration and of little consequence; but if you ignore it, you could find yourself in trouble. For example, you could turn up forty or fifty publications related to your research topic when you do your initial research, only to find that the library does not have any of them on the shelves—or that the ones they do have are out. Often, interlibrary loans can be arranged, but this takes time, and there may be limitations as to who can borrow. You may also find that the library at your campus has unusual or extensive holdings in a specific area. For instance, the University of Alberta's rare book division purchased the complete works of Edward Ward, an obscure eighteenth-century Grub Street writer, thereby creating a rich area of research for anyone who was aware of the acquisition. On the other hand, you may find that your campus library, although generally very good, has some small but distressing gaps in their holdings. If you are to complete your research project successfully, you must think about the resources available to you. Most campus libraries have orientation programs, and it's to your advantage to spend the time to take one. You don't want to find out after you've done all your preliminary work that none of the books you need are actually available.

BEGINNING YOUR RESEARCH — THE CARD CATALOGUE

For most undergraduate research essays, your campus library should provide adequate resources. However, you must understand how to access those resources. In the past, all research projects began with the library card catalogue. Typically, the catalogue was broken into appropriate subsections: there would be a subject catalogue, and an author/title catalogue. If you had an author's name or the title (or partial title) of a work, you would go to the latter catalogue. If you were looking for materials about a particular subject, you would go to the former. The subject catalogue was broken down into specific subjects or categories, with generalized subject descriptions that include more particularized information. The student, armed with a pencil and a box of three-by-five-inch cards, would spend hours thumbing through drawers of catalogue files. The manual catalogue search was always time-consuming—even when the desired authors, titles and subjects appeared in the cards. However, it was often the case that the search items were not represented in the catalogue, and the frustration of finding searchable terms was added to the tediousness of the search itself. Fortunately, this is no longer the case.

Almost all university and college libraries (at this writing, we aren't aware of any exceptions, though there may still be a few hold-outs) have added online, computer-accessible catalogues. Most of these are accessible by means of any home computer and an inexpensive modem (computer communications device). Just by hooking the computer up to the telephone, you can make complicated, high-speed searches of a library's holdings from the comfort of your own home. In fact, you can search any library in your area. For instance, while we were preparing this chapter, we were able to search three university libraries, a college library, and the main branch of our city library—all from our office computers and all within one hour.

It doesn't end there. Most college and universities belong to a mainframe computer service called the Internet. The Internet network is an international service that may be available through your campus computer. With an account on your college's or university's mainframe

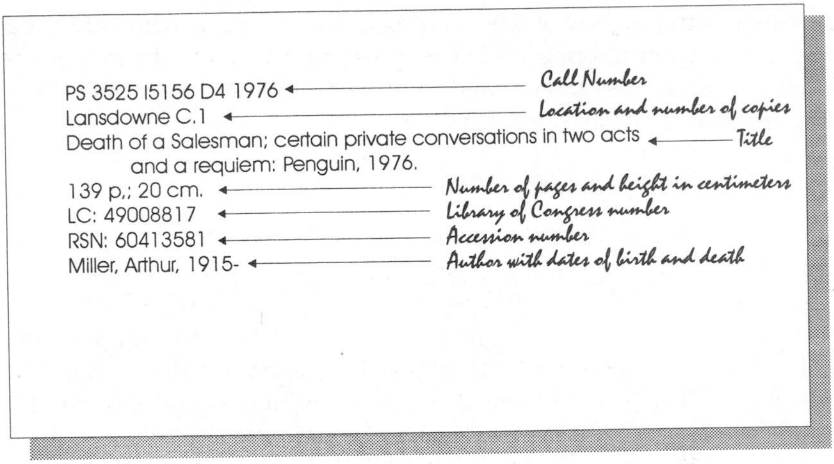

PS 3525 I5156 D4 1976 ←————————— *Call Number*
Lansdowne C.1 ←————————————— *Location and number of copies*
Death of a Salesman; certain private conversations in two acts ←———— *Title*
    and a requiem: Penguin, 1976.
139 p.; 20 cm. ←————————— *Number of pages and height in centimeters*
LC: 49008817 ←————————— *Library of Congress number*
RSN: 60413581 ←————————— *Accession number*
Miller, Arthur, 1915- ←————————— *Author with dates of birth and death*

Figure 8-2: Typical library catalogue card

computer system, you can actually do library searches at institutions across North America and around the world. In many instances, you can get online help with your research problems from research technicians at the host institution. Literally millions of books, articles and other materials are listed for your scrutiny. If your project is important enough, and you have enough lead time, you might even be able to arrange interlibrary loans. Truly, we've entered the information age; and, in the case of the research paper, we've revolutionized our approach to the methodology and level of difficulty of the job.

Let's assume that you're going to begin research for your essay on Arthur Miller's *Death of a Salesman*. If you use the old-fashioned, manual system located at the library, you must physically travel to the library. Each subject, title or author you want to research will require a separate trip to the catalogue. As well, each search is an independent event. As you thumb through the listings, any information that you don't note down on your three-by-five-inch cards will be lost. You can spend far too much time keeping track of catalogue entries of questionable value, or trying to find entries you overlooked during an initial search but later decided you needed. When you find an entry you feel is useful, the file card will contain only basic information about the publication (*see figure 8-2*).

If you use the computer catalogue, more than just the ease of access is altered. Because the automated card catalogue is a giant database (a special form of computer program that optimizes the storage, organization and recovery of information), you can carry out your searches in a complete, logical and integrated manner. Unlike the manual card system, where each search is a separate event, the computer searches can be linked—can build on each other.

Most computer catalogue systems share syntax (the form that the search command takes), even if they do not use exactly the same search terms. If you were looking for works by Arthur Miller, the syntax would be as follows:

[*Command*] [*Index Term*] [*Search Word*]

The *command* tells the computer what primary function you want it to perform. On most systems the word you need would be find, locate, search, etc. You want the computer to find works by Arthur Miller. The second part of your instruction to the computer consists of the *index term*. This a term that limits the universe of the search. These words usually consist of author, subject, title, etc. Since you are looking for works by a single author, you will use the delimiter author. The final element in the command will be the *search word*, the term that will tell the computer what specific information it must match when it performs its search. In this case, you only want the search to save results that consist of works by arthur miller.

Your final instruction would take the form:

find author miller, arthur

The results of your search will include a number of works by Arthur Miller, including *The Crucible* and *Death of a Salesman*. The information, at first, will be the same as that shown on the sample library catalogue entry in figure 8-2. However, on the computer, the basic library card information is only part of what you can find out. If you ask the computer to display more detailed information, you can get a description of the publication's content, the ISBN number, the number of copies of the publication in the library's holdings, the publication's current status ("in" or "out"), and the posted return time if it is already out of the library. As well, many systems will suggest related search parameters (ideas you can use to find other publications that might be of interest to you).

The most useful *index term* when you're beginning your research is subject. When you tell the computer to do a subject search, it will look for any publication that includes the *search words* as part of its description. For instance, suppose you issue the following command:

find subject death of a salesman

The computer will provide you with a list of all publications that have the words "death of a salesman" anywhere in their descriptive information. Here are examples of some of the results of such a search.

The Burning Jungle by Karl Harshbarger: an analysis of Arthur Miller's *Death of a Salesman*.

Teaching English Through Drama to Chinese Students by Marie Osmond: Teaching English as a second language—uses *Death of a Salesman*, Criticism and interpretation.

The Merrill Studies in "Death of a Salesman" by Walter J. Meserve: Studies in *Death of a Salesman*—includes bibliographical references.

Private Conversations on the set of "Death of a Salesman" by Christian Blackwood: VIDEORECORDING—A documentary that goes behind the scenes to examine the making of the film version of Arthur Miller's *Death of a Salesman*. Playwright Miller, Dustin Hoffman, and director Volker Schlondorff discuss the production and the original play.

American Expressionist Drama by Murthy V. Rama: Contains an analysis of three outstanding American plays: O'Neill, *The Hairy Ape*; Tennessee Williams, *The Glass Menagerie*; Arthur Miller, *Death of a Salesman*.

Twentieth Century Interpretations of "Death of a Salesman" edited by Helene Wickham Koon: A collection of critical essays.

As you can see, the computer search turns up quite a variety of titles, some of which would not appear in a manual search of the card catalogue. Unlike a search of the card catalogue (requiring that you make notes on every title that might be useful), the computer search keeps a record of every title found during a single search request. All you have to do to record the results is to ask the host computer to print the search results. Usually, you can get it to print either to a file (for disk storage) or directly to a printer attached to your home computer.

This system is especially useful when you're researching periodicals. Generally, you're required to go through periodical indices by publication and by year. Many libraries have large numbers of periodical indices on a single database. Thus, the computer allows you to research large numbers of periodicals with a single search command.

Searches using the computer are quick, complete and simple. It's possible to explore the holdings of five or six libraries in a matter of minutes without leaving your desk; and your computer can be set up to automatically keep complete records of search results.

It's well worth your time to talk to your library staff about how to use this resource.

ORGANIZING AND DEVELOPING A RESEARCH PAPER

As you do your research, you should keep careful records of what you've found, where you found it, and what additional ideas occurred to you during the research process. Because you may not have a clear idea of your final thesis and path statement at this point, the research process is not only about finding useful material; it's also about narrowing and refining your thesis and about making increasingly discriminating choices in terms of useful material. All of the information you record and organize will be vital to you when you begin to put the actual paper together.

If the organization of research material and ideas is to be handled in a way that facilitates easy translation into a full essay, there must be an organizational system in place from the first brainstorming session to the moment that you sit down at your keyboard to write the essay. Moreover, the system you choose must allow you to move from the initial steps of finding and recording discrete pieces of information, to the subsequent steps of categorizing these pieces of information under the branches of your path and inserting them into the multiple unit model.

There are many systems for organizing your research materials. All have advantages and all have disadvantages. However, one of the most important considerations is that the system be dynamic and flexible. It must allow simple manipulation of information and form. If it doesn't—if you must reconstruct the entire organizational framework to make a simple change—then there's a real chance that you'll become frustrated by the organizational problems and will abandon the organizational process before you should. The three-by-five-inch card system described here offers a dynamic, easily manipulated tool. It will provide a simple, inexpensive means of organizing your research, determining the form your essay will take, and preparing the final version for typing. Moreover, it is consistent with the multiple unit model in terms of visualizing the global structure of your essay.

This is an important point. We don't want you to be misled into thinking that the card system is somehow different or separate from the multiple unit model in concept and function. When you're working with the cards and recording the information we'll describe, you'll really be identifying ideas and bits of material that relate to specific branches or support paths of the research paper's thesis and path statement. If you do the job properly, you'll be able to separate the cards into piles, and create an appropriate sequence within each pile. If you were working with a sufficiently large template, you'd actually be able to take the piles of cards and place them on the appropriate boxes in the template. The cards simply provide a convenient means of recording important materials while you're engaged in the research and organizational phases of the work.

3 x 5 CARD SYSTEM FOR ORGANIZING A RESEARCH ESSAY

Decide what you'll write about, and gather the books and periodicals you'll use to begin your research. Remember that at this point, you probably haven't identified anything resembling a clear, narrow thesis and path statement. At best, you may have a somewhat limited subject area; if your instructor has assigned a closed topic, you may have a reasonable working thesis—or not. In any case, you should begin by doing the following:

1. Get a package of three-by-five-inch cards.

2. Begin by brainstorming and by doing some preliminary research. You should also be doing important narrowing work at this point, directing your reading and research.

3. Write any ideas or quotes on three-by-five-inch cards. Put each idea on a separate card; don't put two quotes or two thoughts on a single card.

4. When you're recording a quotation you may want to use, be sure to include the information you'll need when you type your "Works Cited" and "Works Consulted" pages.

5. When you feel that you've exhausted your ideas on the subject and you've done a reasonable research job, re-examine your focus for adequate narrowing, and begin to organize the paper using your set of cards.

6. Clear off a large space on the floor.

7. Go through your cards and look for themes that could be organized into major development areas (the branches of your path statement). Example: you're writing about clear-cutting, and you find that you have a number of cards dealing with the areas of economics, recreational impact and damage to the ecology.

8. Label a single card with each of the headings (economics, recreational impact, damage to the ecology) and place the label cards on the floor. Lay out the appropriate cards in lines below the label cards.

9. If you have cards left over, see if you can identify any other themes. If you can, repeat step 8. If you don't see themes developing, put the extra cards aside for later.

10. When you have all of the cards laid out, look at each of the development sets in terms of organization. Try to find a logical relationship between the ideas on the cards. Carefully organize the cards into an appropriate sequence. As you put them in order, see if there is information missing. If there is, do more research or more thinking, and record the results on new cards. When you're satisfied that you've gathered all of the missing information, insert the new cards in their proper place in the strings of cards.

11. You may find, after you've reworked the information in a development set, that you have more than one theme—in other words, you need to narrow more. If this is true, make a new label card and split your string of cards into two. Bear in mind that this is likely to affect the form of your final thesis and path statement.

12. When you've fully expanded the development strings, you must prepare the introduction and conclusion. Prepare a label card for each of these sections, and begin to organize a string of content cards for each. Use the same techniques that you used in the development sections.

13. When you have the entire paper laid out, go over each section carefully. Be sure that you have all of the information that you need. Be sure that it's organized in a logical and appropriate manner (considering the nature and focus of your argument). Be sure that you've supported each of your major position statements with proper research. In any instance where you feel more work is necessary, fill out cards that complete the work, and insert them in the appropriate card string.

14. When you're satisfied that everything is ready, pick up the cards (with the "Introduction" label card on top), and take them to your writing desk. You can now flip through them, and you have all of the notes for your first draft. If you have trouble visualizing

the form of the paper after all this, you may need to use the cards to make a large template—this is, after all, what the logically sequenced cards represent.

PROOFREADING AND REVISION

Proofreading entails far more than simply checking spelling, grammar, and punctuation. The proofing process should begin with your first typed draft and continue through your final draft. You should consider the following four-level system of revision only as a guide, and you should keep in mind that a level of revision isn't completed until you've fixed any errors or omissions that occur in your document. It may take four or five passes through a document to complete one revision level.

1. <u>Be sure that all of the parts of the essay are present and correctly structured</u>. You must have a thesis statement and path statement, an appropriate number of development sections and a conclusion. Your first revision should simply assure that each of these parts is present and in the correct order. If you use the three-by-five-inch card method of building the multiple unit model, you should have ensured that this requirement is satisfied before you began to type the essay. However, it's always a good idea to check carefully for structural integrity before you begin more detailed levels of revision.

2. <u>Revise at the paragraph level</u>. Be sure that each paragraph has a topic sentence and that the flow of the paragraph is logical and well paced. Does the material in the paragraph make sense? Is it in the correct order? Have you included all the information necessary for the reader to understand the points you're trying to make?

3. <u>Revise for aesthetics</u>. Once all the parts of the essay are present and in the correct order, you should check for readability—flow of language. You should now look at *how* the prose is written. Is the use of language optimal—have you used the best words to express the ideas you are communicating? Is the rhythm of the piece pleasing? Have you alternated short and long sentences? Can you alter the sentences to make the essay read more smoothly? One of the best ways to conduct this proofing step is to read your essay aloud into a tape player and listen carefully to the playback.

4. Finally, after everything else is completed, <u>revise for spelling, grammar, and punctuation</u>. Remember that you must meet the mechanical as well as the content thresholds.

DOCUMENTING YOUR RESEARCH

One of the requirements of research is that any time you summarize, paraphrase or quote any material that can't be considered "common knowledge," you must acknowledge your sources. This is an ethical (and in most cases, a legal) obligation that you have as a researcher. If you don't meet this obligation, you are plagiarizing. At most educational institutions, the price of plagiarism is high. The plagiarist can expect to fail the assignment on which she plagiarized, will most likely be given a failing mark for the entire semester, and at many institutions, will be expelled. You should also know that some institutions take the view that you don't have to intend to plagiarize to be found guilty of it.

Fortunately, if you've kept records of your library research results, meeting your ethical obligation to your sources and avoiding plagiarizing is easy. All you have to do is mark the text that you're quoting, name the author of the borrowed material and the publication in which it occurred, and indicate where the material appears in the publication.

There are a number of systems used to cite sources in a research paper. The two most important are the system adopted by the Modern Language Association (MLA) and the system adopted by the American Psychological Association (APA). The former will be required for most papers written in the humanities and the later for papers written in the social sciences. Our intention here is not to provide a complete guide to these styles, but rather to give you a sense of general principles. For more information, consult the *MLA Handbook for Writers of Research Papers*, and/or the *Publication Manual of the American Psychological Association*.

As you look over the material below, remember what we said earlier about having elected to present our sample materials single-spaced. If you are strictly following either MLA or APA style, you should know that both systems require you to double space *everything* in a research essay. Also remember to check you instructor's specific requirements.

The MLA System of Documentation

The MLA system (like the APA system) is a parenthetical citation system. The principle upon which it rests is that in the body of the essay, you ought to provide your reader with the minimum (not the maximum) information necessary to allow your reader to track your sources accurately. Generally, you provide your reader with the author's last name and a page reference at the place in your document where the quotation or paraphrase appears. This information is contained inside a set of parentheses. A typical reference using the MLA parenthetical system would look like this:

> Since the material in your research paper rests to a great extent on the scholarship of other writers, you must always give proper credit by citing your sources (Wilbury, 221).

The information in the parentheses is a guide to help the reader find a full reference to the publication from which the quote was taken. That reference will be found in your "Works Cited" page, a full listing of authors and publications you used in the essay. The fictitious source referenced above would appear on the "Works Cited" page like this:

Author. <u>Title</u>. City: Publisher, Date of Publication.

Wilbury, C. <u>Writing Help</u>. Toronto: Full Court Press, 1993.

The rule for your in-document citations is: only include in the parentheses as much information as is necessary for the reader to find the correct source on your "Works Cited" page. Thus, if you are writing a short research essay and you only use a single reference work, then only a page number would appear in the parenthesis:

> Since the material in your research paper comes largely from the work of one writer, you must always give proper credit by citing your source (221).

If you have two entries on your "Works Cited" page, you must include the author's last name and a page number.

> Since the material in your research paper rests to a great extent on the scholarship of other writers, you must always give proper credit by citing your sources (Wilbury, 221).

Finally, if you have two entries on the "Works Cited" page by the same author or by authors with the same name, then you must include the author's last name, a short version of the book's title, and a page number.

> Since the material in your research paper rests to a great extent on the scholarship of other writers, you must always give proper credit by citing your sources (Wilbury, *Documentation* 221).

The exception to these examples occurs when you give the reader information regarding the author's name and the source in the text of your essay. For example:

In his book, *Documentation Methods for College Students*, Wilbury states that ". . . "(221).

The "Works Cited" Page

The "Works Cited" page is located at the end of your essay. It contains a list of all the works you've used as sources in your paper. The entries on the "Works Cited" page are listed by author in alphabetical order. Entries on the "Works Cited" page contain information regarding the author, title and publication details (city of publication, publisher, date of publication). The system for listing books is slightly different from that for listing periodicals. However, you are expected to know that for *each* citation, the first line of the citation begins flush left; all subsequent lines within that citation must be indented five spaces. The first line of the next citation will again be flush left, and so on.

As you examine the examples below, pay close attention to capitalization, punctuation, underlining and order of the elements included in each citation.

Books

Generic Form

Author. <u>Title</u>. City: Publisher, date.

Book with One Author

Campbell, Joseph. <u>The Hero With A Thousand Faces</u>. Princeton: Princeton University Press, 1973.

Book with Two or Three Authors

Bandler, Richard, and John Grinder. <u>The Structure of Magic</u>. Palo Alto: Science and Behavior, 1975.

Book with Four or More Authors

Hodges, John C., et al. <u>Harbrace College Handbook</u>. Toronto: Harcourt Brace, 1990.

Book with No Author

Canadian Society for Literacy. <u>The Threat of Television</u>. Toronto: CSL Press, 1991.

Book with Editors and Editions

Ellmann, Richard, and Robert O'Clair, eds. <u>The Norton Anthology of Modern Poetry</u>. 2nd Ed. New York: Norton, 1988.

Periodicals and Articles

Generic Form

Author. "Title of Article." <u>Title of Publication</u>. Volume Number (Date): Pages on which the article appears.

Magazine Article

Krumm, Bob. "Nymph Fishing Made Easy." <u>American Angler</u>. 15.5 (1992): 25-30.

Journal Article

Ross, Catherine Sheldrick. "Hugh MacLennan's Two Worlds." <u>Canadian Literature</u>. 80 (1979): 5-12.

Newspaper Article

McDonald, Gracie. "Eight Capital Choices." <u>Monday Magazine</u>. 19-25 November 1992: 8-11.

The APA System of Documentation

Like the MLA system of documentation, the APA system is parenthetical. It differs from the MLA in its focus on author and publication date for identification, rather than author and page number.

When you cite a source in APA format, the information inside the parenthesis must include the name of the author, the date of publication, and the page(s) in your reference work on which the quoted material appears (you must proceed the page number with "pp." or "p."). A typical reference using APA would appear as follows:

> Since the material in your research paper rests to a great extent on the scholarship of other writers, you must always give proper credit by citing your sources (Wilbury, 1993, p. 221).

The APA system requires that you always give the name of the author, the date of publication and the page number on which the quoted material appears. This means that, unlike MLA style, the only time you include less information in the parentheses is when you have already given the information in the text of your essay. For example:

> When discussing how to apply the principles of proper documentation, Wilbury (1993) states:
>
>> Since the material in your research paper rests to a great extent on the scholarship of other writers, you must always give proper credit by citing your sources. (p. 221)

The page containing the list of references isn't called the "Works Cited" page in APA format. Instead, it's called "References," and it appears at the end of your document, just as does the "Works Cited" page. As is the case with the MLA system, the method for documenting periodicals is slightly different from that used to document books. Note the differences in components, order, punctuation and the like, as you read through the examples below.

Books

Generic Form

Author. (Date). Title. City: Publisher.

Book with One Author

Campbell, Joseph. (1973). The Hero With A Thousand Faces. Princeton: Princeton University Press.

Book with Two Authors

Bandler, Richard, & Grinder, John. (1975). The Structure of Magic. Palo Alto: Science and Behavior.

Book with Three or More Authors

Hodges, John C., Whitten, Mary E., Brown, Judy & Flick, Jane. (1990). Harbrace College Handbook. Toronto: Harcourt Brace.

Book with no Author

Canadian Society for Literacy. (1991). The Threat of Television. Toronto: CSL Press.

Book with Editors and Editions

Eliot, T.S. (1988). The Wasteland. In Richard Ellmann & Robert O'Clair (Eds.). The Norton Anthology of Modern Poetry (2nd Ed.). New York: Norton.

Periodicals and Articles

Generic Form

Author. (Date). Title of article. Title of Publication, Volume Number (Issue Number): Pages on which the article appears.

Magazine Article

Krumm, Bob. (1992, November). Nymph fishing made easy. American Angler, 15.5: pp. 25-30.

Journal Article

Ross, Catherine Sheldrick. (1979). Hugh MacLennan's two worlds. Canadian Literature, 80: pp. 5-12.

Newspaper Article

McDonald, Gracie. (1992, November 19). Eight capital choices. Monday Magazine: pp. 19-25.

9
Writing Across the Disciplines

In some respects, this chapter is the most important in these materials. So far, we've tried to provide you with a workable approach to undergraduate essay writing. We've also demonstrated how you might use this approach in a variety of contexts to achieve consistently sound results. As well, we've looked briefly at the nature of basic research and the problems of documentation, since academic writing is based on honest inquiry and analysis, together with formal recognition of one's sources. Clear narrowing, an understanding of your audience, the framing of a thesis and path statement, an understanding of content, the ability to achieve transference for your reader—all are essential to the writing of an expository essay. However, it would be wrong to conclude that mastery of the essay form, once achieved, is the only goal or end-product of composition courses or books such as this one. In fact, we want to suggest that the writing and organizational skills and the operative principles you learn to apply in your undergraduate English courses are directly transferable to all other academic disciplines.

If true transferability of understanding and skills is to be a goal, then an English course devoted to essay writing should not focus on how to write only a particular kind of essay in a given subject. After all, mastery of the literary essay form, as an end in itself, doesn't necessarily make one competent to write a case study in business or a physics research report. In the past, there was little apparent concern about this, since the disciplines were often seen to operate independently of each other. Those days are gone, and educational institutions now look increasingly to their English departments to provide students with an understanding of the skills and principles required to write well across the disciplines. If there really is a set of principles and skills upon which clear writing is based, then that set of principles and skills must be the base for clear writing regardless of discipline or specific subject. Moreover, such principles apply not only in the academic world, but in business, industry and the professions.

Much has been written about the problems facing major corporations because of poor communication skills at the management level and about the changes the new technology has caused in industry. The medical and legal professions face small revolutions on a daily basis, and education itself has become increasingly sensitive to the impact of writing and communications technology on curriculum design and delivery. One might therefore properly regard an understanding of the principles and skills of good writing as a prerequisite to success in other fields. This notion of good organizational and writing skills as a prerequisite to success is especially important if we're to believe much of what we hear about a literacy crisis that seems continent-wide. If a literacy crisis—a crisis of communication skills—actually does exist in Canada and the United States, it seems ironic that such a crisis would be occurring just now. At the very time when changes in workplace technology are creating a growing demand for skilled organizers, planners and communicators, the pool of people qualified to assume such positions may be shrinking. We are in the midst of a real change from production-line thinking to information technology. All of us need to develop skills that will help us to make such a transition successfully.

Information-processing technology is developing more quickly than we as individuals can adapt to the technological changes. During this process, different disciplines have grown closer together. This has not occurred because their subject matters have started to merge, though that might happen in some cases. Rather, it has occurred because more and more disciplines are starting to use information-processing models based on technology that is becoming common to *all* disciplines. Computers are everywhere—there are widespread industry standards in word processing, database management, desktop publishing, accounting, graphic design, and so on. Using one or more of these standards, workers in different disciplines have started to handle information in similar ways, using similar technologies and methods, even though the nature of the information is different from discipline to discipline. For example, there were times when people working in anthropology had to store hundreds or thousands of detailed bits of information according to old-fashioned notebook and catalogue procedures. There have long been established methods of paper-copy data storage recognized as appropriate by anthropologists. Similarly, stockbrokers also had paper systems for tracking separate bits of client information and transaction details.

Today, both the anthropologist and the stockbroker may be using a computerized database to identify, sort and cross-reference separate pieces of information—in fact, they might actually be using the same database software, or software that handles information in the same way. Thus, despite the differences in the nature of their work, the anthropologist and the stockbroker must now organize their information according to the capabilities of the computer program. They must begin to think in terms of data searches, computerized cross-indexing, and so on. Each will be able to store and retrieve information more quickly, provided that each understands and can apply the principles of the information-processing model. Nor will their use of the database be much different in principle than it will be for the doctor consulting a biomedical database or a lawyer consulting a legal precedent database. Each of these people will use the same operative principles to deal with information, even though they work in different disciplines. The technology attempts to allow each to use the logical connections between bits of information to access and correlate the information quickly and easily. The technology thus reflects an organizational system with its own internal logic—a model for the effective organization and clear expression of detailed information.

A moment's consideration of the material you've been studying will demonstrate that the organizational principle underlying the multiple unit model is primarily a model for organized thinking, which we've applied to the task of essay writing.

⇨
> *If the purpose of writing is to express clearly to a reader an ordered presentation of ideas, regardless of subject matter or rhetorical approach, then the multiple unit model ought to assist you with writing tasks across the disciplines.*
⇦

In this respect, the multiple unit model provides an organizational system for the clear expression of detailed information, just as does the technology described above. The system itself transfers easily from one discipline to another, since it contains within itself the flexibility to adapt to the content requirements of other disciplines. We've already seen how the multiple unit model can assist you in applying the major rhetorical modes you're required to use as an undergraduate student. Now we'll consider the model's application in a wider range of contexts. In particular, we'll consider examples from the so-called hard sciences, computer technology, business and law—subject areas we've chosen at random to illustrate how you can apply basic principles. We're not primarily concerned here with how to write a lab report or how to write a business memorandum or how to format a floppy disk. Rather, we want to examine some of the general problems within each of the named areas to see how we might apply the multiple unit model as a thinking and organizing strategy that would make the task of writing easier. As we work through this material, keep in mind the following guidelines:

1. The multiple unit model, as an organizational strategy, transfers from discipline to discipline. The components of the model may be adjusted to meet the requirements of a particular assignment or methodology.

2. Every discipline has its own vocabulary, layout formats, analytical methods, usage, and academic perspectives or viewpoints. You must inform yourself about these things in each discipline and learn how to incorporate or apply them in the model. Thus, you will be seen to be speaking the language required for successful writing in each discipline. You must learn on your own the vocabulary and the various acceptable formats for business letters and reports, research proposals, marketing plans, legal memoranda, and the like.

3. In all your writing, regardless of the discipline, you have ongoing obligations: to meet the mechanical threshold and the content threshold; to narrow to a clear and meaningful thesis based on an accurate understanding of an assignment or task; to express a clear path statement; and to develop your thesis and path statement fully in the rest of the document. Your obligations respecting accuracy, believability, consistency, and the like remain constant, as does the need to be sensitive to the audience and its concerns.

4. It may be possible for you to learn to write a particular type of document within the narrow confines of a single discipline. However, it's in your interest to take the larger view and to see those specific tasks as instances in which the general organizational and writing principles we have discussed apply to a defined situation. Such tasks are not different kinds of writing; rather, they involve the same principles, applied in particular ways.

WRITING IN THE HARD SCIENCES

In the applied and natural sciences (the hard sciences), there is a centuries-old tradition of logic, analytical detachment, precision and accuracy that is caught up with the scientific method. There are accepted experimental methodologies in each scientific discipline, and there are clear procedural standards for the presentation of experimental data and for conclusions based on that data. If we consider the nature of scientific research as intellectual activity, we can see that all scientific research is concerned at various times with the rhetorical approaches you've been studying. Researchers may be making inquiry into why a particular reaction or phenomenon occurs the way it does in specific circumstances (cause/effect); or scientists may be looking at the advisability of using one of two processes for doing something (comparison, process). Biologists may be working to classify a new microscopic organism (classification, division). When these scientists must present their results in written form, they must satisfy the procedural standards accepted within the discipline. They must also satisfy the logical requirements of the rhetorical approach governing their research. Furthermore, they must meet the mechanical and content thresholds before any of their colleagues will even read their work.

⇨

> *If the principles of clear writing transfer to each of the scientific disciplines, then the multiple unit model can be used to organize a laboratory report, a presentation, or a formal research paper incorporating hard scientific data.*

⇦

Let's consider an example relating to chemistry. Suppose you must conduct a lab experiment to determine whether a particular chemical reaction will occur in a certain way under controlled circumstances. In order to test your hypothesis that the reaction will indeed occur as you suspect, you'll need to create the controlled environment. Then, you'll have to prescribe a method or process that will produce enough observable data to allow you (or any other informed observer) to make an analysis. You'll also have to be sure that the method you adopt isolates the important aspects of the reaction you're studying so that there are no other variables interfering with the reaction or skewing your data. Once you've identified your methodology, you'll have to apply it in a sequence of documented steps that other researchers must be able to duplicate in order to confirm your findings. As you work through the sequence, you'll have to record not only what you're doing, but also what changes or reactions you observe—and you must do so without leaping to non-analytical conclusions about the nature of those changes or reactions. Next, you'll have to present your analysis and conclusions in "proper" form and in sufficient detail to satisfy readers who work with the scientific method. This will mean providing a summary of your results, a clear statement of the goal or goals of the experiment, material on your methodology, your detailed results, and a detailed discussion containing your analysis.

This doesn't sound much like the process used for producing an English essay. Nonetheless, your task involves the creation of an academic document that must not only withstand scientific scrutiny, but must also meet all the same basic standards as an essay in terms of clarity, organization, level and appropriateness of language, grammar, spelling and punctuation. If we apply the concepts of the thesis, path statement and multiple unit model to the creation of the lab report, we might get something like the layout in figure 9-1.

In the example, we know that the purpose of the lab experiment is to examine a particular reaction according to a specific methodology in order see whether a certain result occurs. However, that is not the purpose of the lab *report*. The purpose of the report is to record the experiment and its results accurately and completely, in an acceptable format. Thus, we can see that the first unit in the model now contains the "Abstract," rather than the "Introduction," and the appropriate heading would actually appear in the final form of the report. In this unit, you might state as the thesis for the lab report your hypothesis for the actual experiment: "The purpose of this experiment is to determine whether reaction x occurs in this way under the following circumstances: ... " The path statement for the document is also present in this unit. It would appear in the final draft of the report in summary form as part of the abstract and would be reflected in the unit headings in the report. You wouldn't need to state the path statement as you would in an essay: while the reader would not know what actual data, analysis, or discussion you would present, he already knows your path statement for the lab report because the order of presentation is predetermined by scientific convention. The branches of your path will be as shown in figure 9-1. The second unit will involve the setting out of your experimental goals or objectives; the third unit will be a detailed description of the process or methods used to conduct the experiment and record the data. The fourth unit sets out all the results and observations made, in a detailed chronological sequence, together with any supporting materials or data summaries. The fifth unit covers discussion and analysis of all the results relative to the objectives of the experiment and sets out your conclusions.

This structure would allow you to meet the expectations of your readers as to form and content in a chemistry lab report. The actual layout would follow the report's internal logic, so that you

The Multiple Unit Model
Writing Across the Disciplines

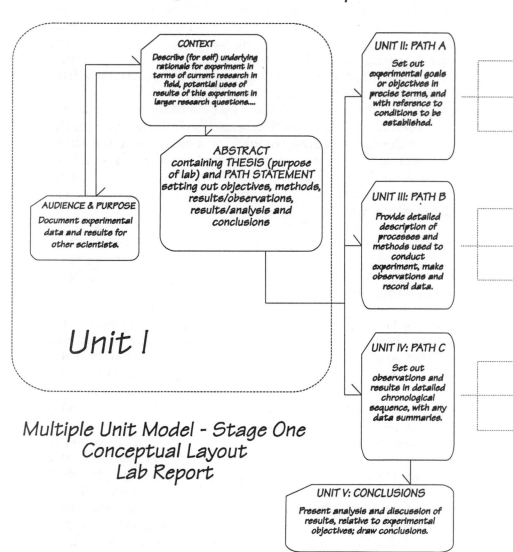

Figure 9-1: Lab Report Layout - Using the Multiple Unit Model

would have a separate cover page, clearly marked subheadings, and the like. If the lab report was lengthy, each branch or section might begin on a new page. The physical structure would be a logical reflection of your path statement's branches. It would be easy to apply your understanding of the operative principles in the same way in a physics lab report, a biology report, or an engineering proposal. What changes from subject to subject is the scientific vocabulary of the discipline. The number, content and labels of the branches of the path change according to the specific task at hand. So, even if your report documents a massive and complex study, each unit of the report might be expanded appropriately (and each would certainly have its own mini-thesis with support paths).

There is another problem that seems to plague writers in the sciences. There is a widely held belief or view that to maintain the degree of clinical objectivity required for accurate scientific observation and recording, one should distance oneself as much as possible from the data and procedures in the experiment. As a result, writing in the sciences is often characterized by gross overuse of the passive voice:

> Various reactions were observed; the data were recorded. Then the next phase of the reaction was triggered, and when it was completed, the additional data were recorded. This data will be analyzed by looking at . . . .

This sort of language, at its best, creates a weak illusion of detachment. It's as if the writer is pretending that he or she had nothing to do with the experiment, the data or the conclusions; that it was all done anonymously. In some circumstances, that might be the case, as in experiments involving many researchers and assistants at once. However, in cases where you're the researcher, you'll be unable to disguise your identity from the reader, or to shift responsibility for the analyses and conclusions from your own shoulders. Therefore, in science courses, as a matter of practical strategy, you should consult your instructors as to their standards and preferences regarding voice and viewpoint in lab writing. If they refer you to a specific set of current guidelines that dictate the use of the passive voice, then follow those guidelines—but make certain that your use of the passive voice doesn't trap you into creating numerous dangling or misplaced modifiers in your writing. If you have the option of avoiding the passive construction, you might want to consider doing so in the interest of clarity and accuracy.

If you become a scientist yourself, you'll run directly into this tension between clear writing and the scientific conventions by which you are supposed to demonstrate apparent objectivity. As writing in the sciences becomes more streamlined and efficient, or as the conventions change, you'll become free to set out your results in as clear and direct a manner as possible, so long as your hypotheses, methodology, observations and conclusions are accurate and verifiable. Remember: true objectivity (which comes from sound hypotheses and procedures, accurate observation and recording of data, and keen analyses of the data) will lead to objective style in your writing. An artificial or "forced" objective style, by itself, is not necessarily an indicator of true objectivity.

Exercise

For this exercise, you'll write a simple lab report based on a little experiment you can try at home. The experiment involves testing four liquids to see whether they are acidic or alkaline in nature. To conduct the experiment, you'll need four clean glasses, a small supply of litmus paper (which can be purchased very inexpensively at many science and hobby shops, or at your college or university bookstore), and four different liquids chosen at random from around your house or apartment. You might choose cleansers, food products, lubricants, or even tap water with different materials dissolved in it. Because litmus paper changes colour in the presence of acid or alkaline compounds, you can use it to determine the nature of each of the liquids. Outline a methodology; then conduct the experiment, being sure to record all your observations. Then, using the example above, prepare a suitable layout, and write the lab report.

WRITING IN COMPUTER TECHNOLOGY

In computer technology, much of the writing that goes on is labeled "technical writing." It frequently relates to the preparation of hardware and software manuals for installation and usage, or to technical reports used by developers, or to instructional materials for various categories of user. As a result, these kinds of technical writing tend to be full of loaded words and terms that have special meaning in the world of computers. The impact of computer technology on our language and culture in the last twenty years has been so great that we've developed whole sets of jargon pertaining to the various activities we can do with computers. Terms like "hacker," "pirate," "clone," "desktop," "window," "network" and "memory" all have specialized meanings, though these words are frequently used improperly. In addition, computer technology depends on artificial communications and intelligence models that provide new and sometimes confusing terms of reference for writers. Explaining the technology clearly can feel like trying to think with someone else's brain. You can use the multiple unit model to help you overcome some of the common writing problems in this field, as long as you keep some common-sense guidelines in mind.

First, much of the development work in computer technology is done by systems professionals and people working in the hard sciences. Many of these people understand symbolic logic and machine language at a level that is simply beyond the average person. As a result, hardware and software manufacturers sometimes have problems producing clearly written maintenance and instructional materials that an ordinary person can understand. The problem is further complicated by the size of the import market: many retailers market products from places where English is not the native language. The documentation for these products is frequently confusing because it was neither written nor translated by someone who was a skilled communicator in English. As the markets have expanded, the ability to understand the technology and to write about it clearly in straightforward language has therefore become highly prized.

If your writing deals with computer technology, keep the basic principles we've been discussing fresh in your mind—remember your obligations to your reader in terms of accuracy and clarity.

> *As a technical writer, you will often stand between the developer or manufacturer and the end user (the buyer) of the hardware or software. This means that you must, in effect, translate difficult concepts and procedures into a series of simple, clear ideas and steps expressed in non-technical language, and you must do so without sacrificing accuracy.*

This isn't an easy task, and it may become more difficult as you develop more expertise in the technology. As you become a more knowledgeable user or programmer, you'll probably spend an increasing amount of time working with other users. Outside your work, you may find yourself socializing with people of like interests and "talking shop" with them. These things are only natural, but they also create a kind of enthusiasm about using computer jargon that you simply cannot afford in your technical writing. Therefore, you must keep firmly before you the end user's requirement for complete clarity, accuracy and simplicity when you write. The technology is complicated enough; don't make matters worse with fuzzy writing. If, after reading a piece of instructional material for a new program, the user can't get the program to work, then the instructional material didn't work and is useless, no matter how elegantly it may have been written.

Before you can write something meaningful in this field, you must be sure that your readers understand the terms you'll be using. If you, as an expert, use technical terminology that other experts will understand, that will be fine—as long as your audience is composed exclusively of other experts. If you have an audience of beginners, even an otherwise clear discussion of process will be meaningless unless you first define every essential term. Thus, when you're writing in computer technology, be certain to define all essential terms, including any which you suspect may be new to your readers and any for which there may be more than a single meaning in context. For example, if you're explaining to a user the process for installing a new hard disk (a high-capacity storage device) in a computer, you may have to define not only "hard disk," but also terms like "slot," "rails," "faceplate," "controller" and "adapter." These words have special meaning when used in reference to the hard disk installation process. In writing about a process where definitions are required, you may have to create a section in the document that covers all definitions. This section should be near the beginning of the document—there is little point to having the reader read on until he or she has seen the definitions of key terms.

It's probably occurred to you that much of the writing in computer technology involves process and cause/effect. This is true: manuals set out procedures or processes for doing things; instructional material sets out a sequence of events and information for you to follow; and completion of the sequence results (theoretically) in learning. Because there are so many processes and causal sequences involved in the way computers work, writers in the field must separate these processes and sequences into smaller units in order to discuss them thoroughly.

⇨
> *Be certain that in a given document you have clearly set out the specific subject or process you intend to cover, and the extent or depth to which you will cover it.*
 ⇦

Because you're working in a subject where precision is critical, you must expressly define the scope of your writing, and then you must give the reader all relevant information on the subject(s) within the defined scope. You can't give partial, incomplete or summary information, since the user is relying on your instructions. Thus, if you have to explain the process of how to set up master pages in a particular desktop publishing software package, you must provide the reader with everything he or she needs to complete the task. To do anything less is to provide partial (and therefore useless) instruction.

Remember that because of the nature of your material, you can incorporate images into your documents to positive effect. Many writers don't consider images to be among the tools available to assist with clear expression. This is a mistake, especially in a society as visually oriented as ours. Computer technology is one of the subject areas in which illustrations are not only appropriate; they're frequently necessary for the reader to be able to understand an instruction or a causal relationship clearly. Images, when properly chosen and integrated into a piece of writing, can help the reader understand and remember a greater amount of detail than he or she otherwise might. They also save the reader from having to visualize complex patterns, screen layouts or component relationships on the basis of text alone. If you're writing a piece of instructional material that refers to the screen layout of a particular piece of software, your readers will be grateful for an illustration clearly showing menu bars, icons, scroll bars, rulers, and the like. An instruction about any of these items will then have much more meaning, and the reader will be able to apply your instructions much more readily.

How can we apply the concepts of the thesis, path statement and multiple unit model to technical writing in computer technology? Suppose that you've been assigned the task of writing a piece of material for people who have just bought their first computer, a machine that's a "clone" of an industry-standard machine. The material, which will be packaged with the computer, is to be included in a binder entitled *Getting Started*. The piece is to be instructional and is to focus on the correct process for using standard operating system commands to format a floppy disk so that it can be used to store data. This is a simple process; you do it regularly. However, you're an experienced user, and what seems commonplace to you is completely new to your audience. You'll have to pretend for a moment that you yourself are new to computers: you must focus on the things you take for granted. If you approached the task in this way, you might apply the multiple unit model to get something like figure 9-2.

In figure 9-2, we can see that this instructional process is reduced to a logical sequence of steps—the usual rules governing process as an approach continue to apply, regardless of the subject matter. As well, there is material covering definitions, since some of the terminology would be unfamiliar or confusing to the novice computer user. The nature of the floppy disk is explained, and the purpose

The Multiple Unit Model
Writing Across the Disciplines

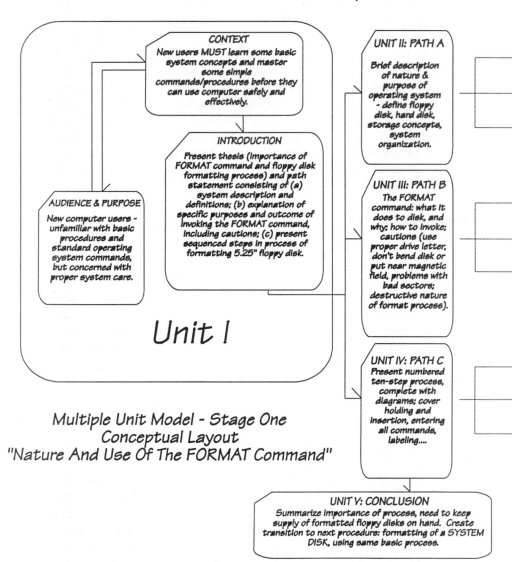

CONTEXT
New users MUST learn some basic system concepts and master some simple commands/procedures before they can use computer safely and effectively.

UNIT II: PATH A
Brief description of nature & purpose of operating system - define floppy disk, hard disk, storage concepts, system organization.

INTRODUCTION
Present thesis (importance of FORMAT command and floppy disk formatting process) and path statement consisting of (a) system description and definitions; (b) explanation of specific purposes and outcome of invoking the FORMAT command, including cautions; (c) present sequenced steps in process of formatting 5.25" floppy disk.

AUDIENCE & PURPOSE
New computer users - unfamiliar with basic procedures and standard operating system commands, but concerned with proper system care.

UNIT III: PATH B
The FORMAT command: what it does to disk, and why; how to invoke; cautions (use proper drive letter; don't bend disk or put near magnetic field, problems with bad sectors; destructive nature of format process).

Unit I

UNIT IV: PATH C
Present numbered ten-step process, complete with diagrams; cover holding and insertion, entering all commands, labeling....

Multiple Unit Model - Stage One
Conceptual Layout
"Nature And Use Of The FORMAT Command"

UNIT V: CONCLUSION
Summarize importance of process, need to keep supply of formatted floppy disks on hand. Create transition to next procedure: formatting of a SYSTEM DISK, using same basic process.

Figure 9-2: Computer Technology - Instructional Material, Using the Multiple Unit Model

and consequences of "formatting" are also covered. The reader is introduced to the concept of removable storage devices. If you were to write the instructional piece based on the template in figure 9-2, you would produce a clear, simple set of instructions, complete with definitions of key terms, and perhaps some illustrations. You would write the piece according to the practices governing process as a rhetorical approach: proper sequencing, adequate transitions, and the like.

We can see, in the layout for this simple piece of instructional material, the emphasis on clarity and simplicity. In addition, the piece would provide information that's relevant to other processes the new computer user will have to learn as well as to her general knowledge of the computer. Thus, the process itself may be part of a larger learning sequence through which the user will eventually move. This is a useful viewpoint in a world where the technology changes almost daily. The technical writer should regard everything he must write as having both an immediate purpose and a role in a larger and longer learning sequence.

Exercise

In this exercise, you'll actually write the instructional piece based on the model in figure 9-2. You may have to do some reading in a basic book on computers. If so, feel free to change the information in the model to suit the new information you find in your research. Remember that you're essentially writing a process paper, though there are some extra factors to consider concerning definitions, and the relationship of the process to larger questions of computer usage for new users.

BUSINESS WRITING

The term "business writing" covers a great many things. On one level, it may include types of documents that are common to businesses of all kinds: letters (inquiries, instructions, collections, complaints, queries, references, confirmations), internal memoranda (covering such things as policy matters, scheduling, general information, internal confirmations, incident documentation), sales or progress reports, proposals, procedural manuals, and business plans. On another level, it may include documents that pertain to specific kinds of business only or to particular business transactions only: feasibility studies, cost-benefit analyses, tax analyses, engagement letters, incentive plans, and the like. All of these types of documentation require you to meet varying content thresholds; all require you to meet a mechanical threshold. All of them require you to be detached and unemotional, even when seeking a remedy for a complaint. Some types of documentation require the participation or assistance of other experts in specialized fields. However, regardless of the nature of a given document, the business writer must meet all the same critical obligations as the student in terms of organization, clarity, consistency, accuracy and completeness. She will have to become informed about standard layouts and conventions pertaining to business usage and will have to pay special attention to the audience. In the business world, the term "audience" may often be synonymous with "target market." The business writer must therefore base all documents on a thorough appreciation of the nature and characteristics of particular readers, and of the importance of accurate and consistent recording of business affairs over time.

When you're writing in the context of business, it doesn't matter whether you are an employee of a large corporation, or the sole proprietor of your own small business. Every time you write something, you're presenting (or representing) your company or business to the reader. You must not only deliver your message clearly to a chosen audience; you must do so from the perspective required of you by your employer or your company's policy or corporate image. You're often not speaking on your own behalf, or in your capacity as a private person, and you must therefore become sensitive to the circumstances surrounding each document you're required to write. Thus, if you're writing a collection letter regarding a delinquent account, you must know what your employer's policy is regarding such accounts and what actions are typically suggested as potential means of obtaining payment. You must also know the history of the particular debtor with your company, since the delinquency may be unusual. Should you threaten legal action against an account if the delinquency is the first for that account in twenty years of doing business? Will you address the problem in the same way if the account has been chronically late in paying over the last eighteen months? Is there any special relationship between the debtor and your company that might influence the way you should handle the problem when you write? These are relevant considerations that you must address *before* committing yourself to paper. Similarly, if you must document, by memorandum, an allegation of sexual harassment made by a worker you supervise, you must know what current company policy says as to form and content for the memorandum, and you must be seen to have taken only the action the policy or the law empowers you to take in the circumstances. Accurate documentation of the incident is in the interest of all parties, including the employer. An expressed assumption of guilt or innocence by you is not in anyone's interest, unless you're specifically authorized to make such a

The Multiple Unit Model
Writing Across the Disciplines

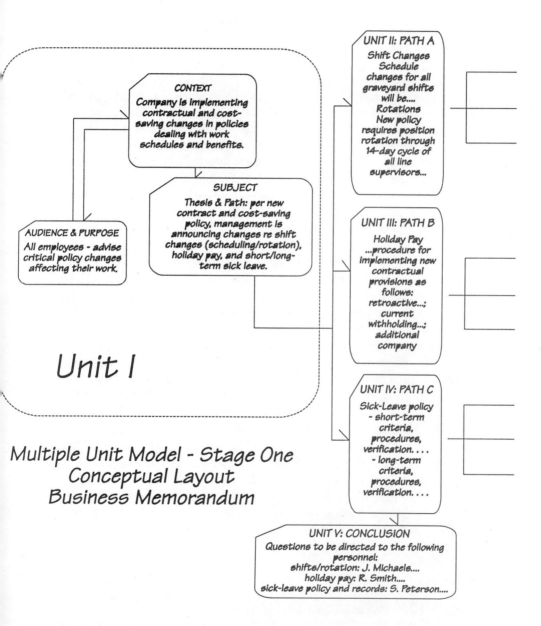

UNIT II: PATH A

Shift Changes
Schedule changes for all graveyard shifts will be....
Rotations
New policy requires position rotation through 14-day cycle of all line supervisors...

CONTEXT

Company is implementing contractual and cost-saving changes in policies dealing with work schedules and benefits.

SUBJECT

Thesis & Path: per new contract and cost-saving policy, management is announcing changes re shift changes (scheduling/rotation), holiday pay, and short/long-term sick leave.

AUDIENCE & PURPOSE

All employees - advise critical policy changes affecting their work.

UNIT III: PATH B

Holiday Pay
...procedure for implementing new contractual provisions as follows: retroactive...; current withholding...; additional company

Unit I

UNIT IV: PATH C

Sick-Leave policy
- short-term criteria, procedures, verification. . . .
- long-term criteria, procedures, verification. . . .

Multiple Unit Model - Stage One
Conceptual Layout
Business Memorandum

UNIT V: CONCLUSION

Questions to be directed to the following personnel:
shifts/rotation: J. Michaels....
holiday pay: R. Smith....
sick-leave policy and records: S. Peterson....

Figure 9-3: Business Memorandum Layout - Using the Multiple Unit Model.

finding. Similarly, you should not include in the memorandum an emotional reaction to the allegation based on your own feelings about sexual harassment, since the matter has not yet been investigated and the rights of various parties (including the alleged victim and the alleged offender) are involved. Thus, you must know what not to say, as well as what to include in the memorandum.

The multiple unit model applies to the creation of business documents, just as it did in the sciences and computer technology. Suppose, for example, that you're required to write a memorandum in which other company employees will be advised of policy changes affecting shifts, holiday pay and sick days. Since the employees will rely on your explanation of the policy in making some personal decisions, you must be clear and accurate. If you apply the multiple unit model to the task, you might get a layout like the one in figure 9-3.

Given this layout, it would be a simple task to draft the memorandum, especially since the physical format must conform to one of the standard business forms of memorandum that most companies use. Similarly, if one were preparing a business plan to launch a new business and attract investors, one might develop a layout like the one in figure 9-4. We've not included much detail in this layout because a business plan can be lengthy and complicated. Still, the layout clearly reveals that the multiple unit model applies to the business plan, just as it did to the memorandum. There are, of course, many possible variations one might make in actually preparing a business plan, but none of them would make a difference to your use of the multiple unit model to create the layout.

In the business world, accurate information has always been valuable as a base upon which to make critical communications and marketing decisions. As technology has made our access to information both faster and more complete, the value of information in decision-making and communications has increased many times. Our ability to respond quickly to changing circumstances has also improved, provided that we can use the changes in technology and new management models to make decisions soundly. This means that when at work, we must keep accurate records of all relevant facts and transactions, and we must document carefully every important event in our working lives. Intelligent decisions can be made only on the basis of accurate and complete information.

Exercise

Figure 9-5 shows an acceptable format for a business letter. In this exercise, you are to use the multiple unit model to prepare a layout for a business letter in which you're making a complaint. In the

The Multiple Unit Model
Writing Across the Disciplines

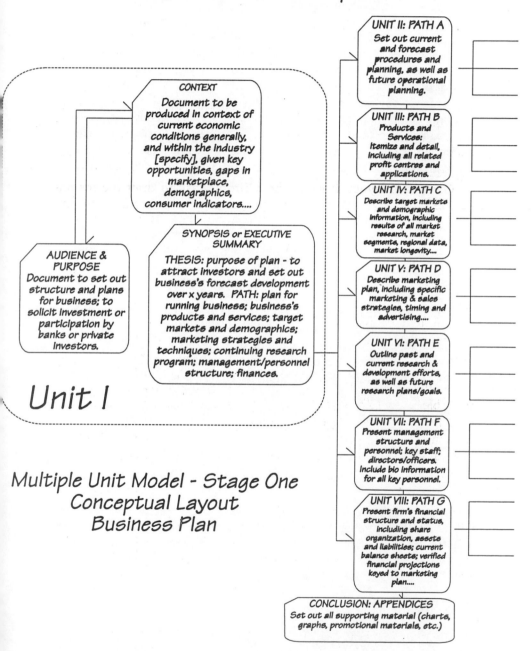

CONTEXT

Document to be produced in context of current economic conditions generally, and within the industry [specify], given key opportunities, gaps in marketplace, demographics, consumer indicators....

AUDIENCE & PURPOSE

Document to set out structure and plans for business; to solicit investment or participation by banks or private investors.

SYNOPSIS or EXECUTIVE SUMMARY

THESIS: purpose of plan - to attract investors and set out business's forecast development over x years. PATH: plan for running business; business's products and services; target markets and demographics; marketing strategies and techniques; continuing research program; management/personnel structure; finances.

Unit I

Multiple Unit Model - Stage One
Conceptual Layout
Business Plan

UNIT II: PATH A

Set out current and forecast procedures and planning, as well as future operational planning.

UNIT III: PATH B

Products and Services: itemize and detail, including all related profit centres and applications.

UNIT IV: PATH C

Describe target markets and demographic information, including results of all market research, market segments, regional data, market longevity....

UNIT V: PATH D

Describe marketing plan, including specific marketing & sales strategies, timing and advertising....

UNIT VI: PATH E

Outline past and current research & development efforts, as well as future research plans/goals.

UNIT VII: PATH F

Present management structure and personnel; key staff; directors/officers. Include bio information for all key personnel.

UNIT VIII: PATH G

Present firm's financial structure and status, including share organization, assets and liabilities; current balance sheets; verified financial projections keyed to marketing plan....

CONCLUSION: APPENDICES

Set out all supporting material (charts, graphs, promotional materials, etc.)

Figure 9-4: Business Plan Layout - Using the Multiple Unit Model

letter, you'll be outlining the causes of your complaint, the measures you've taken to try to correct the problem yourself, and the actions you want the addressee to take on your behalf. Your letter arises from the following facts:

> You recently bought a computer from Incredible Carl's Clone Connection. You went to Carl's to do some research about the kind of computer that would be suitable for your home business. Although you did not know it at the time, you needed a midrange, modestly powered system with a 270-megabyte hard disk drive, a monochrome monitor, a word processor and an accounting package. You also needed a reliable ink-jet printer. At Carl's, you were introduced to a salesman, who asked you some questions about what you wanted the computer for and what your future needs might be. On the strength of the salesman's recommendation, you ended up buying a $6,000 computer system. It came with the most powerful processor on the market; a 20-inch colour monitor; a laser printer; a one-gigabyte hard disk drive; numerous boxes of software, including a desktop publishing program; and Incredible Carl's CarlDOS for Clones. The day after you purchased the system, Incredible Carl himself showed up at your house, spent four hours installing the system, and presented you with a bill for installation in the amount of $75. He left, and since then you have had nothing but trouble. Nothing works for longer than ten minutes. Half the time, the computer will not start up properly. Carl did not install the software properly, and the operating system keeps giving you funny messages and happy faces on the screen.
>
> While trying to correct the problems yourself, you have learned a great deal in a short time, and you now understand what your needs are and what equipment would meet those needs. You have also found that not one other dealer in town charges for installation and that Incredible Carl's record with the ethics committee of the local chamber of commerce is not the best.

After you've prepared the layout, write the letter of complaint to Incredible Carl, being certain to include all necessary details and to ask for the remedies you want. Feel free to invent any details you need, but be clear, detailed, detached and accurate.

WRITING IN THE LAW

If you've ever had to sign a contract of any kind, you've probably had the experience of trying to puzzle through "legalese"—that strange, sometimes incomprehensible mixture of formal English

The Multiple Unit Model
Writing Across the Disciplines

Your Name
Address
City, Province
Postal Code

Date

Name of Addressee
Address
City, Province
Postal Code

Dear _____:

Re: Subject of Letter

_____

_____

_____

_____

_____

_____

_____

_____

Yours sincerely,
[your signature]
Your Name
Enclosures

Physical Layout for Business Letter Exercise

Figure 9-5: Physical Layout for a Business Letter

and legal jargon that leaves most readers scratching their heads and wondering whether they're signing their lives away. People often joke that lawyers use this sort of language to make more work for themselves or that "lawyer" is synonymous with "nit-picker" (or worse). While it's easy to see how one might feel this way, a little closer examination of the way legal language is supposed to work will reveal some interesting truths.

In chapter 1, we suggested that you need to consider the nature of your audience and their expectations, not only in terms of subject matter and specific issues, but also in terms of accuracy and level of language. The audience for which much legal writing is intended is a very specialized audience, consisting primarily of other lawyers, paralegals and judges. People mistakenly assume that legal documents are written primarily for the client's understanding. In fact, they may be written for the client's *benefit*—but the intended audience is often limited to another lawyer or a judge. This audience reads the document to see if it is legally binding; the lawyer or judge may care very little about whether the document is pleasing to read or clear to a layperson, so long as its legal effects are correct. Moreover, the legal systems in the United States, Canada and the United Kingdom are based on the principle of *stare decisis*, or rule by precedent. This means that courts of law in a given jurisdiction are bound by previous decisions of the jurisdiction's higher courts in cases involving similar facts. The reason for the strange and convoluted legal wording in contracts is that most kinds of contracts have been the subjects of court cases for decades or even centuries. Thus, the court systems have examined and re-examined the legal language involved on hundreds of occasions and have made binding decisions as to what those strange terms mean legally. The legalese is present in the documents because its meaning is certain: there can be no dispute if legally binding terms are used. If, as some politicians have suggested, all statutory and contractual language were to be simplified, that might be a good thing for ordinary citizens who want to govern their legal relationships by honesty and common sense. However, every time a contractual dispute went to court or a judge was called upon to interpret a statute, the process of finding legally binding definitions and certainty of terms would have to start again. Centuries of interpretation would have to be repeated, at incalculable cost to those supporting the legal system. This may, in the end, be preferable to legalese, but the decision isn't one to make lightly.

People who must write in a legal context are generally concerned with several things. First, the law is not applied in a vacuum: legal questions arise from complex sets of related facts. Thus, before a legal document of any kind can be written, the writer must gather the facts on which the document will be based. In any particular situation, one may be confronted with a mass of information that relates to different parties and to a variety of issues. Therefore, if you're writing about a legal dispute, you must consider facts that are relevant to the preparation of the document. For example, in a complex construction deal in which there are dozens of subcontractors, one party may be suing the general contractor. If you're preparing a legal memorandum or opinion on the legal obligations of the contractor to the suing party, you'll find dozens of legally significant facts—but some of those facts will relate to other parties or other issues. You must be concerned only with those legally significant facts that relate to your specific focus in the memorandum.

Once you've identified the legally significant matters of fact, you must be able to see how those facts relate to each other to give rise to significant issues of law. One doesn't sue someone based on important facts; one sues because the facts disclose a breach of some legal obligation that a court will recognize. Often, the facts of a case disclose more than one legal issue, and you might have to address some or all of them. The issues must be stated clearly and concisely, in such a way that a legally trained reader would recognize them as objectively described issues, rather than personal interpretations of the facts. After you've clearly defined the issues, you must present, in summary form, the conclusions reached on each of the issues so that the reader can consider the arguments that follow in full knowledge of your legal opinion. Finally, you present the meat of the legal document—the arguments and analyses of applicable statutes and case law that will determine the outcome on each of the issues. Even when writing on behalf of one of the parties, you must carefully consider the arguments likely to be presented on both sides. The statutory and case authorities (which in practical terms are like the supporting material presented in an ordinary research paper) are integrated into the arguments and analyses.

Obviously, there are many kinds of documents you might have to write if you were working in the legal system. Some of these might be form documents that are part of commercial or property transactions. Some might be supporting documents to be used in a criminal proceeding like a bail hearing; and some might be opinion memoranda, or even simple case briefs. You might even be called upon to revise a local or state statute, regulation or bylaw. In every case, you must meet the highest possible standards of clarity and accuracy in order to help people avoid costly and frustrating disputes, and to ensure certainty and fairness in the administration of law. Therefore, since clear and organized thinking and planning would be essential, you could use the multiple unit model as a device for laying out complex discussions of legal issues, or simple case briefs analyzing or illustrating specific legal principles.

The Multiple Unit Model
Writing Across the Disciplines

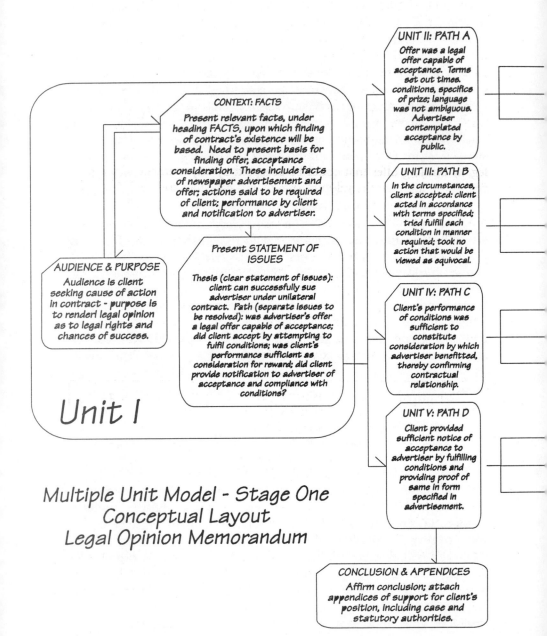

UNIT II: PATH A

Offer was a legal offer capable of acceptance. Terms set out times, conditions, specifics of prize; language was not ambiguous. Advertiser contemplated acceptance by public.

UNIT III: PATH B

In the circumstances, client accepted: client acted in accordance with terms specified; tried fulfill each condition in manner required; took no action that would be viewed as equivocal.

UNIT IV: PATH C

Client's performance of conditions was sufficient to constitute consideration by which advertiser benefitted, thereby confirming contractual relationship.

UNIT V: PATH D

Client provided sufficient notice of acceptance to advertiser by fulfilling conditions and providing proof of same in form specified in advertisement.

CONTEXT: FACTS

Present relevant facts, under heading FACTS, upon which finding of contract's existence will be based. Need to present basis for finding offer, acceptance consideration. These include facts of newspaper advertisement and offer; actions said to be required of client; performance by client and notification to advertiser.

AUDIENCE & PURPOSE

Audience is client seeking cause of action in contract - purpose is to render legal opinion as to legal rights and chances of success.

Present **STATEMENT OF ISSUES**

Thesis (clear statement of issues): client can successfully sue advertiser under unilateral contract. Path (separate issues to be resolved): was advertiser's offer a legal offer capable of acceptance; did client accept by attempting to fulfil conditions; was client's performance sufficient as consideration for reward; did client provide notification to advertiser of acceptance and compliance with conditions?

Unit I

Multiple Unit Model - Stage One
Conceptual Layout
Legal Opinion Memorandum

CONCLUSION & APPENDICES

Affirm conclusion; attach appendices of support for client's position, including case and statutory authorities.

Figure 9-6: Legal Opinion Memorandum Layout - Using the Multiple Unit Model.

Consider an example. Suppose you're a lawyer, and a new client comes to you to find out whether or not he can sue a company over a newspaper advertisement. The advertisement offered a reward or prize to any member of the public who used the company's product as directed, but who didn't get the benefit that use of the product is supposed to provide. The client claims to have complied with the advertisement and to have been denied the reward or prize. You want to provide your client with a written legal opinion of his or her position. You set out to gather the relevant facts: you obtain a copy of the newspaper advertisement and read it carefully; you examine the advertised product and determine the proper method for its use; you question your client carefully as to his manner of use and the alleged failure to get the promised result. You see that, assuming your client is telling the truth, his right to sue will depend on whether the company's advertisement constituted a legally binding offer that could be accepted by any member of the public. You investigate the relevant statute and case law and find that there is some state consumer protection legislation dealing with advertising practices and public offers. In addition, there is a body of case law that clearly defines the sorts of public offers that lead to a contractual relationship when a member of the public meets the terms of the offer. If you want to develop the material for your opinion by using the multiple unit model, you might get a layout like the one in figure 9-6.

In figure 9-6, the multiple unit model provides a clear base from which to write the opinion memorandum. The case is a simple one, the legal arguments straightforward. However, legal issues can become enormously complex very quickly:

⇨

The more effective and consistent one's organizational strategy and layout procedures, the more likely one is to deal with all the important issues in a coherent and balanced way.

⇦

This discussion of writing in the law is not intended to provide you with a basic legal education or to convince you that you ought to become a lawyer. However, if you can see the ways in which you might use the multiple unit model in as specialized a subject as law, then it will be easy for you to find ways to apply it in other areas or disciplines. From this perspective, try the exercise below. It will require you to do some legwork, but it will also help you to use the model as an analytical device in areas that may be unfamiliar to you.

Exercise

For this exercise, you are to prepare a memorandum in response to a request from a hypothetical client. The client has told you that he intends to start a catering business and has asked whether it would be better to run the business as a "sole proprietorship," a "limited company," or a "partnership." To prepare the memorandum, you'll have to do several things. First, you should locate a book that defines each of these terms and gives you some information about their characteristics and suitability for various kinds of businesses. There are quite a few books that try to address legal business concerns for lay audiences; your local library will have some of them. Then you'll need to find out something about the catering business. Exactly what services do caterers provide? Who uses the services? Are there any risks or dangers inherent in the business that might lead to liability? What sort of investment is involved? How many people will be involved in the business? These are all relevant questions. Once you have the answers, you can begin to form your opinion. If you use the multiple unit model to lay out your information and then write the memorandum based on the layout, your memo should not be longer than two to three double-spaced pages. In terms of the format, you can use the following headings in the memorandum: Facts; Statement of Issues; Summary Conclusions; Arguments. When you do the exercise, don't be intimidated by the fact that you're working with legal materials. The law is there to serve you and protect your rights; you merely need to inform yourself as to what those rights are.

CONCLUSIONS

The multiple unit model is a thinking and organizing strategy you can use to apply your writing skills across the disciplines. It's not the only model; it may not even be the best model for you as an individual, depending on your own learning style. However, it will give you a consistent and solid base from which to proceed. In some ways, your appreciation of the philosophy underlying the model and its operative principles is more important than the model itself. For most of us, writing is not a divinely inspired act. Writing is a process in which you, the writer, apply your intellect and your learned skills to the task of creating and controlling the reader's responses to clear, precisely expressed information. When you write an essay in college or university, regardless of the discipline or specific subject matter, you're working with a kind of testing device that requires you to conform to a series of expectations and conventions. Within the form of that testing device, you demonstrate your ability to focus on specific content, analyze it, and present your analysis in a logical way.

APPENDICES:
Common Errors in Student Essays

The materials set out below are the explanations of common errors that we give our students when they're reviewing their graded papers. Each section is keyed to one of the abbreviations listed below. The chances are that your instructor will use a similar code to identify various errors in your writing, or will actually write out the name of the error in full on your paper. In either case, you can use the material below as a place to start your corrections. If you can't find the material you need, or if you need more material on a particular subject, you should consult a complete usage handbook such as the *Harbrace College Handbook*.

THE CODE

Purpose	Purpose of the College Essay
TS	Thesis and Path Statement
U	Unity
C	Coherence
SL	Sequencing and Logic
CD	Concrete Details
PV	Passive Voice
Frag	Sentence Fragment
CS	Comma Splice
FS	Fused Sentence
ROS	Run-on Sentence
FC	Faulty Coordination
SV	Subject (or noun)-Verb Agreement
PR	Pronoun Reference

PA	Pronoun Agreement
(,)	Comma Usage
AP	Apostrophe (Possessives)
CL	Clichés, Hackneyed Expressions & Circumlocutions
WC	Usage and Word Choice
Q	Placement of Punctuation within Quotations
RC	References and Citations
SUP	Supporting Materials
MM	Misplaced and Dangling Modifiers
PO	Paragraph Organization
Para	Faulty Parallelism
Colon	Improper Usage of Colon
Semi	Improper Usage of Semicolon
Rev	Revision/Proofreading Problems
Con	Contractions to avoid
Intro	Problems with Introductory Detail/Context
"You"	Mode of Addressing Reader

General Information and Reminders

Be sure your thesis statement is clear and concise and phrased with your specific audience in mind. Your introductory paragraph will include sufficient indication of your purpose and strategy to let your audience know what they can expect of you. It should also give the reader a sense of the importance of your subject and an understanding of your approach to the subject matter.

The organizational principle for your essay should come from the nature of the assignment and your thesis and path statement. Roughly speaking, if your thesis can be supported by four branches or sections, then the body of your essay should consist of four branches or sections. Each section corresponds to one of the four branches.

When you move from one area of your discussion to another (or even from one sentence to another), you must remember to use appropriate transitional words or phrases. A single word can often be sufficient to connect one idea to another. Your aim should be to create continuity in terms of your argument and the form and flow of your essay.

Your conclusion is not simply a paraphrasing of your thesis. It must be a cogent, clearly reasoned summary of the points you have made in the body of the essay. You should leave your audience with the sense that there is nothing more that needs to be said. You should leave them with the sense that they have been convinced of your point of view; or, at the very least, they should acknowledge that you have made some good points and know your subject area.

Remember: if your ideas aren't clear in your own mind when you write, you won't be able to communicate them clearly to your audience. You may be put to the inconvenience of one or two revisions, particularly if you're not big on rereading. Get a friend to read your essay back to you, as this will help you overcome the mind's ability to fill in blanks you leave by mistake. If your friend is confused by what you have written, you need to do some more work. You may be one of those people for whom 5 percent of the job is writing; the remaining 95 percent consists of rewriting.

Apostrophe (Possessives)

The apostrophe forms the possessive case for nouns and some pronouns. You should add an apostrophe followed by *s* to:

— all singular and plural nouns not ending in *s*: dog's, women's;

— singular proper nouns ending in *s*: Keats's, Sis's (but note that the final "s" can be omitted if the word has a number of them already and would sound awkward, as in Sisyphus';

— indefinite pronouns: someone's, anybody's, etc.

Also, add an apostrophe to plural nouns ending in *s*: families', houses', cars'.

Clichés, Hackneyed Expressions & Circumlocutions

Clichés and trite or roundabout phrases may appear without your noticing them; they make for weak writing. Unnecessary words must be deleted; be prepared to hunt and chop ruthlessly to keep your writing lean and effective:

Wordy	Revised
due to the fact that	because
in the here and now	now
consensus of opinion	consensus
at your earliest convenience	soon
when all is said and done	[omit]
in the eventuality that	if
in all likelihood	probably

Whenever possible, avoid clichés: the straw that broke the camel's back; I didn't know if I was coming or going, etc.

Coherence

When a person is incoherent, he is talking nonsense because there is no apparent logical connection between any of the things he is saying. When you write incoherently, you're not giving the reader the necessary transitions between ideas. This prevents the reader from seeing the logic of your point, your argument or your presentation. If you're incoherent, your paper will appear to jump from idea to idea without rhyme or reason. As a result, your audience will become confused, and you won't have fulfilled your purpose.

People often find it hard to see the lack of coherence in their own work. This is because your mind has a tendency to fill in any blanks you may have left on the page. This is especially true with documents on which you've spent lots of time. You tend to get so close to the subject and so familiar with your own arguments that you end up leaving off the page some critical words, phrases or ideas you have in your head. Remember that your audience wasn't there in your head with you when you were writing! You shouldn't expect the audience to read your mind in order to figure out what's happening in your paper.

One of the easiest ways to spot a coherence problem is to have someone read your own work back to you before you do your final draft. If the person is so confused that she can't keep track of what you're saying (or if you yourself can't see the logic of your argument), you probably have a coherence problem that you can now correct. If there is nobody around to read your paper to you, try recording on an ordinary cassette recorder, being sure to read your paper exactly as you have written it. When you play it back, you'll be able to hear whether you jumped around from idea to idea in a way that is likely to confuse the reader.

Once you have spotted the problem, it's easy to fix; and it doesn't really matter whether the problem is coherence between sentences in a paragraph, or between paragraphs in a paper. You need to use transitional words or phrases, linking expressions that show how you relate each thought to the next (e.g., Moreover, Furthermore, On the other hand, As well, Conversely, However, etc.). If, after selecting and inserting the appropriate transition, you still find that your work appears to jump around, check to see that your ideas in the paragraph or your supporting points in the paper are in a logical sequence. If they're out of order, transitional words won't help, so shuffle the order a bit. In each case, make sure you refer to your thesis and path statement (and your template) as your guideline. It's quite possible that you made a crucial error there when you organized your path statement. If so, you'll need to go back to the very beginning of the process to correct your coherence problem.

The Colon

Generally, you should use a colon to introduce a word, a list, a sentence, or a quotation. The colon should come after an independent clause; however, it doesn't need to be followed by an independent clause. Whatever comes after the colon explains or amplifies the meaning of the clause that came before the colon.

> Among the great Spanish guitar builders have been the following: Ramirez, Lopez, Fernandes and the Sobrinos de Amezcua.

> In his paper, Bill quoted this line: "It is the appearance of individuality that makes life bearable."

> As Jensen says, "Fly-fishing is like prayer: it reaffirms your spiritual foundations."

Note that in the last example the quotation is introduced by a comma because "As Jensen says" isn't a complete sentence; it's a subordinate clause that cannot stand by itself.

Comma Usage

Commas, like all punctuation marks, do a crucial job that your voice does when you speak or do not speak. It's true that there are a few rules you need to remember for when to use commas; but much of the time, there's only one essential point to remember. If you want your reader to make a pause with his or her voice when reading a sentence, the chances are that you'll need to put in a comma (unless the pause is really long—then some other punctuation mark may be required). If you don't want the reader to pause in the sentence, then don't put in a comma.

Apart from this major point, when should you be careful about comma usage? You can use commas to separate items in a list, with the exception of the last item:

> When we went to the store we bought fish, eggs, milk, cereal, bread and cookies.

You can use commas to set off an interruption (an interrupting word or phrase is technically called a parenthetical element):

> The film, I hear, isn't nearly as good as the book.

> My dog, however, attacked the helpless rabbit.

You can also use commas to set off words or phrases that provide additional but non-essential information:

> Our coordinator, terrible Tim, was nowhere to be found.

The student paper, which was assumed to be lost, was at the bottom of the pile.

You will notice that when commas are used this way, they almost always appear in pairs.

Comma Splice

A comma splice occurs when you attempt to join two (or more) independent clauses using only a comma:

I went to the store, I came home again, I had some dinner.

You correct comma splices by making separate sentences of the independent clauses:

I went to the store. I came home again. I had some dinner.

Alternatively, you can correct this error by coordinating the independent clauses in an appropriate way:

I went to the store; then I came home and had some dinner.

There are several variations you could try; but stringing your ideas together and separating them only with commas is not the way to go.

Contractions

Students are regularly told that in expository essays they need to maintain a certain formality of tone. They usually interpret this to mean that they should use polysyllabic jawbreakers and long, flowery sentences. Don't do that. If you want to achieve appropriate tone, you need to be conscious of word choice and other elements of the paper; but the simplest thing you can do to make your tone more appropriate is to eliminate contractions from your work. Don't use "don't"; instead, use "do not." You should always adopt this practice in papers that are intended to follow formal conventions and address "official" expectations.

Faulty Coordination

When you join two (or more) independent clauses in a way that prevents the reader from seeing them as grammatically equal, you may be guilty of faulty coordination. Remember that the decision to make one idea as strong as another (or weaker than another) is a decision you make on the basis of the response you want the reader to have. If you decide that two ideas are of equal importance and you want to put them in one sentence because they're related, then you must be sure to join them in a way that shows they are equal.

For example, if you want to say that you went out to the store, and you also want to say that you came home some time later, there are several ways you could combine these ideas in one sentence. If you want them to have equal weight, you must coordinate them properly:

I went out to the store; some time later, I returned home.

Here, each idea is contained in a separate independent clause, and the clauses are separated by a semicolon, which is a coordinating device. You could just as easily have used "and" or "but," and while the meaning might alter slightly, the two parts of the sentence would continue to have equal grammatical weight.

However, if you want to emphasize one of these ideas over the other, you should leave the one you want to emphasize as an independent clause and change the other one into a subordinate or dependent clause:

I went out to the store, although I did return home some time later.

Clearly, in this sentence the first clause is the independent part— the most important part. You have subordinated the other part to it.

It's important that your reader understand the relative emphasis you want him or her to give to your ideas. When you combine ideas into one sentence, you must decide whether one is more important than the other. You must coordinate or subordinate properly in each case.

Concrete Details

Remember that the undergraduate essay is, among other things, a testing device. Part of the skills base it targets has to do with how interesting and informative the reader finds your work. You might meet the mechanical threshold in an essay; you might even meet the content threshold, in terms of basic knowledge. However, you'll need to make your writing seem more alive and more thoughtful by being selective about the concrete details you introduce into your discussion. Generally, concrete details are easier to understand and remember than abstractions or vague and unsupported generalizations. Handled properly, they can make even a dry subject seem more interesting. Therefore, whenever you're discussing abstractions or general principles, you should always provide specific examples and illustrations. If you have a choice between a concrete word and an abstract one, choose the concrete word. Consider this sentence:

The Puritans were very strict in their adherence to Christian beliefs.

Now see how a few specific details can bring the facts to life:

The Puritans spent their days in back-breaking labour, concentrated Bible study, and frenzied introspection, hoping through their devotion and spiritual self-examination to become pillars of a community rooted soundly in Christian principles.

As always, you can strive for a balance. Just because you're adding concreteness to your work, you shouldn't get the idea that you must get rid of all abstractions. Nor should you get the idea that the point of adding details is to make the reader have fun. The balance comes from seeing that the abstractions are communicated through the use of accurate details, and that the reader will be more willing to keep reading if what you say sounds interesting and informative. Here's a restatement of the some of the principles we mentioned earlier: the object is to convey your precise meaning to the reader, as clearly and directly as possible, in as few words as possible, *without* sacrificing specificity or certainty of meaning.

References and Citations

There are dozens of style manuals available for problems with footnotes, references, and the bibliographic details of your research. Different disciplines frequently insist on adherence to a particular manual or system. For example, at the college where we teach, the English Department insists that students use the MLA (Modern Language Association) parenthetical method of citation; the social sciences require the use of the APA (American Psychological Association) system.

Because you are under a positive obligation—always—to give credit where credit is due, it's up to you to find out what system you must use in every course. To refresh your memory, have another look at chapter 8.

Sentence Fragments

To be complete, a sentence must have both a subject and a verb in an independent clause. If a sentence doesn't meet these requirements, it is a fragment—an incomplete thought. Occasionally, a sentence fragment appears to be acceptable, as in:

Will the government abolish the senate? Not likely.

You'll notice this doesn't happen by accident. Here, the sentence fragment "not likely" is clearly intended to be understood as a short form of "It is not likely that this will happen." The fragment depends upon the material presented immediately before it for its completeness. To that extent, it mirrors the sort of usage we adopt all the time in ordinary conversation. However, even in situations such as the one in the example, where the meaning in context is clear, you're generally wise to avoid the deliberate use of fragments in formal essays.

Unintentional sentence fragments, unlike the example above, usually seem incomplete, rather than merely shortened:

I enjoy living in Seattle. <u>Being a person who likes the sea</u>.

The last sentence is incomplete—where is the subject, the verb? Here you can make the fragment into a complete sentence by adding a subject and a verb:

I am a person who likes the sea.

Alternatively, you could join the fragment to the preceding sentence:

Being a person who likes the sea, I enjoy living in Seattle.

Fused Sentences

This error occurs when you join two independent clauses together without any punctuation between them, and without a coordinating conjunction.

I went to the store I came home then I ate dinner.

The solution to this problem is to break the independent clauses into separate sentences:

I went to the store. I came home. Then I ate dinner.

Alternatively, you could use coordinating conjunctions and appropriate punctuation to tie these thoughts together without weakening any of them:

I went to the store; then I came home and I ate dinner.

I went to the store and I came home; then I ate dinner.

Finally, you could correct the problem by subordinating or weakening one of the clauses and attaching it to one of the others:

Having gone to the store and returned home afterwards, I then ate dinner.

Decide on the solution that most effectively clarifies your meaning.

Introductory Detail and Context

Always remember that you have to provide your reader with enough introductory and contextual detail to make your thesis meaningful or relevant to the reader's knowledge and areas of interest. The introductory material is like a kind of background against which the reader gets to look at your thesis and path statement. If the background material is inappropriate, too vague, unrelated to the thesis, or otherwise defective, your thesis won't work nearly as well—and it may not work at all.

Putting it another way, we can say that the introductory material must contain the "hook"—the critical information that will capture your reader's attention long enough for you to present your thesis. No hook, no readers . . . .

Sequencing and Logic

Your ideas must be presented in logical order—that is, in an order that makes sense in view of your thesis, your audience and your purpose in writing. Keeping your audience in mind, you must choose deliberately an order of presentation that will have the greatest impact. If your subject has a logic of its own, your readers must be advised of that; otherwise, they may jump to wrong conclusions about something you're saying.

Not all subjects are organized on the basis of pure logic. Sometimes you'll be writing to entertain, to describe or to narrate. Even then, you're still under an obligation to find the best sequence in which to present your thoughts. If the object of the game is to create an experience of some kind for the reader and to convince her of your views, then you can't separate thinking about sequencing from thinking about the nature of your audience and your specific purpose. From the very beginning, you should be thinking about the best order for your supporting materials.

Dangling or Misplaced Modifiers

Pecking for worms in the grass, Simon watched the robins.

His grandpa taught him to fish, while still a toddler.

These sentences, though laughable, don't make much sense. The first implies that Simon is pecking for worms in the grass; the second, that his grandpa was still a toddler when he taught the boy to fish. The underlined portion of each sentence is a modifier since it's used to describe another word (or words) in the sentence: "pecking for worms in the grass" describes "the robins," and "while still a toddler" describes "him." You must use modifiers or modifying phrases carefully to avoid confusing your readers. The simplest fix is merely to be sure that the modifier is close to the word it is modifying:

Simon watched the robins pecking for worms in the grass.

While still a toddler, he was taught to fish by his grandpa.

Topic Narrowing

The process of topic narrowing can be difficult until you've practised it enough to be comfortable with it. When you've decided on a general subject area (or one has been foisted on you by an instructor), you can proceed by asking yourself a series of questions relating to an aspect of that topic area. In looking at a subject, consider:

1. How can I define it?

2. Is there a cause/effect relationship I can talk about?

3. Are there mechanisms or processes involved which I could explain?

4. Is there material here which should be catalogued for my audience?

5. What is my relationship to the topic area?

6. What is my audience's relationship to the topic area?

The list of questions you can ask yourself this way could be virtually endless, and you do not need to beat a subject to death. You do need to narrow it sufficiently so that you can make some argument about it or explain some aspect of it reasonably in the space permitted in a normal essay—so let quantity of material be a guide, too. Finally, remember that when you offer your reader the thesis and path statement in a paper, you're effectively taking on an obligation to cover everything that falls within the scope of that thesis and path that you don't expressly rule out.

Paragraph Organization

See, generally, comments on Coherence.

It's possible to write a paragraph that is more or less coherent, but is simply poorly organized. If you run into this kind of problem, you need to consider how to reorganize the material in a paragraph in such a way that the reader is most likely to find your material credible and complete. Check your thesis and path statement, and make sure that your supporting material and your sequencing are consistent with the purpose they represent.

Faulty Parallelism

Parallelism involves the repetition of grammatical elements or components within sentences in order to allow the reader to have a sense about what comes next. Because the repetition creates a kind of rhythm, the reader is better able to keep the overall meaning of a point in mind; he can remember the impact of previous sentences more easily. Putting it another way, we could say that the reader should not be distracted by grammar and structure when he should be concentrating on meaning and message.

> Not parallel: We went to the store, bought some groceries, picked up a video, dropped off the cleaning, paying for it all with cash.

> Parallel: We went to the store, bought some groceries, picked up a video, dropped off the cleaning, and paid for it all with cash.

The Passive Voice

You are using passive voice when the subject of a sentence is the receiver, rather than the doer, of the action expressed by the verb. For example, in the sentence, "I picked up the chalk," the pronoun "I" is the subject of the sentence. It is also the doer of the action, and therefore the sentence is in the active voice. In the sentence, "The chalk was picked up by me," the noun "chalk" is the subject of the sentence; but it is the receiver, rather than the doer of the action. Avoid using the passive voice whenever the active voice is more natural and direct.

The passive voice is properly used when the *receiver* of the action is more important that the doer of the action or the action itself:

> Several valuable old landmarks were destroyed by the vandals.

> The winning coach was hoisted onto the players' shoulders.

But notice the difference in the following sentences when the active replaces the passive:

> Passive: Other games are also played by the guests.

> Active: The guests also play other games.

> Passive: Many agonizing minutes are spent by the student in deciding on a subject for a speech.

Active: The student spent many agonizing minutes deciding upon a subject for the speech.

When you're in doubt, avoid the passive voice—unless you're writing in the sciences and your instructors require it of you.

Pronoun Agreement

A pronoun should agree in number and person with the noun it refers to:

If a student fails an essay, <u>they</u> get upset. (incorrect)

If a student fails an essay, <u>he or she</u> gets upset. (correct)

This is a much more serious problem than it appears to be, since it can badly confuse the reader. Moreover, a skilled reader (like an instructor or marker) is likely to assume that it's evidence of sloppy thinking; she will judge your efforts accordingly.

Pronoun Reference

The link between a pronoun and the noun it refers to must be clear. If the noun doesn't appear in the same sentence as the pronoun, it should appear in the preceding sentence—and the relationship between the noun and the pronoun should be clear and unequivocal.

Since the ball-bearing supply in the warehouse had run out, we borrowed them from the local garage.

Since "ball-bearing" is used as an adjective rather than a noun, it cannot serve as a referent or antecedent for the pronoun "them." You must either replace "them" or change the phrase "ball-bearing supply."

Since the ball-bearing supply in the warehouse had run out, we borrowed ball-bearings from the local garage.

Since the ball-bearings in the warehouse had run out, we borrowed some from the local garage.

When a sentence contains more than one noun, make sure there is no ambiguity about which noun the pronoun refers to:

I took my lunch and a beach ball, and when I got hungry, I ate it.

What does the pronoun "it" refer to—the lunch or the beach ball?

I took my lunch and a beach ball, and when I got hungry, I ate the lunch.

Proofreading and Revision

If you're told that you're not proofreading and revising properly, remember that you are writing in college or university. It isn't appropriate to hand in work that is handwritten or that contains a large number of errors. Try proofreading and revising in the following manner:

1. Be sure that all of the parts of the paper are present and correctly structured. You must have a thesis statement and path statement; an appropriate number of development sections; and a conclusion. Your first revision should simply assure that each of these parts is present and in the correct order.

2. Revise at the paragraph level. Be sure that each paragraph has a topic sentence and that the flow of the paragraph is logical and well paced. Does the material in the paragraph make sense? Is it in the correct order? Have you included all of the information necessary to understand the point you are trying to make?

3. Revise for aesthetics. All of the parts of the paper are now present and in the correct order. The paragraphs are well written and clearly convey the information you intend them to convey. You should now look at *how* the prose is written. Is the use of language optimal? Have you used the correct words to express the ideas you are communicating? Is the rhythm of the piece pleasing? Have you alternated short and long sentences? Can you alter the sentences to make the paper read more smoothly?

4. Finally, after everything else is completed, revise for spelling, grammar, and punctuation. If you know you have problems in this area, you should be doing one complete reread of the paper for each of the known problems. That is, if you have problems with comma splices, you should be doing at least one thorough reread in which you are looking for common splices and ignoring everything else. Try to systematize your proofreading and revision for grammar and mechanics in this way.

Placement of Punctuation within Quotation Marks

A comma or period always goes inside closing quotation marks, except for the comma after the word "said":

She said, "I want to ride on the cable car," but I replied, "You've had enough thrills for one day."

A semicolon or colon always goes outside the quotation marks:

> Sam wants to play a video game; I'd rather watch television.

A question mark, dash or exclamation mark goes inside closing quotation marks if it's part of the quotation, but outside if it isn't:

> Lily asked, "How's your face?"

> Did Sam repeat the order as "Eggs over easy"?

Purposes of the Undergraduate Essay

Remember that in college and university, the undergraduate essay is not merely a vehicle by which you get to express yourself. It's an artificial testing device, designed to allow you to demonstrate your knowledge of a subject and your ability to express yourself according to predetermined conventions and expectations. If you don't familiarize yourself with these conventions and expectations, then your success on essay assignments will be determined by luck rather than skill or hard work.

As a general rule, the undergraduate essay requires you to demonstrate your grasp of a suitably narrowed field of knowledge by making a case (through research, analysis and critical thought) for a specific and very narrow thesis. You must demonstrate your ability to think clearly and logically in the particular discipline and to express your thoughts according to a clear organizational framework that you make apparent to your reader. Moreover, you must demonstrate that you can do all this in concise, grammatically sound English. You'll always have to meet a mechanical threshold that, in college or university, is tantamount to grammatical perfection; you'll always have to meet a content threshold in terms of appropriateness of subject matter, narrowness and clarity of thesis, and soundness of organizational framework.

Make no mistake: because the undergraduate essay is the "coin of the realm" in a great many college and university courses, you *must* ensure that your grasp of the required skills and your understanding of the governing conventions and expectations are sound.

Run-on Sentences

A run-on sentence is one in which you try to combine too many independent clauses and too many distinct thoughts into one grammatical unit. This sort of mistake is confusing and annoying to your reader. It also irritates instructors and markers, who don't expect to see run-on sentences in students' work after grade nine or ten.

> Having gone to the store, I returned home with my purchases and put them away, after which I showered and prepared for

my date with Susan, we were going to the concert at the Royal Theater, where the Nylons, who were our favorite singing group, were playing after a year-long absence due to their Asian concert tour, I hear it was a smashing success, particularly since they received a special award from the Japanese government.

To correct this error, you need to break up the independent clauses and thoughts into appropriate smaller units. Make sure to avoid other errors like the Comma Splice and the Fused Sentence.

The Semicolon

Use a semicolon between two independent clauses, if they are closely related in thought:

The marlin struck like a freight train; I wrenched back on the rod.

Don't hit me; I'm wearing glasses.

Use the semicolon between items in a list if those items contain commas or are lengthy:

John hit the ball out of the park; ran around the bases; bowed to the fans; and took his seat in the dugout.

Use a semicolon to join two independent clauses linked by one of the following words: "consequently," "accordingly," "nevertheless," "however," "hence," "indeed," "moreover," "therefore," "thus," "as a result," or "for example:"

Susan read the book; as a result, she got an "A" on the exam.

These words are called conjunctive adverbs; you should become familiar with their use.

Subject-Verb Agreement

This is a problem that generally creates headaches for non-native speakers of English. It involves a lack of agreement between the noun or pronoun acting as the subject and the form of the verb:

They goes to the store.

John play the guitar very well.

Mom and Dad comes from Oregon.

In each of these examples, the subject of the sentence does not agree with the verb. If the subject of your sentence is the third-person plural pronoun "they," you must make sure that you have chosen the appropriate form of the verb:

They go to the store.

Similarly:

John plays the guitar very well.

Mom and Dad come from Oregon.

This error is all too common. Reread your work carefully to detect this error, as this problem is one that will lead your reader to suspect that your language abilities are much poorer than they are in reality.

Supporting Materials

It seems obvious to say that material you introduce in an essay as support for your argument ought to be relevant and meaningful, but writers seem to have real problems in doing this. When we say that your evidence ought to be relevant and meaningful, what we really mean is that each piece of supporting material you introduce ought to speak directly to the single point or assertion for which you're offering it as support. Moreover, it ought not to be open to misinterpretation as support for some other point or assertion. In addition, it ought to be the best piece of particular support you can find for the point in question, on the theory that sound support depends on introduction of the best evidence, rather than the most evidence.

Remember when you're searching for or introducing supporting materials into a paper that you've got some real credibility issues to consider. You'll have to see to it that the evidence itself is credible and that you make clear and logical connections between the evidence and the point it supports. You'll also have to be sure that the reader identifies the source of the evidence as a credible authority, relative to the focus of your discussion. The consequences of selecting weak or inappropriate supporting materials, or of handling supporting materials poorly, might include problems with unity, coherence, credibility, logic and informative value.

Thesis Statement and Path Statement

This is an area in which we can safely generalize: if you hand in a formal college essay that does not have a clear and narrowly focused thesis statement and path statement (even if the central focus is not called "thesis statement and path statement"), you're almost always certain to receive a poor grade on the assignment. Remember that the undergraduate essay, as a testing device, is governed by conventions and expectations that you must meet in order to succeed with the form. Chief among these expectations or conventions is the requirement that you be able to focus a paper around a clearly defined issue you can handle in the space available to you and that your choice of sub-issues and your organizational framework be readily understood by your audience. This doesn't mean you have to beat your audience on the head with your thesis; but neither can you get by with vague generalizations, fuzzily worded issues, or hidden structural logic.

For purposes of most essays, here's the rule: NO CLEAR, NARROWLY DEFINED THESIS STATEMENT WITH EQUALLY CLEAR PATH STATEMENT = "F."

Unity

Unity is what you get when your essay or paragraph focuses on one clearly defined topic. Your essay must be about the topic and purpose you suggest to the reader in your thesis and path statement. If your essay deals with some other subject or subjects, even if they are related in some way, then your essay will lack unity. If one of your supporting paragraphs deals with material that isn't relevant to your path statement or that supports some point other than the one you're trying to make, your paper will lack unity.

If you have problems with unity, you're not proofreading and revising properly—or perhaps you simply didn't include enough detail at the outline stage, and now you're letting the material get away from you. In either case, go back to your working thesis and path statement. Make sure that your purpose is clear and specific, that you understand it, and that you've mentioned supporting details relating directly to your purpose. Then, re-outline the paper, putting as much detail in at the template stage as is necessary to keep you on topic.

Usage and Word Choice

When you're looking for a particular word to do a particular job in a sentence, remember what we said earlier about "appropriateness." Part of your responsibility to your audience is to select words that will most clearly and accurately convey your meaning. You must become sensitized to the emotional charge of words, as well as to their denotative and connotative meanings; and you must consider whether one word is better than others in view of your specific topic or point of view. For example, if you were writing for a group of pro-choice people on the issue of abortion and you wished them to consider the pro-life view, you would not be well advised to select a word like "murder" in dealing with the issue. This is a sensitive subject, on which your audience already has strong feelings. If you choose words that convey an inappropriate emotional impact, you'll have alienated your audience before you even get to make your case. Review your work, checking word choice against your thesis and path statement. Think about reader response!

At a simpler level, you have a responsibility to use the words you choose in a manner and context that your audience can understand. If a word conveys an inaccurate or incorrect meaning to the audience, you have a usage problem:

I am discussing towards the topic of grammar.

This is faulty use of the word "towards." The sentence should read:

I am writing about the subject of grammar.

Mode of Addressing the Reader

It isn't technically wrong to address the reader as "you"; nor is it technically wrong to speak in the first person (as "I"). There will be times when taking these measures will be appropriate to the context in which you're writing and to your audience and material. In fact, this approach is slowly gaining a measure of approval in the context of the undergraduate expository essay. However, this degree of personal involvement and informality is not yet widely accepted in terms of formal documents, particularly at the university level. Therefore, you should continue to expect that most college and university instructors and markers will continue to view this personal, informal approach as clumsy and amateurish, and will therefore mark you down if you use it in a formal essay.

It's a good idea to check with individual instructors to see if they have a preference in this area. If you're writing a personal essay, a journal, or even an article or book review, you can usually get away with less formality.

INDEX